Transfer Pricing in a Post-BEPS World

EUCOTAX Series on European Taxation

VOLUME 50

Series Editors

Prof. Dr Peter H.J. Essers, Fiscal Institute Tilburg/Center for Company Law, Tilburg University
Prof. Dr Eric C.C.M. Kemmeren, Fiscal Institute Tilburg/Center for Company Law, Tilburg University
Prof. Dr Dr h.c. Michael Lang, WU (Vienna University of Economics and Business)

Introduction

EUCOTAX (European Universities Cooperating on Taxes) is a network of tax institutes currently consisting of eleven universities: WU (Vienna University of Economics and Business) in Austria, Katholieke Universiteit Leuven in Belgium, Corvinus University of Budapest, Hungary, Université Paris-I Panthéon-Sorbonne in France, Universität Osnabrück in Germany, Libera, Università Internazionale di Studi Sociali in Rome (and Università degli Studi di Bologna for the research part), in Italy, Fiscaal Instituut Tilburg at Tilburg University in the Netherlands, Universidad de Barcelona in Spain, Uppsala University in Sweden, Queen Mary and Westfield College at the University of London in the United Kingdom, and Georgetown University in Washington DC, United States of America. The network aims at initiating and coordinating both comparative education in taxation, through the organization of activities such as winter courses and guest lectures, and comparative research in the field, by means of joint research projects, international conferences and exchange of researchers between various countries.

Contents/Subjects

The EUCOTAX series covers a wide range of topics in European tax law. For example tax treaties, EC case law, tax planning, exchange of information and VAT. The series is well-known for its high-quality research and practical solutions.

Objective

The series aims to provide insights on new developments in European taxation.

Readership

Practitioners and academics dealing with European tax law.

Frequency of Publication

2-3 new volumes published each year.

The titles published in this series are listed at the end of this volume.

Transfer Pricing in a Post-BEPS World

Edited by

Michael Lang
Alfred Storck
Raffaele Petruzzi

Wolters Kluwer

Published by:
Kluwer Law International B.V.
PO Box 316
2400 AH Alphen aan den Rijn
The Netherlands
Website: www.wklawbusiness.com

Sold and distributed in North, Central and South America by:
Wolters Kluwer Legal & Regulatory U.S.
7201 McKinney Circle
Frederick, MD 21704
United States of America
Email: customer.service@wolterskluwer.com

Sold and distributed in all other countries by:
Turpin Distribution Services Ltd
Stratton Business Park
Pegasus Drive, Biggleswade
Bedfordshire SG18 8TQ
United Kingdom
Email: kluwerlaw@turpin-distribution.com

ISBN 978-90-411-6710-1

Editors

Prof. Dr Dr h.c. Michael Lang is Head of the Institute for Austrian and International Tax Law of WU (Vienna University of Economics and Business) and academic director of both the LLM Program in International Tax Law and the Doctoral Program in International Business Taxation (DIBT) of this university. He is the president of the Austrian Branch of the International Fiscal Association (IFA) and has been a visiting professor at Georgetown University, New York University, Sorbonne, Bocconi, Peking University (PKU), University of New South Wales (Sydney), and at other universities.

Prof. Dr Alfred Storck is managing director of the WU Transfer Pricing Center at the Institute for Austrian and International Tax Law at Vienna University of Economics and Business (WU) and, since April 2009, a visiting professor at the same institute. The focus of his research and teaching activities is international business taxation and transfer pricing. From 2009 until January 2015, Alfred Storck was an honorary professor for Company Taxation and Managerial Finance at the Institute of Accounting, Controlling and Auditing (ACA) at the University of St. Gallen, Switzerland. Before his activities at both universities, Alfred Storck held various positions in a large multinational company headquartered in Switzerland.

Dr Raffaele Petruzzi, LLM, is managing director of the WU Transfer Pricing Center at the Institute for Austrian and International Tax Law at WU (Vienna University of Economics and Business) and international tax advisor specializing in international corporate taxation and transfer pricing within the transfer pricing department of Deloitte, Vienna (Austria). Since 2007, Raffaele has gained extensive experience in dealing with topics related to international corporate taxation and transfer pricing from both a practical perspective (by working in different countries within big four companies and in the tax department of a multinational) and an academic perspective.

Contributors

Yariv Brauner is a professor of Law with the Levin College of Law at the University of Florida. He joined the Florida faculty in 2006 after teaching at NYU, Northwestern, and ASU. He has been a visiting professor or a guest speaker in various universities in the US and abroad. He is the author of several articles published in professional journals and law reviews and a co-author of US International Taxation – Cases and Materials (with Reuven S. Avi-Yonah and Diane M. Ring), now in its third edition. He has taught multiple courses in the fields of taxation, corporate taxation, international taxation, international trade law, and the law of multinational corporations. He holds an LLB, obtained in 1996, from Hebrew University School of Law and attained his LLM in International Taxation in 1998, and J.S.D. in 2003, from New York University School of Law.

Dr Sven Bremer is Global Head of Group Transfer Pricing at Siemens and has over twenty years of experience in international tax. He is based in Munich. Prior to joining Siemens, Dr Bremer was active for the Big 4 firms in Germany and the United States. He speaks and writes frequently on transfer pricing and international tax topics. Dr Bremer studied at the University of Munich, qualified with the German Tax Advisor Bar Association, and obtained his PhD from the University of Ingolstadt, where he was an assistant professor.

Giammarco Cottani is a partner at 'Ludovici and Partners' tax firm, where he coordinates the transfer pricing practice, with regard to both the prevention and resolution of domestic and international disputes and the assistance in complex audits of large multinational enterprise groups. From 2011 to July 2015, he held the role of advisor to Italy Revenue Agency's Director of Central Assessment on international tax and transfer pricing. He focused on international tax issues related to large multinational groups and SMEs. He was one of the delegates for Italy in the OECD-G20 Action Plan on BEPS. From 2009 to 2011, he was employed as a Transfer Pricing Advisor in the Transfer Pricing Unit of the OECD where he was involved in the introduction of the new Chapter IX of the OECD Transfer Pricing Guidelines concerning business restructuring. He managed more than twenty events in the area of transfer pricing for a number of tax administrations of non-OECD countries. He currently serves as a member of the UN

Sub-Committee Group on transfer pricing which supervises the drafting of the Practical Manual on Transfer Pricing for Developing Countries.

Sébastien Gonnet is a vice president in the Global Transfer Pricing Practice at NERA Economic Consulting. Based in Paris, he specializes in the areas of transfer pricing, intellectual property, and valuation. For a number of years, he has advised multinational companies in transfer pricing system design and implementation, business restructurings, and intellectual property and business valuation not only in Europe, but also in China, in a range of industries including industrial and retail clients and financial institutions. He also acts as an expert economist in advance pricing agreements and tax audits in Europe and China. Before joining NERA Economic Consulting, Sébastien was an economist at KPMG. He holds a Master of Science in Management from HEC, Paris (Ecole des Hautes Etudes Commerciales) and a Master of Science in International Taxation from Paris II Law University.

Dr Christian Kaeser, after four years as an assistant professor of Tax Law at the Universities of Mainz and Valencia, joined a Munich-based tax advisory firm but left to join Siemens AG in 2002. After various appointments in the tax department and a delegation to the US in 2007 and 2008, he was appointed the Global Head of Tax and Corporate Vice President for Siemens in 2009. Kaeser is the chairman of the Tax Commission of the International Chamber of Commerce (ICC) and the president of the German branch of the International Fiscal Association (IFA). He is a member of the scientific council of the largest German tax journal (DStR) and co-editor of 'IStR'. Kaeser is the chairman of the supervisory board of WTS Group AG, a German-based tax advisory group and a member of the scientific council of PwC.

Prof. Dr Guglielmo Maisto founded Maisto e Associati in 1991. He is a professor of International and Comparative Tax Law at the Università Cattolica di Piacenza. He is the president of the Italian Branch of the International Fiscal Association (IFA), a member of the Board of Trustees of the International Bureau of Fiscal Documentation (IBFD) in Amsterdam, a member of the advisory board of the Master of Advanced Studies in International Taxation at Lausanne University, a member of the Practice Council of New York University (NYU) Law's International Tax Program, and a member of the Board of the American Chamber of Commerce in Italy. He represents the Italian Association of Industries (Confindustria) at the OECD Business Industry Advisory Committee. He was also a member of the EU Joint Transfer Pricing Forum.

Antonio Russo is an established practitioner of Transfer Pricing and International Tax law. He is a partner with Baker & McKenzie in Amsterdam and heads the Amsterdam Transfer Pricing Team which has been awarded the International Tax Review Award for the Netherlands Transfer Pricing Firm of the Year in 2005, 2006, 2007, 2010, 2012, 2014, and 2015. Antonio specializes in operating models and transfer pricing systems design and implementation. His area of expertise also encompasses valuation of companies and intangible assets as well as intercompany financial transactions. He has extensive experience in business restructuring and tax planning/restructuring engagements and has performed transfer pricing studies for clients in a wide range of industries. He has also provided assistance to clients developing strategies for the conclusion of (uni- and multilateral) APAs as well as tax audit defenses in EMEA, the Americas, and Asia Pacific. Antonio is a member of Baker & McKenzie's Global Transfer Pricing Steering Committee, the European Tax Steering Committee, and the European Transfer Pricing Leadership Team. Antonio is very active from an academic standpoint, regularly teaching at various universities and institutions: IBFD, University of Leiden, University of Amsterdam, Aarhus University, and the Vienna University of Economics and Business.

J. Scott Wilkie is a partner at Blake, Cassels & Graydon LLP (Toronto, Canada). He is the Vice-Chair of the Permanent Scientific Committee of the IFA. He is a Distinguished Professor of Practice at Osgoode Hall Law School, York University, where he also co-directs the Professional LLM in Tax Law. Scott is an executive fellow at the University of the Calgary School of Public Policy.

Summary of Contents

Table of Contents

Preface

Transfer pricing is currently one of the most relevant and challenging topics in the international tax environment. The annual amount of tax revenue loss that is due to the 'mispricing' of transfer prices has been estimated at several hundred billion dollars by Global Financial Integrity in Washington. As a consequence, the significance of transfer pricing legislations has radically increased.

The economic activities in a globalized business environment involve related parties located in different jurisdictions and, therefore, may be subject to different transfer pricing legislations. Moreover, the increasing complexities regarding the application of the arm's length principle, such as the fundamental principle adopted by most of the transfer pricing rules, are sharply magnifying the relevance of tax controversy around the world on transfer pricing issues.

In this context, the Base Erosion and Profit Shifting (BEPS) project developed by the OECD under the mandate of the G20 leaders was and is intensively working on transfer pricing issues. The effort on this is, indeed, playing a fundamental role in this project, and numerous and radical changes are being proposed to the existing rules and guidelines in the field. The primary goal of this BEPS work is to provide suggestions for reforms which will ensure that transfer pricing outcomes are in accordance with economic activities and value creation.

In detail, the work of the OECD on 'Transfer Pricing, Allocation of Risk and Recharacterization' (Actions 8, 9, and 10 of the BEPS Action Plan) has developed proposals for a substantial revision of the OECD Transfer Pricing Guidelines with regard to a number of closely related topics which are 'at the heart of the arm's length principle'.

The development of further guidance on the transfer pricing aspects of intangibles has increasingly been one of the core topics of the OECD's work on BEPS. The final intent of Action 8 is the development of 'rules to prevent BEPS by moving intangibles among group members'.

The future work on Action 4 will provide further guidance on transfer pricing aspects of related party financial transactions 'including financial and performance guarantees, derivatives (including internal derivatives used in intra-bank dealings), and captive and other insurance arrangements'.

Intra-group services, especially management fees and head office expenses, are among the major areas of concern of the BEPS project. The focus of the OECD is on redrafting the guidelines on 'Special Considerations for Intra-Group Services' and 'Cost Contribution Arrangements'.

Furthermore, the avoidance of Permanent Establishments' (PEs) status of sales activities has also been at the core of the work of the OECD over the past years. The work on Action 7 of the BEPS Action Plan is focusing much of the attention on 'commissionnaire arrangements' and issues of profit attribution to PEs. The aim of the proposal is to deter enterprises from performing significant activities within a country without being subject to tax in that country mainly due to the avoidance of the PE status with these 'commissionnaire arrangements'.

Last, but not least, transfer pricing documentation is a challenge for both taxpayers and tax administrations. The suggested three-tiered approach of the OECD, specifically, a 'Master File', a 'Local File', and a 'Country-by-Country Report' will be the essential elements of documentation that accord with the OECD standards. Many countries are already implementing these requirements into their domestic legislation and, most probably, more will be doing so in the future. The related research, therefore, will explore the new transfer pricing documentation requirements suggested by the OECD and analyze possible methods of implementing them into taxpayers' and tax administrations' operations by way of the use or development of new technology standards.

The WU Transfer Pricing Center at the Institute for Austrian and International Tax Law is conducting research projects to analyze the transfer pricing topics under the focus of the BEPS Action Plan and to develop further suggestions and proposals to improve the results of the project. The current research is based on eight topic-based research papers which are provided by well renowned international experts on transfer pricing. The results of this work were presented and discussed at the first 'Global Transfer Pricing Conference' in February 2016 on location at the WU (Vienna University of Economics and Business). The book is aimed at academics, practitioners (including the business community and advisory firms), international organizations, and government officials who are tax and transfer pricing experts as well as CEOs and CFOs who are interested in this topic. The book will provide an in-depth analysis of the above-described topics, the related BEPS proposals, and suggestions for future solutions to any issues that are raised.

The editors would like to express their sincere thanks to the authors who made it possible to provide this ambitious work. Many thanks are forwarded to Kluwer Law International B.V. for supporting and cooperating with this publication project. Last, but not least, we would like to thank Renée Pestuka, Hedwig Pfanner, and Benedikt Hörtenhuber for their precious support, and Jenny Hill for providing linguistic support to the authors during the publishing process.

Prof. Dr Dr h.c. Michael Lang
Prof. Dr Alfred Storck
Dr Raffaele Petruzzi

CHAPTER 1

The Arm's Length Principle: Between Legal Fiction and Economic Reality

Raffaele Petruzzi[*]

* The author would like to thank Prof. Alfred Storck and Prof. Jeffrey Owens for their valuable inputs and feedback to this chapter. The views expressed in this chapter are solely those of the author.

I. INTRODUCTION

It is the year 1932, and a young American attorney is traveling through twenty-seven countries around the world in pursuit of the 'Holy Grail' of international taxation. His name is Mitchell B. Carroll, and he is looking for the best way to allocate taxable income generated by Multinational Enterprises (MNEs) among different states. After three years of intense work analyzing the legislation and practice of thirty-five countries, Carroll discovered the answer to that question: the arm's length principle.

This principle, considered at that time to be the best solution to the question of how to allocate business income among different jurisdictions, was soon being embedded into many international tax treaties aimed at preventing the double taxation of income and capital. Afterwards, it also became the relevant principle embedded into the transfer pricing rules of many countries around the world.

The importance of this principle was, since its origins, perceived as twofold. On the one side, when embedded into double tax treaties, it had the aim of allocating MNEs' taxable base among different countries in a coherent way: if both countries signing the treaty were applying the principle in the same manner, no economic double taxation would have occurred. On the other side, when embedded into the relevant transfer pricing legislation of a state, often as part of an anti-avoidance rule whereby an MNE would have been refrained from distorting the 'fair' distribution of its income among different subsidiaries in order to shift it from high tax jurisdictions to low tax jurisdictions, the principle had the aim of setting a standard for such a 'fair' distribution.[1]

The arm's length principle was originally conceived as a legal fiction, whereby different parts of the same entity (i.e., head office and its permanent establishment(s))[2] as well as different entities belonging to the same MNE were considered as separate legal entities pursuing their own interests. This legal fiction, nevertheless, soon had to face the economic reality of the business environment, whereby becoming a more economic principle.

This chapter presents these issues by first analyzing the historical background, where the origins of the arm's length principle are introduced and described.[3] Subsequently, the view of the arm's length principle as a legal fiction is represented.[4] Afterwards, the developments of the principle to reflect the economic reality are investigated.[5] Finally, several conclusions and proposals for the future interpretation of the principle are introduced.[6]

1. Petruzzi, R., *Transfer Pricing and EU Law: The Effects of SGI on Thin Cap GLO*, Diritto e pratica tributaria internazionale (1/2013), pp. 77-95.
2. In this chapter, for reasons of simplification, reference to the topic of allocation of profits to permanent establishments, unless otherwise stated, will generally consider the view expressed by the Authorized OECD Approach and the thereby defined 'separate legal entity' approach.
3. See Section 2.
4. See Section 3.
5. See Section 4.
6. See Section 5.

II. THE HISTORICAL BACKGROUND

The expression 'at arm's length' seems to originate in the seventeen century[7] in the discipline of archery where it was referring to 'holding the bow at arm's length'.[8] However, this expression was introduced many years later in the vocabulary of numerous tax specialists as the result of a process that endured almost twenty years.

Transfer pricing rules were conceived for the first time in 1915 in the United Kingdom (UK). At that time, the finance Act was awarding the UK Commissioners with the power of assessing the income taxes of non-residents when 'either no profits or less than the ordinary profits' were generated in the course of their business with resident persons who were considered to be related by 'close connection' and 'substantial control'.[9] Two years later, the United States (US) also introduced similar regulations under their War Revenue Act which allowed the tax administration to consolidate the accounts of two or more related trades or businesses 'whenever necessary to more equitably determine the invested capital or taxable income'.[10] Interestingly enough, the UK rules first and the US rules afterwards were making reference to concepts such as 'ordinary', 'equitably', and 'accurate' in order to define 'how much' taxable income could be assessed by the tax administration when applying those rules.

Several years later, in 1927, the first Draft Model Convention for the Prevention of Double Taxation and Evasion was elaborated by the League of Nations,[11] whereby introducing the concept of 'permanent establishment' in order to allocate taxing rights

7. See http://dictionary.reference.com/browse/arm-s-length (accessed 6 Jan. 2016).
8. Koomen, M., *Transfer Pricing in a BEPS Era: Rethinking the Arm's Length Principle – Part I'*, International Transfer Pricing Journal 22 (4/2015), p. 147.
9. See Section 31(3) of the Finance (No. 2) Act of 1915 which was specifically phrased as follows:

> Where a non-resident person not being a British subject or a British, Indian, Dominion, or Colonial Firm or Company, or branch thereof, carries on business with a resident person, and it appears to the Commissioners by whom the assessment is made that, owing to the close connection between the resident and the non-resident person, and to the substantial control exercised by the non-resident over the resident, the course of business between those persons can be so arranged, and is so arranged, that the business done by the resident in pursuance of his connection with the non-resident produces to the resident either no profits or less than the ordinary profits which might be expected to arise from that business, the non-resident person shall be chargeable to income tax in the name of the resident person as if the resident person were an agent of the non-resident person.

10. See Regulation 41, Articles 77-78, promulgated under the War Revenue Act of 1917. A number of years later, these regulations were followed by the first transfer pricing rules which provided the United States Commissioner with the authorization to consolidate the accounts of affiliated corporations 'for the purpose of making an accurate distribution or apportionment of gains, profits, income, deductions, or capital between or among such related trades or business' (Revenue Act of 1921, Chapter 136, Section 240(d), 42 Stat. 260 (1921) (re-enacted in Revenue Act of 1924, Chapter 234, Section 240(d), 43 Stat. 288 (1924), and Revenue Act of 1926, Chapter 27, Section 240(f), 44 Stat. 46 (1926))) in order to avoid the international tax avoidance opportunities available to MNEs (see Avi-Yonah, R.S., *The Rise and Fall of Arm's Length: A Study in the Evolution of U.S. International Taxation*, Finance and Tax Law Review 9 (2006), pp. 310 et seq.).
11. For this purpose, in 1922 the League of Nations nominated the Committee of Technical Experts in order to analyze issues related to double taxation and tax evasion.

related to business income. This concept was including, *inter alia*, 'affiliated companies'.[12] Once identified whether profits could have been taxed in the source state (based on the existence, or not, of a permanent establishment), the subsequent issue was 'how much' of those profits could have been taxed by this state. At that time, the answer to this question, otherwise referred to as a 'system of apportioning the income according to its source', was suggested to be found either by analyzing the accounts of the permanent establishment (so-called separate accounting approach) or by agreement between the competent authorities of the contracting states.[13] The system of apportioning the income according to its source was considered as depending on the businesses involved and on the rules of the specific countries involved.[14]

However, the separate accounting approach was soon abandoned in 1928 when the new Draft Model Convention for the Prevention of Double Taxation and Evasion[15] declared the agreement between the competent authorities of the contracting states as the only method of apportionment. The reason for this appears to be founded in the committee's lack of time to address this issue more closely.[16] Nonetheless, a unani-

---

12. League of Nations, *Report on Double Taxation and Tax Evasion, Presented by the Committee of Technical Experts on Double Taxation and Tax Evasion*, C.216.M.85, London, 12 Apr. 1927, p. 10. Based on the wording of Article 5 of the proposed Draft of a Bilateral Convention for the Prevention of Double Taxation, 'The real centres of management, affiliated companies, branches, factories, agencies, warehouses, offices, depots, shall be regarded as permanent establishments.'
13. League of Nations, *Report on Double Taxation and Tax Evasion, Presented by the Committee of Technical Experts on Double Taxation and Tax Evasion*, C.216.M.85, London, 12 Apr. 1927, p. 10. Based on the wording of Article 5 of the proposed Draft of a Bilateral Convention for the Prevention of Double Taxation, 'Should the undertaking possess permanent establishments in both Contracting States, each of the two States shall tax the portion of the income produced in its territory. In the absence of accounts showing this income separately and in proper form, the competent administrations of the two Contracting States shall come to an arrangement as to the rules for apportionment.'
14. League of Nations, *Report on Double Taxation and Tax Evasion, Presented by the Committee of Technical Experts on Double Taxation and Tax Evasion*, C.216.M.85, London, 12 Apr. 1927, p. 15. Based on the wording of the Commentary to Article 5 of the proposed Draft of a Bilateral Convention for the Prevention of Double Taxation:

    > These rules will vary essentially according to the undertakings concerned; in certain States account is taken, according to the nature of the undertakings, of the amount of capital involved, of the number of workers, the wages paid, receipts, etc. Similarly, in cases where the products of factories are sold abroad, a distinction is often made between 'manufacturing' and 'merchanting' profits, the latter being the difference between the price in the home market and the sale price abroad, less cost of transport. These criteria are, of course, merely given as indications.

15. League of Nations, *Report on Double Taxation and Tax Evasion, Presented by the Committee of Technical Experts on Double Taxation and Tax Evasion*, C.562.M.85, London, 31 Oct. 1928. In the 1928 Model the reference to 'affiliated companies' was removed.
16. Indeed, it was stated that:

    > The Committee held an exhaustive discussion, which revealed the complexity of the question and the numerous obstacles which face any attempted solution. Nevertheless, while fully realising the difficulty of the task, the Fiscal Committee is of opinion that the moment has come to deal with the real substance of the question, since, until this is settled, one of the principal causes of double taxation will continue to exist. The

mous decision was taken by the General Meeting to establish a standing fiscal committee dealing, *inter alia*, with the question of taxation of business income.[17]

This question was first analyzed in a report by the American economist Thomas S. Adams.[18] By addressing to various countries the question 'What are the methods for determining the income of branches of foreign business concerns doing business in your country?', Adams discovered that the separate accounting approach was the most frequently employed methodology. However, when the accounts were ascertained to be 'inadequate or misleading', they were corrected in order to estimate the taxable profits by means of different methods such as formulary apportionments, 'a comparison with the earnings of local undertakings engaged in similar business', several external indicators (e.g., salaries or rental payments), or as a lump sum. However, the ultimate result of Adams' report was that the problem under analysis was characterized by more complexity than originally believed.[19]

At this point, the task of providing a suggestion for answering the question of the proper amount of tax base to allocate to the state of the permanent establishment was entrusted to the American attorney Mitchell B. Carroll.[20] By analyzing the legislations of thirty-five countries, twenty-seven of which were 'personally visited' by himself,[21] Carroll successfully completed a survey on the 'Methods of Allocating Taxable Income' around the world ('Carroll Report').[22]

> Committee decided to concentrate chiefly on this point' (League of Nations, *Report to the Council on the Work of the Second Session of the Committee*, C.340.M.140.1930.II, Geneva, 22 31 May 1930).

See also Wittendorff, J., *Transfer Pricing and the Arm's Length Principle in International Tax Law* (Kluwer Law International, The Netherlands, 2010), p. 88.

17. Wittendorff, J., *Transfer Pricing and the Arm's Length Principle in International Tax Law* (Kluwer Law International, The Netherlands, 2010), p. 88.
18. League of Nations, *Fiscal Committee: Report to the Council on the Work of the Committee – First Session*, C.340.M.140.1930.II, Geneva, 31 May 1930.
19. Indeed, it was stated that:

> Double taxation which may result from the taxation of companies, appears to constitute both a serious and complex problem. As members of the Committee were unable to agree on a solution, the Committee decided to resume its examination as its next session' (League of Nations, *Fiscal Committee: Report to the Council on the Work of the Committee – First Session*, C.340.M.140.1930.II, Geneva, 31 May 1930).

See also Wittendorff, J., *Transfer Pricing and the Arm's Length Principle in International Tax Law* (Kluwer Law International, The Netherlands, 2010), p. 89.

20. League of Nations Fiscal Committee, Report to the Council on the Fourth Session of the Committee. C.399.M.204. 1933.II.A., Geneva, 15-26 Jun. 1933.
21. 'Mr. Carroll reported to the Committee on the enquiry which he had conducted in a large number of countries on the lines indicated in the Committee's previous report. He personally visited twentyseven countries, in order to study their legislation on the spot and to collaborate with the experts responsible for making special reports on each country. In other countries, the corresponding members of the Committee drew up reports on the basis of a questionnaire prepared for their guidance. With their help, and the valuable assistance afforded to Mr. Carroll by the International Chamber of Commerce and its national committees, the survey was successfully completed' (League of Nations Fiscal Committee, Report to the Council on the Fourth Session of the Committee. C.399.M.204. 1933.II.A., Geneva, 15-26 Jun. 1933).
22. Mitchell B. Carroll, *Methods of Allocating Taxable Income*, League of Nations (Geneva, 1933).

The Carroll Report was structured into thirteen chapters, eleven of which were describing the legislation, jurisprudence, and practice of the surveyed countries while the last two were dedicated to the practical conclusions on the topic by the author. The final aim of this report was to conceive a system for allocating or apportioning the income of business enterprises which should have been 'fair, practical, logical and suitable for all types of undertakings' by 'taking into account both the legitimate requirements of fiscal administrations and the needs of industry and international trade'.[23]

The Carroll Report identified several critical aspects that are still currently valid. *Inter alia*, it was emphasized that each business was distinguished by specific characteristics, making them unique from each other,[24] international business structures were becoming increasingly complex,[25] tax administrations were concerned with the phenomena of profit shifting via improper transfer prices,[26] and differences in the tax laws of various countries were a further factor adding complexity to the topic of the cross-border allocation of business income.[27]

The following methods were determined to be implemented in the various jurisdictions in order to allocate or apportion profits:

- the 'method of separate accounting', whereby the basis of the assessment was constituted by the tax returns and accounts of the branches;[28]
- the 'empirical methods', whereby the assessment was made 'by comparing the given enterprise with similar enterprises, or taking into account turnover, assets and other readily ascertainable factors';[29] and
- the 'method of fractional apportionment', whereby the assessment was made 'by dividing total net income in the ratio of certain factors – for example, assets, turnover, pay-roll or a fixed percentage'.[30]

---

23. Carroll Report, p. 9.
24. 'There are practically no two businesses of exactly the same type, size or organisation. Each enterprise reflects the brain and personality of its owner or its principal officers, and the profits depend largely on their initiative, skill and wisdom. The factors conducing to profits vary with each enterprise. It is extremely difficult therefore to decide on the best methods of sub-classifying industrial and commercial enterprises in order to consider in sufficient detail methods of allocation or apportionment applicable to them' (Carroll Report, p. 11).
25. Carroll Report, p. 11.
26. 'Tax-collectors complain that sometimes enterprises take the rate of tax in various countries into consideration, and fix the transfer price from the factory to a selling establishment at so high a figure as to show little or no profit in the books of the sales branch. Through the arbitrary fixation of inter-establishment billing prices or charges for interest, royalties, services, etc., profits can be shifted from place to place, the purpose frequently being to transfer them to the country with a low rate of tax or no income-tax at all.' (Carroll Report, p. 12).
27. 'The allocation of the income of the previously mentioned and other types of enterprises is complicated, not only by the diversity in their methods of operation, but also by the incredible differences in the tax laws of the various countries. No two income-tax systems are exactly the same, and it is impossible to classify them' (Carroll Report, p. 14).
28. Carroll Report, p. 45.
29. Carroll Report, p. 45.
30. Carroll Report, p. 46.

Moreover, three ways were identified and adopted into the national tax systems to reassess the taxable income due to the relationship between foreign enterprises and local subsidiaries:

(1) readjustment on basis of independent persons – i.e., the legal fiction is respected, but the relations between the two are examined in order to divide the joint profit between them in the measure that each would have earned had the two been dealing with each other as independent persons;
(2) assessment of the parent in the name of the subsidiary as agent;
(3) assessment on basis of economic unity – i.e., merging the subsidiary with the parent on the theory that they both constitute a single economic unit, or that the subsidiary is merely an organ of the parent.[31]

In the conclusions, after establishing that the taxing powers exercised by a state on a foreign corporation should have been limited to the income from sources 'clearly within its territory',[32] the following principles were established by the Carroll Report:

- The fundamental difference between transactions among different related companies, on the one hand, and transactions between one part of a company and its branch, on the other, is that the former are characterized as 'legal transactions'.[33]
- In both cases (i.e., transactions among different related companies and transactions between one part of a company and its branch) should have been treated as being transactions between 'independent enterprises'.[34]

The final outcome of the Carroll Report was the establishment of the 'fundamental principle' based on which 'permanent establishments must be treated in the same

31. Carroll Report, p. 110.
32. Carroll Report, p. 170.
33. Carroll Report, p. 176.
34. 'The subsidiary must ordinarily have an adequate capital, and the nature of its activities and its contractual relations with outsiders and other corporate units of the enterprise will determine its income. If its income is diverted to other units of the enterprise in any manner, the tax authorities, as a general rule, have only to examine the inter-company transactions, appraise their terms and results in the light of sound legal and business principles, or by comparison with independent companies engaged in similar activities under similar circumstances, and recapture any profit that may be shown to have been diverted. Obviously, if the diverted profit is retrieved after it has already been taxed as income of another unit, double taxation will result, unless the administration of the other country is willing to reduce its assessment and refund a proportionate amount of the tax.

As the conduct of business between a corporation and its subsidiaries on the basis of dealings with an independent enterprise obviates all problems of allocation, it is recommended that, in principle, subsidiaries be not regarded as permanent establishments of an enterprise but treated as independent legal entities; and if it is shown that inter-company transactions have been carried on the subsidiary on the basis of what it would have earned had it been dealing with an independent enterprise.

Branch establishments, moreover, should be treated in so far as possible as independent entities, in order that the income allocated to a branch may be equivalent to that which would have been derived by an independent enterprise. The type of establishment which may most readily be treated as an independent enterprise is what is termed an "autonomous establishment"' (Carroll Report, p. 177).

manner as independent enterprises operating under the same or similar conditions, with the corollary that the taxable income of such establishments is to be assessed on the basis of their separate accounts'.[35]

Therefore, in 1933, the League of Nations established the arm's length principle as the most appropriate method to allocate taxable rights related to business income between different countries and embedded this principle into Article 3 (concerning the attribution of profits to permanent establishment)[36] and Article 5 (concerning the attribution of profits between 'associated enterprises')[37] of the Draft Convention on the

35. 'In view of the diversity of national laws and the extreme complexity and variety of the individual cases that arise, the Committee thought it advisable to prescribe only general principles. Mr. Carroll's very detailed report can be usefully consulted as a guide for the application of those principles to the complex cases that are encountered in practice. The fundamental principle laid down is that, for tax purposes, permanent establishments must be treated in the same manner as independent enterprises operating under the same or similar conditions, with the corollary that the taxable income of such establishments is to be assessed on the basis of their separate accounts. In these circumstances, there was no need for the draft Convention to embody details as to the methods of accounting, which may legitimately vary with different enterprises' (League of Nations Fiscal Committee, Report to the Council on the Fourth Session of the Committee. C.399.M.204. 1933.II.A., Geneva, 15-26 Jun. 1933).
36. Article 3 of the proposed 'Draft Convention' was stating the following:

> If an enterprise with its fiscal domicile in one contracting State has permanent establishments in other contracting States, there shall be attributed to each permanent establishment the net business income which it might be expected to derive if it were an independent enterprise engaged in the same or similar activities under the same or similar conditions. Such net income will, in principle, be determined on the basis of the separate accounts pertaining to such establishment. Subject to the provisions of this Convention, such income shall be taxed in accordance with the legislation and international agreements of the State in which such establishment is situated.
>
> The fiscal authorities of the contracting States shall, when necessary, in execution of the preceding paragraph, rectify the accounts produced, notably to correct errors or omissions, or to re-establish the prices or remunerations entered in the books at the value which would prevail between independent persons dealing at arm's length.
>
> If an establishment does not produce an accounting showing its own operations, or if the accounting produced does not correspond to the normal usages of the trade in the country where the establishment is situated, or if the rectifications provided for in the preceding paragraph cannot be effected, or if the taxpayer agrees, the fiscal authorities may determine empirically the business income by applying a percentage to the turnover of that establishment. This percentage is fixed in accordance with the nature of the transactions in which the establishment is engaged and by comparison with the results obtained by similar enterprises operating in the country.
>
> If the methods of determination described in the preceding paragraphs are found to be inapplicable, the net business income of the permanent establishment may be determined by a computation based on the total income derived by the enterprise from the activities in which such establishment has participated. This determination is made by applying to the total income coefficients based on a comparison of gross receipts, assets, number of hours worked or other appropriate factors, provided such factors be so selected as to ensure results approaching as closely as possible to those which would be reflected by a separate accounting (League of Nations Fiscal Committee, Report to the Council on the Fourth Session of the Committee. C.399.M.204. 1933.II.A., Geneva, June 15th to 26th, 1933).

37. Article 5 of the proposed 'Draft Convention' stated the following:

> When an enterprise of one contracting State has a dominant participation in the management or capital of an enterprise of another contracting State, or when both

Allocation of Business Income between States for the Purpose of Taxation. This method was favored by most countries at that time.[38]

Since that moment,[39] the arm's length principle has been the preferred method for allocating business income between head offices and permanent establishments and also between related companies both in the OECD Model Tax Convention on Income and on Capital (OECD Model) and in the United Nations Model Double Taxation Convention between Developed and Developing Countries (UN Model) as well as being the relevant principle embedded in most transfer pricing rules around the world.

III. THE ORIGINS OF THE ARM'S LENGTH PRINCIPLE: THE LEGAL FICTION

Income tax law is, per se, a fiction.[40] Income tax law, indeed, establishes legal fictions in order to tax transactions which happen in reality. Otherwise stated, 'Income tax law cannot tax economic transactions directly. Rather, it taxes the legal forms that we use to represent economic transactions.'[41]

Within the general fiction of income tax law, many other fictions have been adopted: the concept of 'corporation', the limited responsibility of a corporation's shareholders, the distinction between debt and equity among a corporation's form of

enterprises are owned or controlled by the same interests, and as the result of such situation there exists, in their commercial or financial relations, conditions different from those which would have been made between independent enterprises, any item of profit or loss which should normally have appeared in the accounts of one enterprise, but which has been, in this manner, diverted to the other enterprise, shall be entered in the accounts of such former enterprise, subject to the rights of appeal allowed under the law of the State of such enterprise' (League of Nations Fiscal Committee, Report to the Council on the Fourth Session of the Committee. C.399.M.204. 1933.II.A., Geneva, June 15th to 26th, 1933).

38. League of Nations, *Taxation of Foreign and National Enterprises: Vol. IV, Methods of Allocating Taxable Income*, C.425(b).M.217(b).1933.II.A, Geneva, 1933.
39. The first tax treaty that included the arm's length principle was the United States-France Tax Treaty negotiated in 1930 and signed in 1932.
40. Prof. John Prebble refers to this phenomenon as 'Ectopia'. See Prebble, J., 'Ectopia, Formalism, and Anti-avoidance Rules in Income Tax Law', in: Krawietz, W., MacCormick, N. & von Wright, G.H. (eds.), *Prescriptive Formality and Normative Rationality in Modern Legal Systems* (Berlin: Festschrift for Robert S. Summers, Duncker & Humblot, 1994), pp. 367-383; Prebble, J., '*Philosophical and Design Problems That Arise from the Ectopic Nature of Income Tax Law and Their Impact on the Taxation of International Trade and Investment*', Chinese Yearbook of International Law and Affairs 13 (1995), pp. 111-139; Prebble, J., *Can Income Tax Law Be Simplified?*, NZ Journal of Taxation Law and Policy 2 (1996), p. 187; Prebble, J., *Should Tax Legislation Be Written from a Principles and Purpose Point of View of a Precise and Detailed Point of View?*, British Tax Review 112 (1998).
41. Prebble, J., *Fictions of Income Tax*, Victoria University of Wellington Legal Research Paper No. 29/2011, Electronic copy available at: http://ssrn.com/abstract=1604978, p. 3.

financing, and the notion of 'groups', *inter alia*, are concepts which would not, per se, exist in reality but do find their tangible base for existence into contractual legal arrangements.[42]

Among these fictions, the arm's length principle is also a legal fiction[43] which embeds and builds upon other fictions.[44] The generally recognized authoritative statement of the arm's length principle is contained into Article 9, paragraph 1, of the OECD Model:

> Where
>
> a) an enterprise of a Contracting State participates directly or indirectly in the management, control or capital of an enterprise of the other Contracting State, or
> b) the same persons participate directly or indirectly in the management, control or capital of an enterprise of a Contracting State and an enterprise of the other Contracting State,
>
> and in either case conditions are made or imposed between the two enterprises in their commercial or financial relations which differ from those which would be made between independent enterprises, then any profits which would, but for those conditions, have accrued to one of the enterprises, but, by reason of those conditions, have not so accrued, may be included in the profits of that enterprise and taxed accordingly.

The perspective of the arm's length principle as a legal fiction was already obvious when the principle was first identified and generally accepted in 1933.[45] This

42. Prebble, J., *Fictions of Income Tax*, Victoria University of Wellington Legal Research Paper No. 29/2011, Electronic copy available at: http://ssrn.com/abstract=1604978, p. 3.
43. Wilkie, J.S., *Reflecting on the 'Arm's Length Principle': What is the 'Principle'? Where Next?*, in: Schön, W. & Konrad, K.A. (eds.), *Fundamentals of International Transfer Pricing in Law and Economics* (Munich: Springer, 2012), pp. 137-156.
44. To some extent, it could even be stated that the arm's length principle is a fiction on top of a fiction since, as shown below, it aims at treating two integrated parts of the same MNE – i.e., two corporations, fictitious themselves – as separate and independent elements. Moreover, when applied to PEs, the arm's length principle is a fiction on top of a fiction on top of another fiction since it aims at treating two parts of the same integrated corporation – fictitious itself – as two corporations – second fiction – which are separate and independent – third fiction.
45. The abovementioned Carroll Report was, indeed, stating the following:

> Enterprises carrying on business in two or more countries, especially if countries have different language, currency and economic conditions, very frequently organise a company in each country in conformity with the requirements of its commercial or company law. Thus, instead of extending its operations into each country through a branch of its own organisation, the parent enterprise conducts its operations through a subsidiary, which, in law, is a separate legal entity. The parent must therefore, in strict law, deal with the subsidiary company as if it were a separate legal person. In other words, the legal transactions between the parent and the subsidiary should be conducted in the same manner as similar transactions between independent legal persons. As long as the intercompany transactions are carried on under the same circumstances and conditions and on the same terms as they would be between two entirely separate and independent persons, dealing with each other in an open market, and in a manner which is graphically described as at 'arm's length', the tax authorities in general respect the separate legal existence of the subsidiary company and tax it on the basis of its own declaration as supported by its properly kept separate accounts. To verify this declaration and accounts, the tax authorities may enquire into the current of

principle, indeed, was based on the legal fiction of treating two parts of a single enterprise (a legal fiction, itself) or two enterprises belonging to the same group of companies (another legal fiction) as 'separate legal entities' pursuing their own interest. The assessment of this legal fiction was based on the analysis of the 'legal arrangements' between the different enterprises (or 'dealings', in the case of permanent establishments). The result of this assessment should have been performed by a 'comparison' of 'conditions [...] made or imposed between the two enterprises in their commercial or financial relations [and] [...] those which would be made between independent enterprises'.

When analyzing these factors, it is evident how the arm's length principle should have worked and how consistent and 'fair' the results of its application should have been. In the 'real' world, indeed, where income tax law and all of its embedded fictions are generally accepted and included into the reality, separate legal entities as well as legal arrangements do commonly exist (and are clearly observable); therefore, a comparison of 'conditions made or imposed' between non-independent enterprises and those between independent enterprises should have been applicable, at least in principle.

The application of the arm's length principle was fundamentally based on three pillars: the fiction of separate legal entities (the so-called separate entity approach), the relevance of the contractual arrangements, and the comparability of the transaction. According to the separate entity approach, two parts of a single enterprise or two enterprises belonging to the same group of companies should have been treated as separate legal entities pursuing their own interests. The Organisation for Economic Co-operation and Development (OECD) already provided a clarification of this concept in its first guidelines issued in 1995 ('1995 Guidelines'):[46]

> By seeking to adjust profits by reference to the conditions which would have obtained between independent enterprises in comparable transactions and comparable circumstances (i.e., in 'comparable uncontrolled transactions'), the arm's length principle follows the approach of treating the members of an MNE group as operating as separate entities rather than as inseparable parts of a single unified business.[47]

Second, concerning the relevance of contractual arrangements, the analysis of the 'legal arrangements' between the different enterprises (or 'dealings', in the case of

business between the local subsidiary and the parent company or other subsidiary companies of the parent, which may for convenience be termed associated companies, and scrutinise carefully the results of interlocking transactions. If this is difficult, they may resort to a comparison with similar enterprises and make an empirical assessment upon the basis of turnover, or in accordance with one or another of the empirical methods described above in discussing the allocation of profits of local branches of foreign enterprises (Carroll Report, p. 46).

46. OECD, *Transfer Pricing Guidelines for Multinational Enterprises and Tax Administrations* (Paris: OECD, 1995). For reason of simplification, the 1995 Guidelines referred to hereinafter also include the amendments made by the updates in 1996 (DAFFE/CFA(96)2), 1997 (DAFFE/CFA(97)27 and DAFFE/CFA/WD(97)11/REV1), 1999 (DAFFE/CFA(99)31), 2008 (CTPA/CFA(2008)30/REV1) and 2009 (CTPA/CFA(2009)51/REV1).
47. 1995 Guidelines, para. 23.

permanent establishments) should have been based on the legal structure adopted by the related parties involved in the transaction since the focus of the analysis should have been primarily on the assessment of the arm's length 'pricing' of the transaction. This was previously clarified by the OECD in its 1979 Report ('1979 Report')[48] when it was established that, in cases 'other than exceptional', the actual transactions should have been recognized as starting point of the assessment of the arm's length nature of an intra-group transaction.[49] In the 1979 Report, indeed, it is evident throughout the wording of the entire document how the scope of the adjustments and the focus of the attention was the 'price' of a transaction rather than the overall structure.[50]

Finally, in regard to the comparability of the transaction, the assessment of the arm's length nature of the transaction should have been performed by a 'comparison' of 'conditions made or imposed' between non-independent enterprises and those between independent enterprises. In this context, the 1979 Report was indeed referring to the comparable uncontrolled price as 'the most appropriate to use and in theory the easiest' since the arm's length principle would have 'ideally required direct reference to prices in comparable transactions between enterprises independent of each other or between the group and unrelated parties'.[51]

IV. THE EVOLUTION OF THE ARM'S LENGTH PRINCIPLE: THE ECONOMIC REALITY

A. General Background

As emphasized in the previous section, the arm's length principle was conceived as a legal fiction. Nevertheless, the principle soon evolved to reflect the economic reality of the transactions between related parties.

When the above-mentioned 1979 Report was included into the 1995 Guidelines, it was recognized, for the first time, how 'transfer pricing is not an exact science but does require the exercise of judgment on the part of both the tax administration and taxpayer'.[52] Those guidelines were already embedding an increasing amount of economic considerations into the interpretation of the principle and had to recognize how this interpretation was often unable to produce a unique and objective result.

The 1995 Guidelines were subsequently revised and updated several times between 1996 and 2008.[53] However, a substantial revision of these guidelines was made in 2010 when the OECD radically amended Chapters I-III and inserted a

48. OECD, *Transfer Pricing and Multinational Enterprises* (Paris: OECD, 1979).
49. 1979 Report, para. 23.
50. This aim is clear, *inter alia*, in the wording of the 1979 Report, para. 23, where it is stated that 'the aim in short is, for tax purposes, to adjust the price for the actual transaction to an arm's length price'.
51. 1979 Report, para. 11.
52. 1995 Guidelines, para. 1.12.
53. See the updates in 1996 (DAFFE/CFA(96)2), 1997 (DAFFE/CFA(97)27 and DAFFE/CFA/WD(97)11/REV1), 1999 (DAFFE/CFA(99)31), 2008 (CTPA/CFA(2008)30/REV1) and 2009 (CTPA/CFA(2009)51/REV1).

completely new Chapter IX addressing 'business restructurings'.[54] As a result of this update, the following changes were implemented in the 2010 OECD Guidelines (2010 Guidelines):[55]

- The hierarchy of transfer pricing methods, whereby the transactional profit methods were considered to be 'last resort methods' compared to the traditional transaction methods, was removed. Consequently, the 'most appropriate method to the circumstances of the case' became the relevant criteria to select the method to apply.[56]
- The guidance on comparability analysis was substantially extended and embedded into a new Chapter III.[57]
- Additional guidance was provided for the application of transactional profit methods.[58]
- As mentioned above, a new chapter was introduced entirely dedicated to issues related to business restructurings.[59]

Between the two updates, the OECD also worked on the issue of attribution of profits to permanent establishments which resulted, first in 2008 and then in 2010, in the issuing of the so-called Authorized OECD Approach (AOA).[60]

---

54. The OECD also updated the Foreword, the Preface, the Glossary, Chapters IV-VIII and the annexes (see CTPA/CFA(2010)47).
55. OECD, *Transfer Pricing Guidelines for Multinational Enterprises and Tax Administrations* (Paris: OECD, 2010). These changes were implemented as the result of two OECD reports: the report on transfer pricing aspects of business restructurings (OECD, *Report on Transfer Pricing Aspects of Business Restructurings*, 22 Jul. 2010) and the report on the review of comparability and profit methods (OECD, *Review of Comparability and Profit Methods*, 22 Jul. 2010). For further details on these revisions, see Lucas Mas, M.O. & Cottani, G., '*OECD Proposed Revision of Chapters I-III of the OECD Transfer Pricing Guidelines: Business Comments on Selected Issues*', International Transfer Pricing Journal 17 (4/2010); Oosterhoff, D. & Wingerter, B., *The New OECD Guidelines: The Good, the Bad and the Ugly*, International Transfer Pricing Journal 18 (2/2011); BNA Report, *Proposed Revision Of Chapters I-III of the OECD Transfer Pricing Guidelines*, Bloomberg BNA (June 2010).
56. 2010 Guidelines, para. 2.2.
57. 2010 Guidelines, Chapters I and III.
58. 2010 Guidelines, Chapter II.
59. 2010 Guidelines, Chapter IX.
60. OECD, *Report on the Attribution of Profits to Permanent Establishments* (Paris: OECD 2008); OECD, *2010 Report on the Attribution of Profits to Permanent Establishments* (Paris: OECD 2010). For the analysis of some relevant aspects of this document, see Baker, P. & Collier, Richard, *2008 OECD Model: Changes to the Commentary on Article 7 and the Attribution of Profits to Permanent Establishments*, Bulletin for International Taxation (May/June 2009), pp. 199-203; Bobbett, C. & Avery Jones, J.F., '*The Proposed Redraft of Article 7 of the OECD Model*', Bulletin for International Taxation (January 2010), pp. 20-27; Pijl, H., *Interpretation of Article 7 of the OECD Model, Permanent Establishment Financing and Other Dealings*, Bulletin for International Taxation (June 2011), pp. 294-306; Kamphuis, E., *Significant People Functions and Functional Ownership: The New Motto in Transfer Pricing*, Tax Management Transfer Pricing Report (17/2008); Moerer, O. & Russo, A., *Questioning the Comparability of Capital Structures under the Thin Capitalization Approach to PE Profit Attribution*, Tax Management Transfer Pricing Report (20/2011); Oosterhoff, D., *The True Importance of Significant People Functions*, International Transfer Pricing Journal (March/April 2008), pp. 68-75; Bennett, M., *The Attribution of Profits to Permanent Establishments: The 2008 Commentary on Art. 7 of the OECD Model Convention*, European Taxation (September 2008), pp. 467-470; Schnitger, A., *Comments on the*

The current work of the OECD on the Base Erosion and Profit Shifting (BEPS) project[61] with specific reference to Actions 8, 9, and 10 is further revising the 2010 Guidelines and intending to embed more economic considerations into the interpretation of the arm's length principle.

The following sections will analyze how the arm's length principle has been evolving from its origins of 'legal fiction' into a more 'economic principle'. The focus will be placed on the above-identified three pillars: the separate entity approach,[62] the relevance of contractual arrangements,[63] and the comparability of the transaction.[64]

B. The Separate Entity Approach

As mentioned in the previous section, one of the fundamental pillars on which the arm's length principle is based is constituted by the 'separate entity approach': entities within a group (as well as different parts of the same entity, i.e., permanent establishments) should be considered as separate from each other rather than belonging to the same group or entity. This concept has always been embedded into the guidelines provided by the OECD and ultimately confirmed, as well, by the AOA as well as the 2010 Guidelines.

The AOA was based on the fundamental 'separate legal entity approach' recognizing that a permanent establishment is a 'separate and independent enterprise engaged in the same or similar activities under the same or similar conditions'.[65] Additionally, the 2010 Guidelines were making reference to the separate entity approach in the newly introduced Chapter IX when addressing the concept of 'group-level business reasons' of a restructuring.[66]

However, this principle, embedded into the legal fiction of the arm's length principle, in some cases, appeared to be 'modified' in order to reflect the 'economic reality' of specific situations. The OECD had previously seemed to slightly modify this principle in the 1995 Guidelines. Indeed, when dealing with the topic of intra-group services, the 1995 Guidelines introduced the concept of 'incidental benefits attributable solely to [...] being part of a larger concern' (so-called implicit support):[67]

> Similarly, an associated enterprise should not be considered to receive an intra-group service when it obtains incidental benefits attributable solely to its being

Klaus Vogel Lecture – Problems Arising under Domestic Tax Law Due to the Introduction of the Authorised OECD Approach, Bulletin for International Taxation (April/May 2013), pp. 211-215; Kofler, G. & van Thiel, S., *The 'Authorised OECD Approach' and EU Tax Law*, European Taxation (August 2011), pp. 327-333.

61. OECD, *Action Plan on Base Erosion and Profit Shifting* (Paris: OECD Publishing, 2013); OECD, *Addressing Base Erosion and Profit Shifting* (Paris: OECD Publishing, 2013).
62. See Section 4.2.
63. See Section 4.3.
64. See Section 4.4.
65. AOA, Part I, para. 8.
66. 2010 Guidelines, para. 9.178.
67. 1995 Guidelines, para. 7.13.

> part of a larger concern, and not to any specific activity being performed. For example, no service would be received where an associated enterprise by reason of its affiliation alone has a credit-rating higher than it would if it were unaffiliated, but an intra-group service would usually exist where the higher credit rating were due to a guarantee by another group member, or where the enterprise benefitted from the group's reputation deriving from global marketing and public relations campaigns. In this respect, passive association should be distinguished from active promotion of the MNE group's attributes that positively enhances the profit-making potential of particular members of the group. Each case must be determined according to its own facts and circumstances.

Another modification of the separate entity approach could also be ascertained in the above-mentioned AOA. The underlying separate legal entity approach was disregarded when the issue of creditworthiness of a permanent establishment was analyzed. In this context, the OECD stipulated that a permanent establishment should have had the same creditworthiness of the enterprise it belongs to,[68] thereby disregarding treating the two as being separate legal entities. The following two justifications were provided, in that context, by the OECD:

(a) 'The authorised OECD approach is based on the factual situation of the enterprise, which is that the capital, risks, etc. are fungible, so it would be inconsistent to grant all the benefits of synergy to the head office'.[69]
(b) 'There are factors other than capital such as reputation, profitability, management quality, risk diversification that also affect creditworthiness. Again it is hard to understand why all these factors should be treated as belonging to one part of the enterprise'.[70]

However, the AOA also provided a number of examples of when an exception to this modification (therefore, realigning the principle to the separate legal entity approach) could have been made.[71]

Finally, the guidance introduced in 2010 in the context of business restructuring were also making often reference to the concept of 'group synergies'.[72]

68. AOA, Part I, paras. 30, 33 and 99-104.
69. AOA, Part I, para. 101.
70. AOA, Part I, para. 102.
71. AOA, Part I, para. 100 identifies an exception in cases:

> where for regulatory reasons the capital attributed to the PE of one jurisdiction is not available to meet liabilities incurred elsewhere in the enterprise' and AOA, part II, para. 30 illustrates an exception in cases 'where assets located in a specific jurisdiction are not available to meet claims outside the jurisdiction or have been earmarked to support a particular financial instrument in order to give that instrument the desired rating by a credit rating agency.

72. 2010 Guidelines, paras. 9.57-9.58.

1. *The Separate Entity Approach in the Post-BEPS World*

The BEPS Project has been addressing the topic of the separate entity approach in various occasions. In this context, it seems that the above-mentioned principles and guidance introduced in 2010 in the context of business restructuring have been now extended to all intra-group transactions.

Under the work on BEPS Action 8, the proposed amendments to Section D of Chapter I of the 2010 Guidelines have dedicated an entire new section to the topic of 'MNE group synergies'.[73] In this context, after explaining the concept of group synergies,[74] the OECD clarifies that certain synergistic benefits may possibly be derived from being part of a group. For this purpose, it should be distinguished between synergistic benefits deriving solely from being part of a group (i.e., the above-mentioned incidental benefits)[75] and synergistic benefits deriving from 'deliberate concerted group actions'.[76] This distinction is of fundamental relevance since, while the former type of benefits should not require an arm's length compensation, the latter type should do so. In order to distinguish the two types of benefits, a comprehensive functional and comparability analysis should be performed.

Therefore, the OECD provides for the application of this concept to all types of intra-group transactions by embedding the concept of group synergies (which was already referred to in Chapter IX on business restructurings) in the first chapter of the proposed new guidelines. This amendment would initially suggest that a 'group approach' might more often prevail over the separate entity approach (since group synergies inherently exist only between associated enterprises). However, the fact that the OECD stipulates that synergies deriving from deliberate concerted group actions should be divided among the members of the group who contribute to their creation[77] seems to demonstrate that the separate entity approach should still be respected. On the other side, prevalence of the group approach over the separate entity approach is still preserved in the event of incidental benefits.

---

73. OECD, *Aligning Transfer Pricing Outcomes with Value Creation, Actions 8-10 – 2015 Final Reports*, OECD/G20 Base Erosion and Profit Shifting Project (Paris: OECD Publishing, 2015), paras. 1.157-1.173. 'Group synergies' are also defined in para. 6.30.
74. OECD, *Aligning Transfer Pricing Outcomes with Value Creation, Actions 8-10 – 2015 Final Reports*, OECD/G20 Base Erosion and Profit Shifting Project (Paris: OECD Publishing, 2015), para. 1.157.
75. OECD, *Aligning Transfer Pricing Outcomes with Value Creation, Actions 8-10 – 2015 Final Reports*, OECD/G20 Base Erosion and Profit Shifting Project (Paris: OECD Publishing, 2015), para. 1.158. Typical examples of these could be a credit rating improvement deriving solely to being part of a group (see paras. 1.164-1.166) or 'simple recognition of group membership or the use of the group name merely to reflect the fact of group membership' (see para. 6.81).
76. OECD, *Aligning Transfer Pricing Outcomes with Value Creation, Actions 8-10 – 2015 Final Reports*, OECD/G20 Base Erosion and Profit Shifting Project (Paris: OECD Publishing, 2015), para. 1.159. Typical examples of these are illustrated in paras. 1.167, 1.170-1.173.
77. OECD, *Aligning Transfer Pricing Outcomes with Value Creation, Actions 8-10 – 2015 Final Reports*, OECD/G20 Base Erosion and Profit Shifting Project (Paris: OECD Publishing, 2015), para. 1.162.

C. The Relevance of Contractual Arrangements

The second pillar on which the arm's length principle is based is the relevance of 'contractual arrangements': the 'legal arrangements' established between the different enterprises (or 'dealings' in the case of permanent establishments) would define the legal structure adopted by the related parties involved in the transaction, whereas the focus of the assessment of the arm's length principle should have been primarily based on the 'pricing' of the transaction.

As mentioned before, this was already clarified in the 1979 Report which established that the contractual arrangements between associated enterprises should have been the starting point of an analysis aimed at defining the arm's length price of a transaction. The possibility of not recognizing the actual transactions undertaken was granted to the tax administration only in exceptional cases. However, the same 1979 Report also mentioned the possibility of considering the 'underlying reality behind an arrangement' without, however, further investigating and thoroughly explaining when this should have been the case.[78] Nevertheless, that report was already making clear how the contractual characterization of the transaction was not the relevant factor determining the deductibility of interest expenses in regard to the question of 'loans versus equity contributions'.[79]

Additionally, when referring to the topic of intangibles (with specific reference to license fees, as well as payments related to Cost Contribution Arrangements – 'CCAs'[80]) and, more extensively, to the topic of services,[81] the deductibility of the related intra-group costs was subject to the presence of a 'real benefit'. Moreover, the 1979 Report mentioned that, in some cases, a transaction which is, 'in law', a sale of goods could be considered to be a provision of services by examining the specific functions performed by the parties involved.[82]

The 1995 Guidelines increased the emphasis on this point. On the one hand, these guidelines were placing more emphasis on the analysis of the 'conditions' rather than on the mere 'pricing' of a transaction. Additionally, even if the 'exceptionality' for

78. In this regard, the wording of the 1979 Report, para. 24, was the following:

> Associated enterprises are, however, able to make a much greater variety of contracts and arrangements than can unrelated enterprises because the normal conflict of interest which would exist between independent parties is often absent. Associated enterprises may and frequently do conclude arrangements of a specific nature that are not or are very rarely encountered between unrelated parties (cost contribution arrangements for research and development expenditure as discussed in Chapter III of the report would be one example). This may be done for various economic, legal or fiscal reasons dependent on the circumstances in a particular case. Moreover, contracts within an MNE could be quite easily altered, suspended, extended or terminated accordingly to the overall strategies of the MNE as a whole and such alterations may even be made retroactively. In such instances tax authorities would have to determine what is the underlying reality behind an arrangement in considering what the appropriate arm's length price would be.

79. 1979 Report, paras. 183-191.
80. 1979 Report, paras. 89, 112.
81. 1979 Report, paras. 151-159.
82. 1979 Report, para. 35.

non-recognition of the transaction actually undertaken was still present, the OECD dedicated much more time explaining in which cases this non-recognition could have occurred.[83] These cases were identified as the following:

(a) 'where the economic substance of a transaction differs from its form';[84] or
(b) 'where, whilst the form and substance of the transaction are the same, the arrangements made in relation to the transaction, viewed in their totality, differ from those which would have been adopted by independent enterprises behaving in a commercially rational manner and the actual structure practically impedes the tax administration from determining an appropriate transfer price'.[85]

In those circumstances, it would have been 'appropriate and legitimate for a tax administration to consider disregarding the structure' of the transaction; therefore, the tax administration was empowered by Article 9 to adjust the conditions of intra-group arrangements[86] by means, *inter alia*, of reference to 'alternatively structured transactions between independent parties'.[87] However, the OECD specified that there was a substantial difference between restructuring a transaction that is considered to be 'generally inappropriate', and using alternative structures as comparable which instead could have been considered as useful.[88]

Additionally, the 1995 Guidelines, when introducing extensive reference to the comparability factors,[89] mentioned the 'contractual terms of a transaction' (which could also be eventually found in correspondence and communications) as relevant indicia for the performance of the functional analysis.[90] However, in absence of written terms, the contractual relationships could have been derived from 'conduct' and 'economic principles' of the parties.[91] Moreover, even when those terms existed in writing, it would still be necessary to analyze that they were reflecting the 'conduct of the parties'.[92]

The relevance of contractual arrangements, however, seemed to be radically weakened, first, by the above-mentioned AOA and then by the 2010 Guidelines. In regard to the changes introduced by the AOA, the OECD provided relevance to the functional analysis by introducing the concept of 'significant people functions' as a key factor in the absence of existing contracts as the relevant basis for allocating income

83. 1995 Guidelines, paras. 1.36-1.41.
84. 1995 Guidelines, para. 1.37. This circumstance was explained by using the example of the 'loans versus equity contributions' topic, which was removed in the 1995 Guidelines.
85. 1995 Guidelines, para. 1.37.
86. 1995 Guidelines, para. 1.38.
87. 1995 Guidelines, para. 1.40.
88. 1995 Guidelines, para. 1.41.
89. See section below.
90. 1995 Guidelines, para. 1.28.
91. 1995 Guidelines, para. 1.28.
92. 1995 Guidelines, para. 1.29.

between an enterprise and a permanent establishment located in a different country.[93] This concept was introduced in order to supplement the fact that a permanent establishment, differently from an enterprise, is a 'mere fiction' (i.e., not even a legal one)[94] and, therefore, the assessment of the profits to be attributed could not be based on the analysis of the legal framework.[95] Hence, the identification of the significant people functions was selected as the relevant criteria in order to attribute assets 'economically owned',[96] risks inherent in or created by, and 'free' capital attributable to a permanent establishment.

At the same time, the 2010 Guidelines introduced a new chapter addressing business restructuring.[97] In this context, the functional analysis assumed more relevance when assessing intra-group arrangements; however, more focus was placed on the 'risk factor'. Indeed, the allocation of risks among different parties was defined as being an essential element of the functional analysis and, for the purpose of defining this allocation, contractual terms where considered as the 'starting point' of the analysis.[98] However, the analysis of the contractual terms should have been supplemented by an assessment of the following questions:

(a) whether the conduct of the related parties was in line with the risks contractually allocated;
(b) whether this risk allocation was at arm's length; and
(c) what the outcome was of this risk allocation.[99]

In order to answer these questions, the OECD referred to new concepts such as 'control over risk' and 'financial capacity to assume the risk'.[100] Additionally, extensive guidance supplemented by numerous examples was provided for this purpose.[101] The consequences of the risk allocation should have ultimately been that the party to which the risks were allocated should, on the one hand, bear the costs related to the managing, mitigating, and realization of such risks and, on the other, be compensated with greater expected returns.[102]

93. This notion was different in the case of enterprises operating in the financial sector. In this case, reference was made to the concept of 'key entrepreneurial risk-taking functions'.
94. AOA, Part I, para. 12.
95. AOA, Part I, paras. 13-14.
96. The 'economic ownership' is defined by the AOA as:

> the equivalent of ownership for income tax purposes by a separate enterprise, with the attendant benefits and burdens (e.g., the right to the income attributable to the ownership of the asset, such as royalties; the right to depreciate a depreciable asset; and the potential exposure to gains or losses from the appreciation or depreciation of the asset) (AOA, part I, footnote 4).

97. 2010 Guidelines, Chapter IX.
98. 2010 Guidelines, para. 9.11.
99. 2010 Guidelines, para. 9.12.
100. 2010 Guidelines, para. 9.21.
101. 2010 Guidelines, Chapter IX, Part I.
102. 2010 Guidelines, para. 9.39.

Moreover, when identifying the transactions in the scope of the business restructuring, the OECD made clear reference to the relevance of functions performed, assets used, and risks assumed by the parties involved, although a review of the legal 'rights and obligations' should always be considered.[103] The emphasis of elements different from the contractual arrangements was also emphasized with regard to the issue of 'indemnification' whereby an analysis of the 'options realistically available', the 'remuneration of the transactions', the 'financial conditions of the termination', the 'substance of the arrangement', the 'actual conduct of the parties', and the 'significant investments underlying the transactions' should have contributed to answering the question of whether independent enterprises would have agreed on any indemnification clause.[104]

However, the most obvious proof of the change by the OECD towards a radically decreased reliance on the contractual arrangements was embedded into a special section of Chapter IX of the 2010 Guidelines.[105] This section was, indeed, entirely dedicated to analyzing the topic of 'Recognition of the actual transaction undertaken', and it did so by providing extensive guidance. From this section, it was clear that the tax administration was empowered, for transfer pricing purposes, with the possibility of non-recognizing intra-group transactions. However, as already established by paragraph 1.65 of the 2010 Guidelines,[106] this non-recognition should have been limited to 'exceptional cases'.[107]

The OECD provided, in this context, extensive guidance regarding the meaning of 'exceptional'. In general, this term was considered to be the equivalent of 'rare' or 'unusual'.[108] Additionally, the abovementioned two circumstances of: (a) economic substance of a transaction differing its form, and (b) diverging characterization or structure of the transaction from the one that would have been adopted by independent parties were considered as representing this exceptionality.[109] This second circumstance should have been tested by referencing concepts such as 'normal commercial behaviour' (and 'behaviour test'), options realistically available, 'economically interrelated' transactions, and 'group-level business reasons'.[110]

The consequences of the non-recognition of a transaction were identified by either: (a) disregarding the characterization and re-characterizing the transaction or (b) adjusting the conditions of the agreement in a 'commercially rational manner'.[111]

103. 2010 Guidelines, paras. 9.53-9.56.
104. 2010 Guidelines, paras. 9.106-9.113.
105. 2010 Guidelines, Chapter IX, Part IV.
106. Presented before as para. 23 of the 1979 report and as para. 1.37 of the 1995 Guidelines.
107. 2010 Guidelines, para. 9.168.
108. 2010 Guidelines, para. 9.168.
109. 2010 Guidelines, para. 9.169.
110. 2010 Guidelines, paras. 9.171-9.179.
111. 2010 Guidelines, paras. 9.183-9.184.

1. *The Relevance of Contractual Arrangements in the Post-BEPS World*

Also in this case, the BEPS Project has been addressing the topic of the relevance of contractual arrangement in various occasions. As with the previous topic, in this context, it appears that the above-mentioned principles and guidance introduced in 2010 in the context of business restructuring is now extended to all intra-group transactions.

First of all, under the work on BEPS Actions 8, 9, and 10, the concept of 'delineation of the actual transaction undertaken' has been introduced. This concept, however, was already embedded into the principles of the above-mentioned Chapter IX of the 2010 Guidelines under a different terminology and would now be incorporated into the first chapter of the proposed new guidelines in which it would apply to all types of transactions and not only to business restructurings.

On this topic, the proposed amendments to Section D of Chapter I of the 2010 Guidelines clearly state that the review of contractual arrangements are only the starting point of the analysis.[112] The relevant transfer pricing analysis will, indeed, be derived from the definition of the actual conduct of the associated enterprises which will be defined by reference to the economically relevant characteristics of the actual transaction.[113] As a consequence:

> If the characteristics of the transaction that are economically relevant are inconsistent with the written contract between the associated enterprises, the actual transaction should generally be delineated for purposes of the transfer pricing analysis in accordance with the characteristics of the transaction reflected in the conduct of the parties.[114]

Interestingly enough, in this context, the OECD makes reference to the concept of 'material differences' between contractual terms and conduct of the parties in order to provide for a standard of when the delineation of a transaction should occur.[115]

Therefore, for the purposes of delineating the actual transaction undertaken, the performance of a functional analysis seems to be of vital importance. In this situation, the OECD spends a considerable number of pages in defining the 'risk factor' related to this functional analysis[116] by explaining new concepts such as 'risk management',

112. OECD, *Aligning Transfer Pricing Outcomes with Value Creation, Actions 8-10 – 2015 Final Reports*, OECD/G20 Base Erosion and Profit Shifting Project (Paris: OECD Publishing, 2015), para. 1.42. This is confirmed also in para. 1.81.
113. OECD, *Aligning Transfer Pricing Outcomes with Value Creation, Actions 8-10 – 2015 Final Reports*, OECD/G20 Base Erosion and Profit Shifting Project (Paris: OECD Publishing, 2015), paras. 1.43-1.50.
114. OECD, *Aligning Transfer Pricing Outcomes with Value Creation, Actions 8-10 – 2015 Final Reports*, OECD/G20 Base Erosion and Profit Shifting Project (Paris: OECD Publishing, 2015), para. 1.45.
115. OECD, *Aligning Transfer Pricing Outcomes with Value Creation, Actions 8-10 – 2015 Final Reports*, OECD/G20 Base Erosion and Profit Shifting Project (Paris: OECD Publishing, 2015), para. 1.46.
116. OECD, *Aligning Transfer Pricing Outcomes with Value Creation, Actions 8-10 – 2015 Final Reports*, OECD/G20 Base Erosion and Profit Shifting Project (Paris: OECD Publishing, 2015), paras. 1.56-1.106.

'financial capacity to assume risk', 'control over risk', 'risk mitigation', 'economic significance of risk',[117] and a detailed definition of 'risk' itself.[118] Additionally, it introduces a detailed six-step analysis in order to assess the relevant risks of a transaction, which party bears those risks, and, consequently, which party should be entitled to the related profit or loss (otherwise defined as 'unanticipated returns' and 'unanticipated losses').[119] To achieve this, it is specified that, in order to determine whether the contractual assumption of risk is consistent with the conduct of the parties, it would be relevant to ascertain: (a) that the parties follow the contractual terms, and (b) whether the party which assumes the risk (b1) exercises control over the risk and (b2) has the financial capacity to assume risk.[120]

However, it is also stated that, in this situation, risks are not necessarily more important than functions and assets.[121] Furthermore, the analysis of characteristics of property and services, economic circumstances, and business strategies will prove relevant for the purposes of delineating the actual transaction undertaken. After delineating the actual transaction undertaken (and identifying the substance of the commercial and financial relationships), the OECD emphasizes that the pricing of the transaction should follow such delineation.[122] Nevertheless, the transaction between related parties could also be disregarded (as it has always been, as previously indicated under the OECD guidelines).

The guidance on the recognition of the accurately delineated transaction and, consequently, on any disregarding of transactions between related parties has been considerably changed by the work on BEPS Actions 8, 9, and 10. While the exceptionality of the circumstance that such disregarding should occur has been confirmed,[123] the description of when this exceptionality materializes has been amended. For this purpose, the OECD has replaced the two above-mentioned circumstances (i.e., (a) economic substance of a transaction differing its form and (b) diverging characterization or structure of the transaction from the one that would have been adopted by independent parties) with the following:

117. Some of these concepts, however, were already embedded in the principles established in Chapter IX of the 2010 Guidelines.
118. Whereby the different concepts of 'Strategic risks or marketplace risks', 'Infrastructure or operational risks', 'Financial risks', 'Transactional risks', and 'Hazard risks' are described.
119. OECD, *Aligning Transfer Pricing Outcomes with Value Creation, Actions 8-10 – 2015 Final Reports*, OECD/G20 Base Erosion and Profit Shifting Project (Paris: OECD Publishing, 2015), paras. 1.71-1.106.
120. OECD, *Aligning Transfer Pricing Outcomes with Value Creation, Actions 8-10 – 2015 Final Reports*, OECD/G20 Base Erosion and Profit Shifting Project (Paris: OECD Publishing, 2015), para. 1.86.
121. OECD, *Aligning Transfer Pricing Outcomes with Value Creation, Actions 8-10 – 2015 Final Reports*, OECD/G20 Base Erosion and Profit Shifting Project (Paris: OECD Publishing, 2015), para. 1.59.
122. OECD, *Aligning Transfer Pricing Outcomes with Value Creation, Actions 8-10 – 2015 Final Reports*, OECD/G20 Base Erosion and Profit Shifting Project (Paris: OECD Publishing, 2015), paras. 1.119-1.121.
123. OECD, *Aligning Transfer Pricing Outcomes with Value Creation, Actions 8-10 – 2015 Final Reports*, OECD/G20 Base Erosion and Profit Shifting Project (Paris: OECD Publishing, 2015), para. 1.121.

> The transaction as accurately delineated may be disregarded, and if appropriate, replaced by an alternative transaction, where the arrangements made in relation to the transaction, viewed in their totality, differ from those which would have been adopted by independent enterprises behaving in a commercially rational manner in comparable circumstances, thereby preventing determination of a price that would be acceptable to both of the parties taking into account their respective perspectives and the options realistically available to each of them at the time of entering into the transaction.[124]

In this context, it is specified that it should be relevant 'to consider whether the MNE group as a whole is left worse off on a pre-tax basis'.[125] Therefore, it now appears clear that, in order to understand whether a transaction could be disregarded, the relevance is placed on the analysis of the 'commercial rationality' of the arrangement.[126]

Finally, the topic of the relevance of contractual arrangement has also been analyzed during the work on BEPS Action 8 on 'Intangibles'.[127] In this context, the OECD has clearly stated that, when analyzing the question, for transfer pricing purposes, of who has ownership of intangibles, a six-step analysis should be performed[128] whereby legal ownership and contractual arrangements are only the starting point.[129] The relevance is, indeed, placed on the functional analysis and intended to identify the member(s) who: (a) 'perform and exercise control' over the functions, (b) 'provide funding and other assets', and (c) 'assume the various risks' associated with the Development, Enhancement, Maintenance, Protection, and Exploitation (so-called DEMPE) of the intangible.[130]

D. The Comparability of the Transaction

The third pillar on which the arm's length principle is based consists of the comparability of the transaction: the assessment of the arm's length nature of a transaction

124. OECD, *Aligning Transfer Pricing Outcomes with Value Creation, Actions 8-10 – 2015 Final Reports*, OECD/G20 Base Erosion and Profit Shifting Project (Paris: OECD Publishing, 2015), para. 1.122.
125. OECD, *Aligning Transfer Pricing Outcomes with Value Creation, Actions 8-10 – 2015 Final Reports*, OECD/G20 Base Erosion and Profit Shifting Project (Paris: OECD Publishing, 2015), para. 1.122.
126. OECD, *Aligning Transfer Pricing Outcomes with Value Creation, Actions 8-10 – 2015 Final Reports*, OECD/G20 Base Erosion and Profit Shifting Project (Paris: OECD Publishing, 2015), para. 1.123.
127. OECD, *Aligning Transfer Pricing Outcomes with Value Creation, Actions 8-10 – 2015 Final Reports*, OECD/G20 Base Erosion and Profit Shifting Project (Paris: OECD Publishing, 2015), Chapter VI.
128. OECD, *Aligning Transfer Pricing Outcomes with Value Creation, Actions 8-10 – 2015 Final Reports*, OECD/G20 Base Erosion and Profit Shifting Project (Paris: OECD Publishing, 2015), para. 6.34.
129. OECD, *Aligning Transfer Pricing Outcomes with Value Creation, Actions 8-10 – 2015 Final Reports*, OECD/G20 Base Erosion and Profit Shifting Project (Paris: OECD Publishing, 2015), paras. 6.32-6.72.
130. OECD, *Aligning Transfer Pricing Outcomes with Value Creation, Actions 8-10 – 2015 Final Reports*, OECD/G20 Base Erosion and Profit Shifting Project (Paris: OECD Publishing, 2015), para. 6.48.

should be performed by a 'comparison' of 'conditions made or imposed' between non-independent enterprises and those between independent enterprises.

As previously mentioned, the 1979 Report placed relevance on the comparable uncontrolled price method by emphasizing it as the most appropriate way to achieve an arm's length result. However, the cost plus method, the resale price method, or 'other methods' were already suggested in that report as being beneficial when no comparable uncontrolled transactions were available.[131]

Moreover, regarding alternatives to the 'pure' application of the arm's length principle (in terms of comparability of the transaction), the use of global formulary apportionments (so-called, at that time, global method) and of 'safe havens' was highly criticized and ultimately discouraged by the OECD.[132] However, this idea found a deviation in the case of attribution of profits to permanent establishments. Indeed, Article 3 of the 1933 proposed 'Draft Convention' was stating that, in certain circumstances, a formulary apportionment could have been used to attribute profits to permanent establishments.[133] This concept survived in paragraph 4 of Article 7 of the OECD Model until 2010 when the changes developed within the AOA were embedded.

The relevance of the comparability of the transaction and of the 'comparability analysis' was emphasized in the 1995 Guidelines which stressed the need for a comprehensive examination of the comparability factors that were identified as characteristics of property or services, functional analysis, contractual terms, economic circumstances, and business strategies.[134] However, at the same time, the OECD included an extensive reference to two other methods into its guidelines[135] (i.e., the 'profit split method' and the 'Transactional Net Margin Method' (TNMM)), which, however, should have been used in 'exceptional situations'.[136]

---

131. 1979 Report, paras. 12-13, 45-75.
132. 1979 Report, paras. 14-16.
133. Article 3 of the proposed 'Draft Convention' stated the following:

> If an establishment does not produce an accounting showing its own operations, or if the accounting produced does not correspond to the normal usages of the trade in the country where the establishment is situated, or if the rectifications provided for in the preceding paragraph cannot be effected, or if the taxpayer agrees, the fiscal authorities may determine empirically the business income by applying a percentage to the turnover of that establishment. This percentage is fixed in accordance with the nature of the transactions in which the establishment is engaged and by comparison with the results obtained by similar enterprises operating in the country.
>
> If the methods of determination described in the preceding paragraphs are found to be inapplicable, the net business income of the permanent establishment may be determined by a computation based on the total income derived by the enterprise from the activities in which such establishment has participated. This determination is made by applying to the total income coefficients based on a comparison of gross receipts, assets, number of hours worked or other appropriate factors, provided such factors be so selected as to ensure results approaching as closely as possible to those which would be reflected by a separate accounting (League of Nations Fiscal Committee, Report to the Council on the Fourth Session of the Committee. C.399.M.204. 1933.II.A., Geneva, June 15th to 26th, 1933).

134. 1995 Guidelines, paras. 1.15-1.35.
135. 1995 Guidelines, paras. 3.1-3.57.
136. 1995 Guidelines, para. 2.49.

The 2010 Guidelines, as previously mentioned, introduced radical changes concerning the topics of transfer pricing methods and the comparability analysis. In regard to the transfer pricing methods, the preference for the traditional transaction methods over the transactional profit methods was removed. Although the former methods were still recognized as the 'most direct' to assess the arm's length principle,[137] the selection process should have aimed at finding 'the most appropriate method for a particular case'.[138] In this context, further guidance was provided for the application of the transactional profit methods.[139] Therefore, the increased reliance on the latter methods over the traditional transaction methods, typically characterized by greater dependence on the comparability analysis, was a major shift by the OECD towards less relevance of the comparability of the transactions.

At the same time, the 2010 Guidelines placed more emphasis on the comparability analysis by dedicating an entire new chapter to the topic[140] wherein the OECD suggested a well-developed nine-step approach in order to identify reliable comparables.[141]

1. *The Comparability of the Transaction in the Post-BEPS World*

As for the other two topics analyzed in the previous sections, the BEPS Project has been dealing with the topic of the comparability of the transaction in various occasions. As a result of this work, on the one hand, the application of methodologies which rely heavily on the comparability analysis seems to be less dependent from this analysis and, on the other, the use of methods less reliant on such a comparability analysis seems to have gained more relevance. Regarding the first point (i.e., the decreasing dependence from the comparability analysis of methodologies which rely heavily on this analysis), the application of the comparable uncontrolled price method appears, in certain cases, to be less dependent on the perfect application of the comparability analysis.

Under the work on BEPS Action 10, the OECD has provided relevance to the use of quoted prices in the context of applying the comparable uncontrolled price method to commodity transactions.[142] Quoted prices, referred to as the prices 'of the commodity in the relevant period obtained in an international or domestic commodity exchange market',[143] are mostly used in developing countries. Reference to these prices in order to assess the arm's length price of a transaction in the context of applying the

137. 2010 Guidelines, para. 2.3.
138. 2010 Guidelines, para. 2.2. This change was anticipated in the wording of the AOA (see AOA, Part I, para. 41).
139. 2010 Guidelines, Chapter II.
140. 2010 Guidelines, Chapter III.
141. 2010 Guidelines, para. 3.4.
142. OECD, *Aligning Transfer Pricing Outcomes with Value Creation, Actions 8-10 – 2015 Final Reports*, OECD/G20 Base Erosion and Profit Shifting Project (Paris: OECD Publishing, 2015), paras. 2.16A-2.16E.
143. OECD, *Aligning Transfer Pricing Outcomes with Value Creation, Actions 8-10 – 2015 Final Reports*, OECD/G20 Base Erosion and Profit Shifting Project (Paris: OECD Publishing, 2015), para. 2.16A.

comparable uncontrolled price method seems to place less emphasis on the comparability of the transaction under review by replacing it with a method based more on proxies for the sake of providing the system with more simplification.

This point has also been confirmed by the work on BEPS Action 10 concerning low value-adding services. In this context, the OECD has suggested a 'simplified approach' in order to determine the arm's length nature of so-called low value-adding intra-group services.[144] After accurately defining this category of services,[145] a simplified methodology has been suggested which provides for a simplified benefit test, the determination of the relevant cost base as a pool of all costs related to those services, the allocation of these costs with allocation keys, and the application of a profit mark-up of 5% for each service that does not need to be justified.[146] As a result, the application of the cost plus method to these types of transactions will be less reliant on the comparability analysis.

Concerning the second point (i.e., the increasing relevance of methods less reliant on a comparability analysis), on the one hand, more relevance appears to be attributed to the use of the profit split method and, on the other, more emphasis has been attributed to the use of other methods.

During the work on BEPS Action 10, the OECD has provided relevance to the use of the profit split method. This work, which should be finalized in 2016 and 2017, aims at revising the 2010 Guidelines in the context of the application of the profit split method with particular reference to a number of specific topics, i.e., most appropriate method, highly integrated business operations, unique and valuable contributions, synergistic benefits, profit splitting factors, and the use of profit split to determine TNMM range, royalty rates, and other payment forms.[147] Additionally, the profit split method has also been suggested as one of the most useful methods when transactions involving intangibles are concerned.[148]

The work on BEPS Action 8 has instead suggested the use of methods alternative to the five classical methods as a valid one.[149] To this end, valuation techniques have

---

144. OECD, *Aligning Transfer Pricing Outcomes with Value Creation, Actions 8-10 – 2015 Final Reports*, OECD/G20 Base Erosion and Profit Shifting Project (Paris: OECD Publishing, 2015), paras. 7.43-7.65.
145. OECD, *Aligning Transfer Pricing Outcomes with Value Creation, Actions 8-10 – 2015 Final Reports*, OECD/G20 Base Erosion and Profit Shifting Project (Paris: OECD Publishing, 2015), paras. 7.44-7.51.
146. OECD, *Aligning Transfer Pricing Outcomes with Value Creation, Actions 8-10 – 2015 Final Reports*, OECD/G20 Base Erosion and Profit Shifting Project (Paris: OECD Publishing, 2015), paras. 7.52-7.63.
147. OECD, *Aligning Transfer Pricing Outcomes with Value Creation, Actions 8-10 – 2015 Final Reports*, OECD/G20 Base Erosion and Profit Shifting Project (Paris: OECD Publishing, 2015), pp. 55-61.
148. OECD, *Aligning Transfer Pricing Outcomes with Value Creation, Actions 8-10 – 2015 Final Reports*, OECD/G20 Base Erosion and Profit Shifting Project (Paris: OECD Publishing, 2015), paras. 6.148-6.152.
149. OECD, *Aligning Transfer Pricing Outcomes with Value Creation, Actions 8-10 – 2015 Final Reports*, OECD/G20 Base Erosion and Profit Shifting Project (Paris: OECD Publishing, 2015), para. 6.136.

been suggested as useful tools.[150] Based on these techniques, transfer prices could be estimated as the result of 'the calculation of the discounted value of projected future income streams or cash flows derived from the exploitation of the intangible being valued'.[151] However, when employing such techniques, careful consideration must be paid to specific concerns, e.g., accuracy of financial projections, assumptions regarding growth rates, discount rates, useful life of intangibles and terminal values, and assumptions regarding taxes.

V. CONCLUSIONS AND PROPOSALS

This chapter has presented the origins of the arm's length principle and its evolution over the past decades. The previous sections have demonstrated how this principle, originally conceived as a legal fiction to allocate business income among different jurisdictions, has soon developed into an economic principle reflecting the economic reality of the transactions.

This development is evident when analyzing the three pillars on which the principle is based: the separate entity approach, the relevance of contractual arrangements, and the comparability of the transaction. In regard to the separate entity approach, the arm's length principle appears to have preserved this pillar. However, over the years, the inclusion of concepts such as implicit support, same creditworthiness between head offices and permanent establishments, and group synergies has, in some circumstances, modified the strength of this factor thereby depriving it, to some extent, of its fundamental importance.

Concerning the relevance of contractual arrangements, the work first conducted by the OECD in 2010 and subsequently within the BEPS Project seems to place more emphasis on the commercial rationality of the transactions undertaken, rather than on their legal structure. In this context, the performance of a comprehensive functional analysis (with a specific focus on functions performed in the case of permanent establishments and risks assumed in the case of associated enterprises) is being provided with increasing relevance. As a result, the possibilities of adjusting the conditions of intra-group arrangements under the application of the arm's length principle may plausibly radically increase in the future.

As far as the comparability of the transaction is concerned, on the one side, the OECD has been placing more emphasis and provided more guidance on the performance of the comparability analysis (with particular emphasis on the functional analysis). However, on the other side, the evolution of transfer pricing methodologies suggested as alternatives to the traditional transaction methods as well as the newly

150. OECD, *Aligning Transfer Pricing Outcomes with Value Creation, Actions 8-10 – 2015 Final Reports*, OECD/G20 Base Erosion and Profit Shifting Project (Paris: OECD Publishing, 2015), paras. 6.153-6.178.
151. OECD, *Aligning Transfer Pricing Outcomes with Value Creation, Actions 8-10 – 2015 Final Reports*, OECD/G20 Base Erosion and Profit Shifting Project (Paris: OECD Publishing, 2015), para. 6.153.

proposed approaches to apply the comparable uncontrolled price method and the cost plus method in specific situations might also suggest less reliance in the future on this third pillar.

As a result, the arm's length principle has evidently become an economic principle whereby business rationales and market principles might increasingly influence its functioning. This point is further substantiated by the inclusion in the OECD Guidelines since 2010[152] of concepts such as 'reasonable expectations', 'options realistically available', 'profit potential', 'substance', and 'actual conduct of the parties' which typically do not require any legalistic consideration. Even more, the work on BEPS Actions 8, 9, and 10 has further stressed the relevance of this point by providing emphasis on new concepts such as 'economically relevant characteristics', 'deliberate concerted group actions', 'anticipated/unanticipated returns' (and 'anticipated/ unanticipated losses'), and 'anticipated (or *ex ante*) remuneration (as opposed to 'actual (or *ex post*) remuneration').

Therefore, currently, at the outset of a post-BEPS world, the following relevant questions could be raised: Is the arm's length principle still a solid and reliable standard? How will its future look in a post-BEPS world? What are the issues and challenges it will face? What are the possible solutions to these issues and challenges?

First, it must be clarified that the arm's length principle is and, based on the author's opinion, most probably will keep being the relevant international standard in the long-term future when allocating business income among different jurisdictions. On the one hand, this principle is already embedded into probably all double tax treaties currently in force, and any deviation from this principle will require a process which would necessitate a considerable amount of time to be completed. On the other hand, the currently suggested alternatives to this principle (i.e., the use of global formulary apportionment) would not provide a solution that would resolve all existing issues. The introduction of such an alternative, indeed, as already clarified by the OECD guidelines, although embedding some advantages into the system (e.g., administrative convenience and certainty to taxpayers;[153] closer representation of the economic reality;[154] and reduction of compliance costs for taxpayers[155]), incorporates numerous issues which would be difficult to solve in order to make it a globally recognized standard: the difficulties in granting efficient implementation that would ensure avoidance of double taxation and guarantee single taxation;[156] the difficulties in reaching a general consensus regarding the formula to be used;[157] the significant political and administrative complexity that would require cohesive international cooperation;[158] the subjectivity in defining the global formula (implying arbitrary

152. Some of these concepts where already referred to into the 1995 Guidelines; however, the 2010 Guidelines and the work on BEPS Actions 8, 9 and 10 has increased the emphasis on them.
153. 2010 OECD Guidelines, para. 1.19.
154. 2010 OECD Guidelines, para. 1.19.
155. 2010 OECD Guidelines, para. 1.20.
156. 2010 OECD Guidelines, para. 1.22.
157. 2010 OECD Guidelines, para. 1.23.
158. 2010 OECD Guidelines, para. 1.24.

decisions disregarding specific market conditions);[159] the negative distortions deriving from exchange rate movements;[160] high compliance costs and data requirements;[161] the substantive valuation issues related to all relevant factors to allocate the tax base within the MNE group;[162] the inflexibility in accounting for specific characteristics of single entities such as geographical differences and separate companies efficiencies;[163] the questions about the relevance of imposing withholding taxes on cross-border payments, causing the rejection of many rules in the DTCs;[164] the difficulties in administrating the relationships between group members included in the formulary apportionment as well as group members who are excluded from it.[165]

In addition to the deficiencies of the existing proposed alternative to the arm's length principle, the relevance of this principle as a globally recognized international standard should be emphasized by the advantages that it embeds:[166]

- *No disincentive of foreign direct investments*: reference to the arm's length principle would better reflect the economic reality and reasoning of specific situations.
- *Prevention of the phenomena of tax avoidance and/or aggressive tax planning*: the arm's length principle would be flexible enough to ascertain any aggressive tax planning scheme.
- *Fair and balanced allocation of taxing powers between different states*: the arm's length principle would allocate the taxable base between different states in a fair manner.
- *Avoidance of double taxation and of less-than-single taxation*: the arm's length principle, which is implemented in the existing double tax treaties, would allow avoiding the phenomena of double taxation or less-than-single taxation.
- *Allowance of a coordinated approach (implying a reduction of the administrative burden on cross border transactions)*: an internationally coordinated approach could plausibly be more easily achieved since, as mentioned in the previous point, the arm's length principle has already been internationally agreed upon and implemented in the existing double tax treaties.
- *Stability and certainty of law*: when applied correctly and without distortion, the arm's length principle has the potential of providing stability and certainty of the law.

159. 2010 OECD Guidelines, para. 1.25.
160. 2010 OECD Guidelines, para. 1.26.
161. 2010 OECD Guidelines, para. 1.27.
162. 2010 OECD Guidelines, para. 1.28.
163. 2010 OECD Guidelines, para. 1.29.
164. 2010 OECD Guidelines, para. 1.30.
165. 2010 OECD Guidelines, para. 1.31.
166. Petruzzi, R., *Transfer Pricing Aspects of Intra-Group Financing* (Kluwer Law International, The Netherlands, 2016).

- *Compatibility with tax treaties*: the adoption of the arm's length principle would be compatible with the existing double tax treaties.[167]
- *Compatibility with primary and secondary EU law*: the adoption of the arm's length principle would be in accordance with the principles established by the jurisprudence of the Court of Justice of the European Union (EUCJ).
- *Enforceability*: rules based on the arm's length principle would be, in most cases, easily enforceable since the principle has already been embedded in many countries' legislations.
- *Avoidance of conflicts between different types of rules*: any reference to the arm's length principle would avoid conflicts, for example, with national transfer pricing rules based on this principle.

These points, in the author's opinion, considerably contribute to ensuring that the arm's length principle remains a solid and reliable standard. However, in the post-BEPS world, this principle may not look the same as when it was conceived and developed over the past decades.

As emphasized above, this standard will increasingly embed economic considerations, making its functioning highly influenced by business rationales and market principles. The three pillars on which it is fundamentally based (i.e., the separate entity approach, the relevance of contractual arrangements, and the comparability of the transaction) may be less dependent on the initially conceived legal fiction and more on the economic reality of the transactions.

Nevertheless, this circumstance will potentially raise substantial issues and challenges that will need to be inevitably addressed. Indeed, the increasing relevance of economic considerations over the application of the principle could potentially increase the risk of distortions and manipulations to the principle itself. These distortions and manipulations could be intentionally pursued and exploited by all parties involved in the application of the principle, i.e., both taxpayers and tax administrations.

Therefore, the relevant question ultimately resulting from this assessment would be basically aimed at identifying any possible solution to these issues and challenges. In the author's view, the possible solution to these challenges could be identified in the interpretation of the arm's length standard on a principle-based approach. Otherwise stated, when applying this standard, continuous reference should be made to the above-identified fundamental pillars on which it is based and to the final aim of the standard itself, specifically, the determination of what third parties would do in circumstances which are similar to those of the intra-group transaction.

In order to apply this solution, any interest-oriented interpretation of the principle should be genuinely avoided. In other words, considerations that are based only on the subjective interest (either from the taxpayers or from the tax administrations) to

167. This aim could only be reached, thus far, with the arm's length principle which has already been implemented in Article 9 of probably all double tax treaties currently in force. The compatibility of the other solutions with double tax treaties can be ambiguous and, in some cases, should still be tested.

interpret the arm's length principle in order to maximize the personal benefit (i.e., respectively, a minimization of the overall tax burden or a maximization of the collected tax revenues) should be disregarded. To achieve this, tools that are aimed at granting some simplification to the system in exchange of a 'minimum taxation' of the profit generated by a transaction (e.g., safe harbor rules) should be carefully reviewed and analyzed before their implementation.

Additionally, any solution provided either by the taxpayers or by the tax administrations should be conceived with the consideration that the same (or similar) solution should be uniformly applied to all intra-group transactions characterized by the same (or similar) circumstances. Further work on the implementation of instruments such as simultaneous tax examinations, multilateral Advance Pricing Agreements (APAs), and, in general, any cooperative compliance tool is urgently needed. In this respect, the publication of the outcomes of the solutions achieved by these tools will contribute to reducing this interest-oriented interpretation of the principle.

Moreover, the arm's length principle should be applied in a consistent manner. One of the outcomes of this approach would be that any reference to expressions such as 'exceptional (or non-ordinary) circumstances' as well as to concepts including 'generally inappropriate', 'not compulsory', and 'material differences' should be reconsidered and reviewed. Furthermore, any deviation between similar cases should be removed. This can be accomplished by applying the arm's length principle in the same way to transactions between related companies as well as to dealings between head offices and their permanent establishments.[168]

In detail, as far as the separate entity approach is concerned, its relevance should be further emphasized and confirmed. The arm's length principle, indeed, is finally aimed at identifying not what the market does (even if market considerations might always be useful in the process of its interpretation), but rather what related parties would do if they were not related. Therefore, the importance of concepts such as implicit support, same creditworthiness between head offices and permanent establishments, and group synergies might be reviewed.

In regard to the relevance of contractual arrangements, the emphasis on the commercial rationality of the transactions undertaken goes, rightly, in the direction of disregarding fictitious structures which would not occur if the related parties were not related. However, further guidance might be required in order to provide certainty on when the possibilities of adjustment of the conditions of intra-group arrangements under the application of the arm's length principle could materialize.

Finally, concerning the comparability of the transaction, although this pillar should continue to be fundamentally applied in the presence of identifiable comparable situations, the recourse to alternative methodologies (e.g., the use of financial valuations) or the application of traditional transaction methods less based on a pure comparability-based approach (e.g., by identifying more proxies to such a

168. On this point see, *inter alia*, Tavares, R.J.S. & Owens, J., *Human Capital in Value Creation and Post-BEPS Tax Policy: An Outlook*, Bulletin for International Taxation 69 (10/2015), pp. 590-601.

comparability) could prove beneficial to both taxpayers and tax administrations and, therefore, could be extended to all types of transactions.

Overall, it is difficult to imagine and predict how the arm's length principle will evolve in the post-BEPS world and how any further future amendment to the currently proposed new guidelines will look like in the future. However, a constant debate between all relevant players involved in the application and amendment of the arm's length principle will surely grant significant support to achieve interpretations that are ideal and commonly shared.

CHAPTER 2

Risks Redefined in Transfer Pricing Post-BEPS

Sébastien Gonnet[*]

* The author would like to thank *Pim Fris*, Special Consultant at NERA, for his valuable contribution to this chapter. The views expressed in this chapter are solely those of the author and are not necessarily the opinions of NERA Economic Consulting.

I. INTRODUCTION

Mandated by Actions 9 and 10 of the Base Erosion and Profit Shifting (BEPS) Action Plan, the Organisation for Economic Co-operation and Development (OECD) has developed a substantial revision of the OECD Transfer Pricing Guidelines (TPG) with regard to a number of closely related topics that are 'at the heart of the arm's length principle'. Among others, the changes introduced emphasize the importance of identifying the commercial and financial relationships inside Multinational Enterprises (MNE) and accurately delineating the actual transactions against that relational background while also including guidance on risk definition and allocation among entities of an MNE.

This chapter summarizes the revisions to section D of Chapter I of the TPG which focuses on risk definition and allocation. It proceeds with a critical review of the OECD revisions in consideration of other sections of the TPG, notably Chapter VI on intangibles and Chapter IX on business restructurings and of the OECD guidance on Permanent Establishments (PEs). The chapter then introduces an economically sound and BEPS-compliant *process as a guide* for multinational companies to design arm's length transfer pricing systems by taking into account an appropriate place for risk allocation. This process is thereafter illustrated through a case study. The chapter concludes by providing insight into specific areas of current concern for MNEs following the updated guidance on risk allocation.

Before taking a more detailed examination at the risk in post-BEPS transfer pricing practice, it may be beneficial to state a number of things about transfer pricing and the role of risk in a broader sense. To begin with, strictly speaking, transfer pricing is not a tax matter. Although it has a significant *impact* in regard to tax, it is basically a management-control concept: historically, it served a major role in performance measurement and management for multinational enterprises at a time that markets were primarily defined by country borders, and MNEs operated in country-based structures. All of this has gradually changed as the importance of country borders has faded when conducting business and as developing communication and information technologies widened the span of management control thus enabling the adoption of integrated business models. Today, business enterprises effectively operate as global players. No longer is the country-by-country rhythm the beginning point for conducting international business as, instead, it is now performing and managing global business operations. Consequently, country-related profits no longer had any relevance for performance management purposes, and transfer prices lost their relevance as a fundament for management control.

Although markets and business had globalized, taxation of businesses had not kept pace; global profits (per business unit or industry group) had to be converted and adapted exclusively for purposes of calculating national corporate income tax bills. Once tax authorities realized this, rules, methods, and practices were introduced exclusively for tax purposes, losing the old connection with management-control concepts now considered outdated, and transfer pricing became the playing field of tax experts. What followed was a revolution in transfer pricing practice that, driven by the increasing absence of comparable transactions, shifted the focus from transactions to entity profits as the pretext for comparability. The question of whether this shift still afforded an opportunity for a correct application of the arm's length principle was eclipsed in the unstoppable evolution of transfer pricing practice towards a quasi-exclusivity of the 'new method', introduced as the Comparable Profits Method in the US and embraced (hesitantly at first) by OECD in its 1995 TPG as the Transactional Net Margin Method (TNMM). This practice soon evolved into one based on stereotypical, functional profiles for group entities that did little justice to how commercial and financial relations really evolved between entities inside MNE operations. The BEPS initiative has provided a new stimulus to capture those *relations* in realistic terms, referring to roles and responsibilities of entities in the joint value creation inside an MNE business. It is useful to remember that Article 9 of OECD Model Tax Convention (MTC) defining the arm's length principle primarily refers to (commercial and financial) relations and not to transactions and most certainly not to entity profits. Where it was concluded earlier that transfer prices lost their relevance for management-control purposes, transfer pricing practice can most certainly benefit from the concepts employed in management control to delineate those roles and responsibilities within the relational context. The analytical framework presented further in this chapter will rely on those concepts. What is the place of risk in this new context?

The most fundamental definition of an enterprise could be the following. It is an organization of capital and labor that enters into economic exchanges in society (the market), accepting the risks involved in doing so with the intention of generating profits and thus securing its continuity. As the fundamental challenge in operating a business is about accepting and managing risks, it may be obvious that risk is a key element of that part of economic science that addresses the management of enterprise. In this context, it is all the more amazing to find that, during the 1990s into the 2000s, transfer pricing practice developed a perception of risk that bore virtually no relationship with economics. Risk was captured in contractual stereotypes that perfectly matched the requirements of applying TNMM but lost connection with realities inside MNE businesses.

With the BEPS mission being founded on the concept of value creation by MNEs, the challenge for businesses is to develop a transfer pricing system for a specific MNE based on the arm's length principle with roles of entities in the joint value creation as its essential reference. How would third parties have formulated their relationship in the circumstances of the specific MNE? Simple, straightforward tests of either comparable prices or comparable profits no longer deliver the answers required. In the transfer pricing practice, as it has taken shape post-BEPS, the contributions of individual entities to those processes of joint value creation decide the bargaining power that entities can be deemed to have in the simulation of arm's length bargaining processes. Roles and responsibilities assigned to entities defined by group management are the beginning point of analysis. These can, for different purposes, be confirmed and documented in contracts; however, business reality, not the contract, is the driver.

In this context, the new, post-BEPS landscape for transfer pricing, and particularly the redefined place of risk, will be reviewed and assessed.

II. THE NEW OECD RISK FRAMEWORK

The OECD provides the summary below of the objectives of Actions 9 and 10 of the BEPS Action Plan and corresponding outcome:

> Actions 9 and 10 mandate the development of:
>
> i. 'rules to prevent BEPS by transferring risks among, or allocating excessive capital to, group members. This will involve adopting transfer pricing rules or special measures to ensure that inappropriate returns will not accrue to an entity solely because it has contractually assumed risks or has provided capital. The rules to be developed will also require alignment of returns with value creation.'
> ii. 'rules to prevent BEPS by engaging in transactions which would not, or would only very rarely, occur between third parties. This will involve adopting transfer pricing rules or special measures to clarify the circumstances in which transactions can be recharacterised.'
>
> The guidance ensures that:
>
> - actual business transactions undertaken by associated enterprises are identified, and transfer pricing is not based on contractual arrangements that do not reflect economic reality contractual allocations of risk are respected only when they are supported by actual decision-making
> - capital without functionality will generate no more than a risk-free return, assuring that no premium returns will be allocated to cash boxes without relevant substance
> - tax administrations may disregard transactions when the exceptional circumstances of commercial irrationality apply

The following section elaborates on the subject of risks in transfer pricing that are at the core of the OECD final guidance on revisions to Chapter I of the TPG. It is followed by a comparison of the new wording against the wording on risks of TPG's Chapter IX and OECD guidance with respect to PEs.

A. Risks under the New Chapter I of the TPG

In the new TPG's Chapter I, the OECD introduces a six-step process[1] for analyzing risks:

1. Identify economically significant risks in the relevant relational context.
2. Determine how risks are contractually assumed.
3. Determine through a functional analysis which enterprise(s) assume and manage risks, i.e.,
   - perform(s) control functions and risk mitigation functions,
   - encounter(s) upside or downside consequences of risk outcomes, and
   - have(s) the financial capacity to assume the risks.

1. Paragraph 1.60.

4. Determine whether the contractual assumption of risks is consistent with the conduct of the parties by analyzing whether:
   - the associated enterprises follow the contractual terms; and
   - the party assuming risk exercises control over the risk and has the financial capacity to assume the risk.
5. Where the party assuming risk does not control the risk or does not have the financial capacity to assume the risk, allocate risk to the party exercising control and having the financial capacity to assume the risk.
   - In case of multiple associated enterprises exercising control and having the financial capacity to assume the risk, the risk should be allocated to the associated enterprise exercising the most control.
6. Price the transaction (accurately delineated) taking into account the financial and other consequences of risk assumption.

The above process (termed as 'new OECD risk process' in the remainder of the chapter) clarifies the existing TPG by:

- emphasizing the importance of accurate delineation of transactions;
- providing a new categorization of risks which broadens the understanding of risks within an MNE (see below);
- recognizing that risks also entail an upside element and not just a downside;
- promoting an alignment between risk management functions, funding capabilities, and actual assumption of risks; and
- enriching the existing TPG framework in which the TNMM oriented 'typical process' might potentially have favored artificial risk allocation in the past.

As stated in the introduction by the OECD, the new OECD risk process (and related new definitions) aims at directly addressing transfer pricing structures attributing high returns to low functionality based on a contractual allocation of risks that are considered artificial. In this respect, the new OECD risk process established by the OECD is certainly more approximate to the corresponding wording of Chapter IX than that of the former Chapter I and has certain similarities with the Authorized OECD Approach (AOA) on the attribution of profits to PEs. The following section elaborates on these similarities.

The consistency between the new OECD risk process and the OECD guidance on intangibles as expressed by the OECD itself in the Summary of the Intangibles Report should also be noted:

> The chapter places the guidance on intangibles within the wider context of the guidance on accurately delineating the transaction and the analysis of risks contained in the first chapter of this Report relating to 'Guidance on Applying the Arm's Length Principle', which is relevant in dealing with the difference between anticipated and actual returns to intangibles. The framework for analysing risks contained in the chapter 'Guidance on Applying the Arm's Length Principle' depends on a very specific and meaningful control requirement, which takes into account both the capability to perform relevant decision-making functions together with the actual performance of such functions. If an associated enterprise contractually assuming a specific risk does not exercise control over that risk nor has the financial capacity to assume the risk, then the framework contained in the chapter 'Guidance on Applying the Arm's Length Principle' determines that the

risk will be allocated to another member of the MNE group that does exercise such control and has the financial capacity to assume the risk.[2]

B. Risks under Chapter IX of the TPG

Chapter IX of the TPG provides a framework for understanding risks in the context of business restructuring[3] that needs to be supported and substantiated by the new OECD risk framework. The OECD suggests beginning with the contractual arrangements between the related parties that are concerned but to also review the conduct of the parties, the arm's length nature of the risk allocation, and the consequences of such risk allocation. Key concepts for a contractual allocation of risk in order to pass a reality test include:

- The control over the risks: *'control' should be understood as the capacity to make decisions, to take on the risk (decision to put the capital at risk), and decisions on whether and how to manage the risk, internally or using an external provider. This would require the company to have people – employees or directors – who have the authority to, and effectively do, perform these control functions.*[4]
- The financial capacity*: whether the risk-bearer has, at the time when risk is allocated to it, the financial capacity to assume (i.e., to take on) the risk.*[5]

Even though approximate, the new OECD risk framework has certain substantial differences with the existing Chapter IX framework:

- The new Chapter I wording tends to be more explicit with specific definitions of 'risk management' and 'risk mitigation'.
- The new OECD risk framework also appears to place more emphasis (than Chapter IX) on the financial capacity to assume the risk. Chapter IX indeed provides that such financial capacity is a 'relevant, although not determinative factor'.

Such differences may justify future reconsideration and possibly the wording adaptations of OECD Chapter IX. The new OECD risk process also has a direct impact on the 'Authorised OECD Approach' (AOA) introduced by the OECD in the context of attribution of profits to PEs.

2. Actions 8-10 – 2015 Final Reports, Intangibles, Revisions to Chapter VI, p. 63.
3. A business restructuring under Chapter IX is a 'cross-border redeployment by a multinational enterprise of functions, assets and/or risks' (para. 9.1).
4. Paragraph 9.23.
5. Paragraph 9.29.

C. Risks under Authorized OECD Approach

The OECD Report on the attribution of profits to permanent establishments[6] addresses the attribution of profits without questioning when a PE actually exists. It advocates the use - as part of the AOA - of the functionally separate entity approach as the fundamental starting point for dealing with profit attribution to PEs.

As a component of the AOA, a two-step process is required to determine the profits attributable to a PE:

- Step 1 consists of a functional and factual analysis in order to hypothesize the PE as a distinct and separate entity and to identify its role in the context of the total enterprise.
- Step 2 consists of determining the profits by applying the arm's length principle by analogy to what would occur between distinct legal entities.[7]

Within Step 1, Significant People Functions (SPF) are identified to attribute risks and economic ownership of assets to the PE. The vital aspect of the SPF concept is the capability to assume responsibility. This very closely resembles the notion of 'control' as it is being employed in Chapter IX and now in the new OECD risk process.

With all of the similarities between the above notions related to PE and the new Chapter I phraseology, it remains puzzling what the meaning is of certain subtle differences in wording, while the AOA emphasizes the need for 'active decision-making', the new OECD risk process refers to 'decision-making'.

The similarities previously mentioned are, in fact, both logical and essential as, in the context of MNE business models, the difference between entities and other forms of presence in different countries (PEs) is often hypothetical and a situation whereby none of the competing parties has an advantage at the outset is essential in terms of attributing income based on involvement in value creation. It would, moreover, be beneficial if the recognition expressed in the TPG that business realities must be appreciated in terms of economic substance rather than contractual definitions is also extended to the issue of deciding when a PE is considered as existing. The changes to the PE definition resulting from Action 5 remain at the level of contractual definitions and seem to disregard the fact that the more refined analysis of roles in the processes of joint value creation in the MNE allows insight in the economic substance that may be more decisive in answering the PE question than contracts.

D. Critical Review

When comparing the new OECD risk framework with Chapter IX and the AOA, it can be concluded that the OECD has attempted to enhance the existing toolkit available to tax authorities for reviewing the internal allocation of risks within MNEs; allocation of

6. OECD Report on the attribution of profits to permanent establishments, 22 Jul. 2010.
7. Pim Fris, Dr. Emmanuel Llinares & Sébastien Gonnet, *PEs and Transfer Pricing: The Playing Field in International Taxation Redefined*, Tax Planning International Transfer Pricing 12 (2008).

risks is a key reference for testing the ultimate allocation/attribution of profits between the individual entities of the MNE. The OECD now provides a new risk framework where contracts are assumed as a starting point but respected only in certain conditions. In order for an entity to be faced with the upside and/or downside impact of certain risks, it is now vital that this entity performs related risk management functions and has the financial capacity to assume such risks. If not, tax authorities employing the new OECD risk framework may be in a position to reallocate risks to the entity actually performing such risk management functions and having the financial capacity to assume the risks.

The new OECD risk process may prove as advantageous for tax authorities when strongly criticizing extreme circumstances where risk follows neither the functions nor the financial capacity; cash boxes illustrate good examples of such situations. For these extreme situations, what is ambiguous is how, in practice, tax authorities will leverage from the process and concretely apply it:

- How will the tax authorities determine which entity(ies) has control or where the financial capacity resides?
- How will the tax authorities allocate risks to such entity(ies)?

When drafting the new OECD risk process, the OECD seems to be considering certain exceptional and extreme situations where risks are clearly identifiable (and quantifiable) and where the artificiality of the allocation is also obvious.

However, what about the rest, i.e., the non-extreme situations? In most situations, defining risk, identifying risk management, and financial capacity are not obvious and free from ambiguity. The most challenging exercise is certainly the identification of risk management and control. Currently, MNEs are becoming much less organized with a unique decision center, hosting most (if not all) decision makers of the group. It is increasingly the case that companies are decentralizing a number of important responsibilities, operate with regional hubs, take decisions within a network, or establish global councils to take the most important strategic decisions for the group as a whole. Where is the control when personnel hosted by a number of different legal entities make important decisions that entail significant upside or downside consequences for the entire enterprise?

The above description illustrates the fundamental bias in the current transfer pricing practice. It is the TP (tax) function inside an MNE that is expected to ensure that business satisfies the requirements of the testing process as explained in the TPG and applied by tax authorities. In fact, however, the responsibility of the TP (tax) function is far wider and more fundamental than that as it must design and manage the transfer pricing system of a company that should express and be aligned with how the company actually operates. How a company operates can be captured not so much in functions as in processes; the processes allow entities of an MNE to enter into the collaborative exercise of joint value creation. An enterprise is creating value if it is successful in being profitable and securing continuity. The perspective of a future stream of profits in excess of the cost of funding represents this value – as yet intangible!

The new OECD risk framework indeed appears to focus on only people and control on a contemporaneous basis while the arm's length principle refers to commercial and financial relationships between entities within a group. In order to design an arm's length transfer pricing system, it is necessary to map the relative position of group entities involved in the process of jointly creating value by taking into account functions (with people as a key element) as well as risks and assets. Such an analysis cannot be focused exclusively on people and made on only a contemporaneous basis:

- History of an entity matters (for instance, its history in terms of cost assumption, assumption of capital expenditures investments, start-up losses).
- Legal rights of an entity should also be taken into account.
- Intangibles should not be disregarded. They generally result from a long process that an MNE has been establishing for years or even decades and have a long lifetime.

The new OECD risk process tends to invite tax authorities to review risk allocation from a purely controlling perspective as defined in the TPG, ignoring the fact that an arm's length negotiation between entities would take into account their bargaining positions that are being extensively influenced by their history, their legal rights, and the intangibles they have built over time. In fact, these elements only emerge when paying sufficient attention to the relationships between parties in a broad sense. Any attempt to define 'actual transactions' without proper attention to the relational starting point is a dubious one.

The new OECD risk process, therefore, may prove misleading for tax authorities and may create risks for MNEs considering its focus on only the people perspective. This can be illustrated by a simple example. A leading MNE in a sector where brand and reputation can be claimed to be the number one Critical Success Factor (CSF) can face risks associated with the brand which range from strategic risks (less appeal to the brand vis-à-vis customers) to financial risks (a lower financial performance, higher rates of unsold products, etc.). The brand has been established over time by the Central Group entity which has been developing the brand architecture and has financed related brand promoting investments. Over the past years, however, the Group has created a strategy involving closer proximity to the markets, and marketing teams are now widespread in regional companies around the world. Regional teams are afforded the capabilities to make key decisions regarding brand advertising and promotion in their regions, events, and PR strategy and to locally adapt the brand.

These facts and circumstances create uncertainty as to how tax authorities might apply the new OECD risk process in this specific situation, notably in the countries where regional marketing teams are hosted. Tax authorities may be tempted to claim that regional teams control key brand-related strategic and financial risks and, as such, they should be entitled to related upside/downside. If so, how would local tax authorities quantify the related upside/downside of regional brand management? Notably in comparison to the central brand management activities? Is it appropriate for local tax authorities to review the set-up on an incidental contemporaneous basis only?

Should tax authorities ignore the history (brand management hosted historically centrally), the legal rights (trademarks rights at central level), and intangibles (processes involved with managing the brand result from years of elaboration and also relate to the Company's culture and DNA)?

This basic example demonstrates that the new OECD risk process raises a number of questions. By focusing on control, the process seems to disregard important aspects that would be taken into account in an arm's length negotiation between independent parties, i.e., history, legal rights, and intangibles.

In addition to creating risk exposure for MNEs in terms of unforeseen tax liabilities (with the potential negative impact on the reputation of the company), the new OECD risk process may also simply prove to be impractical and quasi-impossible for MNEs to manage. Isolating the 'risk management' functions of a certain risk is certainly not a straightforward exercise. For instance, brands are often reflected in every activity of a company, and these activities ultimately relate to customer experience. When the OECD suggests that, for a certain economically significant risk, the risk management functions must be identified, it makes the assumption that companies are simple and basic organizations: the R&D team should be held responsible for technology-related risks, the marketing team should be held responsible for brand-related risks, management should be held responsible for strategic risks, etc. The reality is much more complex. Errors within certain departments may have a significant impact on other parts of the organization, thus explaining why companies place such increasing emphasis on processes and culture/values; risks can arise from different parts of the organization.

Another illustration concerns retail brands that spend tens of millions of Euros to promote their brand. The image and value of the brand can be severely impacted by mistakes made in the suppliers' countries, for instance, if the company's suppliers do not respect local law and/or ethics and sustainability standards. In these cases, where is the control of such risks? Is it at the level of the group company which establishes processes and standards for supplier selection? Is it at the level of the local entity which performs the suppliers' selection at the basic level? Is it at the level of the communication team which manages the consequences of a scandal?

It should be noted that all of the questions raised above are not hypothetical. They simply need to be answered – by the MNE. They *need* to be answered and *can* be answered; however, it must be recognized that the TPG only addresses one element of the situation. The TPG explains how tax authorities approach transfer pricing for their testing purposes, which are basically always ex-post; the MNE needs to do more than anticipating and according with those tests.

The examples given tend to confirm that the new OECD risk framework will certainly achieve the tax authorities' goals of tackling extreme situations by providing updated tools to the tax authorities to deny risks and rewards allocated to cash boxes. For all other situations, the process as stipulated by the OECD may open areas of dispute between tax authorities and tax payers regarding what the economically significant risks are, where the control is, and to which party (and how) such risks should be allocated. More worryingly, the new OECD risk process ignores important aspects at the core of arm's length by overly focusing on human involvement as an allocation criterion. This process is very much static and contemporaneous. It tends to ignore history, legal rights, and intangibles that are gradually established.

In that context, MNEs should still carefully review the above risk process as this is how tax authorities will likely review risk allocation within MNEs and more generally transfer pricing systems. This process is very much meant as a tool to assist tax authorities in reviewing (and challenging) certain situations. It is not meant to help MNEs in designing an arm's length transfer pricing system.

Designing a transfer pricing system for an MNE necessitates more:

- First, it is company-specific: each industry is specific and, within an industry, each company has its own specificities (notably in terms of the business model and organization). This means that each company needs to design, develop, and implement its own solutions to risk allocation.
- Second, the new OECD risk process, as discussed extensively, is testing-only and thus too limited to serve as a full reference for MNEs in designing their TP policies.
- Third, it tends to ignore important aspects of what would be an arm's length negotiation between entities (for instance, history, legal rights, and intangibles).
- Fourth, the new OECD risk process does not include a perspective on how to actually define an arm's length transfer pricing policy in regard to risk allocation.

Below is a proposed framework to help MNEs design and defend an arm's length transfer pricing system. It is based on the concept of value creation: the NERA Value Chain Analysis framework (VCA framework). Such framework is, in our opinion, BEPS-compliant; more specifically, it is compliant with the results of Actions 8-10 and embeds a comprehensive understanding of risks in accordance with the new OECD risk process. However, while the OECD wording is a tool for tax authorities to tackle extreme risk misallocation situations, the VCA framework is broader and should help any MNE categorically design and defend arm's length transfer pricing systems.

The following section presents the VCA framework and describes to which extent such a framework is compliant with the new OECD risk process.

III. A PROPOSED FRAMEWORK FOR UNDERSTANDING RISKS IN AN MNE[8]

The analytical framework leading up to an appropriate definition of a company's transfer pricing system includes:

8. Pim Fris, Sébastien Gonnet & Ralph Meghames, *Understanding Risk in the Enterprise: The Key to Transfer Pricing for Today' s Business Models*, International Transfer Pricing Journal, vol. 21, no. 6 - 11/12 (2014).

- analysis of how value is created in the intercompany relationships;
- identification of the responsibilities of individual parties and entities;
- assessment of the relative bargaining position of individual entities in regard to the contributions to value creation and risks carried; and
- definition and implementation of transactional conditions including a coherent contractual allocation of risks.

This framework allows the mapping of the responsibilities of the individual parties for the different concerned risk categories. It begins with an understanding of how value is created within an enterprise and relates the enterprise's functions, risks, and assets (including intangibles) to the individual value drivers. It subsequently establishes the role and responsibilities of the transacting parties considering the identified functions, assets, and risks in regard to their ability to control such risks and their role in the development of (intangible) assets. As a final step, it should be established how, in this pattern of value creation in the enterprise and allocation of roles therein to individual group entities, prices would be determined between parties that have no shareholding ties.

A. Step 1: Analyzing Value Creation

The first step of the proposed framework involves the identification and analysis of the enterprise's value chain.

A value chain analysis consists of understanding how value is created in the enterprise. This requires identifying the key value drivers that influence the most critical success factors and that can be held accountable for the enterprise's major risks and for developing, maintaining, and enhancing the enterprise's intangibles. Value chain analysis is at the center of discussions and preoccupations in transfer pricing at the global level because of the current complex business environment.

The OECD report on BEPS had noted:

> The rise of global value chains has also changed the notion of what economies do and what they produce. It is increasingly less relevant to talk about the gross goods or services that are exported, while it is increasingly relevant to talk about tasks and stages of production. In a world where stages and tasks matter more than the final products being produced, global value chains also challenge orthodox notions of where economies find themselves on the value-added curve. From an economic point of view, most of the value of a good or service is typically created in upstream activities where product design, R&D or production of core components occur, or in the tail-end of downstream activities where marketing or branding occurs. Knowledge-based assets, such as intellectual property, software, and organizational skills, have become increasingly important for competitiveness and for economic growth and employment.[9]

9. OECD (2013), *Addressing Base Erosion and Profit Shifting*, OECD, Paris.

B. Step 2: Linking the Enterprise's Functions, Risks, and Assets (IP) with Value Creation

The second step involves linking of enterprise's functions, risks, and assets (including intangibles) with value creation as identified within the enterprise's value chain.

Certain functions, certain risks (in accordance with the new OECD classification introduced above), and certain assets (including intangibles) of the enterprise correspond to each value driver, i.e., each step in the value creation process. In this mapping process, risks are naturally associated with functions that are influencing the risks.

A simplified illustration of the association between a value driver, functions, risks, and assets is illustrated in Figure 2.1:

Figure 2.1 Value Chain Analysis (Steps 1 & 2)

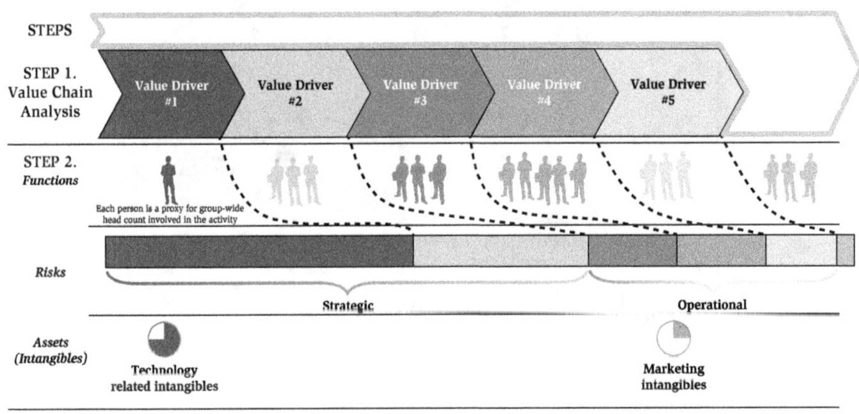

The VCA framework involves an extensive understanding of business risks as suggested by the new OECD risk process. Risks under the VCA framework are aligned with the categories outlined in the Actions 8, 9, and 10 BEPS report with two notable exceptions:

- The intellectual and human capital risks included in the VCA framework are not present in the new OECD classification.
- The transactional risks are included in the new OECD classification and not within the VCA framework.

The intellectual capital risks (including human capital risks) emerge from challenges related to a company's talent and leadership as well as its choices to differentiate itself from the competition. The related technological, intellectual, and human capital systems are key to realizing the promises of the strategic choices. Failure will have a negative impact on continuity. In the opinion of the author, this risk category should be added to the new risk categorization proposed by the OECD.

Risk management in an enterprise is addressing the impact of volatility (both downside and upside); it is relevant to distinguish the source of volatility as well as its impact. The Figure 2.2 captures these elements in the VCA framework risk categories.[10]

Figure 2.2 The Enterprise View of Risk: Managing the Impact of Volatility

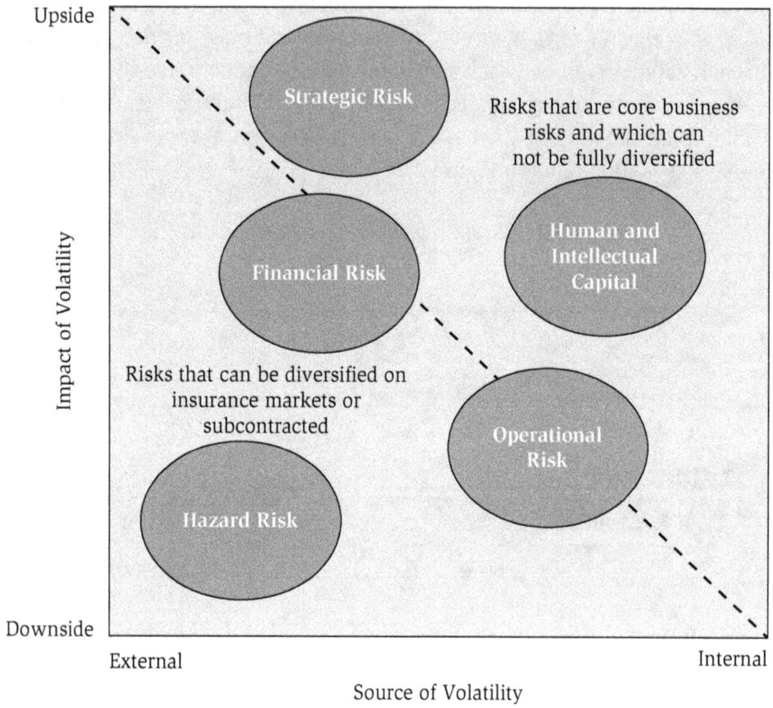

The value chain together with the related mapping of the underlying functions, risks, and assets provides an understanding of the enterprise's value creation process, how this value creation is stimulated by functions within the entities of the enterprise, the related risks associated with the performance of said functions, and the assets (primarily intangibles) related to said functions and risks.

C. Step 3: Mapping Roles, Responsibilities, and Control of the Individual Group Entities

The third step establishes the role and responsibilities of the group entities/transacting parties in the identified functions, their assumption of risks regarding their ability to control such risks, and their role in the development of (intangible) assets.

10. The opinion presented here is based on and adapted from D. Nadler & A. Slywotzky, *Risk and the Enterprise: Creating a Risk-Competent Company in an Age of Volatility*, MMC Viewpoint, issue 1 (Marsh & McLennan Companies, 2008).

In an intra-group context, a company can only be held liable for elements that it can reasonably take responsibility for, that is, for what it is equipped to manage. In that respect, the management-control concept of responsibility profiles can help define the role and responsibilities of group members involved in intra-group transactions. The responsibility profiles as given in Table 2.1 can be used.

Table 2.1 The Entity Responsibility Profiles

Transfer Pricing Responsibility Profiles Paradigm	
Investment Centers	Investment centers are profit centers, which are also responsible for investing in new products, services or work processes in order to enhance future profitability. It also assumes responsibility for the continuity of the enterprise
Profit Centers	Profit centers are responsible for achieving the maximum profit levels by increasing revenues and/or decreasing costs
Revenue Centers	Revenue centers are responsible for maximizing sales volumes while not exceeding the budgeted operating cost level
Cost Centers	Cost centers are responsible for operating as efficiently as possible and producing the budgeted quantity according to the agreed quality specifications and delivery terms
Expense Centers	Expense centers are responsible for delivering outputs according to the agreed quality specifications and delivery terms and within expense budget limits

It is one thing to identify which player contractually bears the risk associated with a certain transaction; however, it is another to identify the player that is able to control, i.e., take responsibility for managing this risk. The concept of 'control' is crucial in this context just as it is in the new OECD risk process.

Embedded in the full-scope VCA, the new OECD risk process is more relevant for the following reasons:

- It begins with a holistic perspective on what creates value within a Company considering its chosen business model in a certain industry while the OECD testing process starts with the transactions.
- It identifies the responsibility profile of entities based on its human capabilities (control) and also on its role within the MNE by taking into account a full-scope view on functions, risks, and assets and not only on a contemporaneous basis.
- It is the relevant starting point for mapping the relative contribution of entities in the total value creation process and assessing the relative bargaining power of entities.

In order to determine which entity has 'control' over risk, the 'SPF',[11] and important functions[12] are crucial.

The vital aspect of the SPF concept is the capability to assume responsibility for risks. This notion was developed in the context of permanent establishments and is potentially also relevant in situations where it is questionable as to whether a contractual allocation of risk between entities is realistic.

However, it should be remembered that the notion of control is not necessarily possessed by the 'significant people' referred to here. The role of management in a company ranges from strategy definition (long term) through responsibility allocation or delegation in the design of the business model (medium term) to operational management responsibilities (with year-to-year reporting) allowing 'control' and evaluation by the management level that allocated the responsibility to the operational managers. A team or an entity can be reputed as performing an SPF only to the extent that people in the team or entity have the actual resources and competences to manage and take responsibility for the underlying risks and assets. 'Control' of how good the team or entity performs its operational role, notably in the form of 'active decision-making' in relationship to the assumption of risks and ownership of assets, rather suggests the strategic level. This is reflected in Chapter IX (context of business restructurings) where paragraph 9.23 clarifies that:

> in the context of par. 1.49, 'control' should be understood as the capacity to make decisions to take on the risk (decision to put capital at risk) and decisions on whether and how to manage risk, internally or using an external provider. This would require the company to have people – employees or directors – who have the authority to, and effectively do, perform these control functions.

In the context of the 'important functions' (introduced as an expression in the discussion draft for Chapter VI, dealing with intangibles), the key criterion is also 'control' which obviously refers to a group's value creation in a wide sense, embracing all risk categories. Important functions as elaborated in Chapter VI just seem to have a more limited focus as the concept is applied only in the context of the generation of intellectual property. 'Intangibles', however, form a broader universe than merely intangible property depending up how they are defined by the Guidelines as intangibles or as comparability factors.

The two terms, SPF (at an operational level) and important functions (at a more strategic level), are comparable as they both emphasize the distinction between performing certain activities versus the control issue. That is exactly what can be captured by using the responsibility profiles previously introduced in combination with the different risk categories in the enterprise view on risk.

11. OECD Report on the attribution of profits to permanent establishments, 22 Jul. 2010.
12. OECD Revised Discussion Draft on Transfer Pricing Aspects of Intangibles, July 2013.

D. Step 4: Assessing Bargaining Positions in the Internal Pricing Process

The fourth and final step of the proposed framework consists of the translation of contributions of group entities/transacting parties to value creation while considering the responsibilities attributed to them in their respective bargaining positions in the process of establishing transfer prices.

Transactions are the materialization of the commercial and financial relationships between different parties. Both commercial and financial relationships between independent and associated enterprises can take many distinctive forms. They can be incidental, involving one or a limited number of transactions, or can be broad and of long duration. Furthermore, relationships constitute a different context depending upon the impact that the decision to enter into the transactional arrangement will have in terms of additional investments in capacity, i.e., in assets and people.

If one of the parties has invested heavily and that investment becomes obsolete earlier than foreseen, then the impact on the price of the transaction between the parties will be different depending upon the relationship. If the relationship is purely transactional, this would be the risk of the investing party. However, in the context of a long-term cooperative relationship, parties will re-assess their terms and conditions if and as long as they both wish to continue their relationship. In other words, they will find a way to share the consequences of an unforeseen event and of the risks arising from it.

Figure 2.3 The Relational Pricing Dynamics

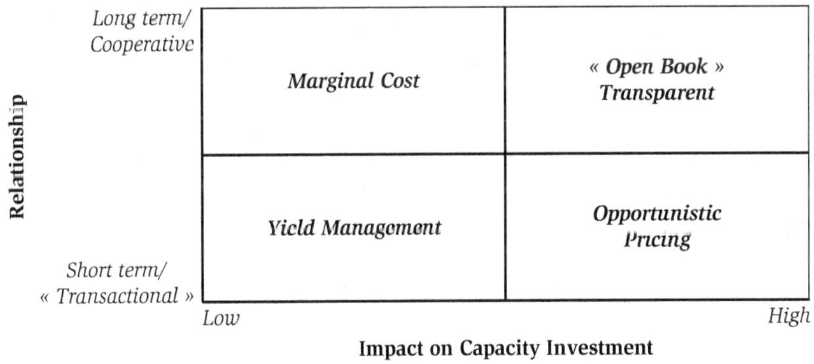

The relational context dictates the dynamics of the ultimate allocation of jointly achieved results to the individual parties involved (the basic transfer pricing system design). In this respect, methods play a different role than the one identified for testing purposes. In the detailed design, the different relevant parameters of the system can be stipulated based on the bargaining positions and solidified by, potentially, a broad range of further economic analyses. Benchmarking may give relevant orientation; however, ultimate justification may have to be delivered by analytical tools such as an analysis of external long-term relationships, investment-based models, game theory, compensation-based models, surveys, and bargaining analyses.

In summary, the analytical process previously described effectively helps to assess the respective contributions by the transacting parties in an intra-group context to the joint value creation and to derive the relative bargaining position of each of them. The information on the bargaining power of the entities involved is essential for concluding an appropriate pricing system for internal transactions and allows evaluating whether or not, in the complex reality within the MNE, third parties would enter into the transactions with the prevailing terms and conditions. Only if that conclusion is justified can the prices for intercompany transactions be considered to be 'at arm's length'.

IV. CASE STUDY

The case study aims at illustrating how the above VCA framework may help MNEs in the design and documentation of transfer pricing policies in the post-BEPS context. It emphasizes that a crucial process of understanding value creation and risks within the entire enterprise combined with rigorous economic analyses provide the foundations for MNEs to (re)design and defend their transfer pricing policy.

This case study section is composed of an introduction of the background of the case followed by a summary of the application of the VCA framework and is concluded by the application of an economic analysis in regard to the VCA findings.

A. Background

The Company operates within an industrial sector and exclusively as a B2B business. Within the sector where the Company operates (industrial with B2B distribution), brands may or may not be valuable intangible assets.

Functions involved in the development and maintenance of the Company's brand (the 'Brand') are centrally controlled and performed (including some local execution) but fully funded by the local operational entities through a management fee recharge.

The case aims at:

- determining whether the Brand is actually a valuable intangible asset for this Company in this sector;
- if so, identifying which entities are involved in the Development, Enhancement, Maintenance, Protection, and Exploitation (DEMPE[13]) of the Brand;
- in regard to the above, assessing whether the existing transfer pricing system is arm's length, BEPS proof, and compliant with the new OECD risk process; and
- if a change in transfer pricing system is needed, designing the new transfer pricing system for the Brand.

13. OECD/G20 BEPS Project, Intangibles, para. 6.32 'ownership of intangibles involving the development, enhancement, maintenance, protection and exploitation of intangibles'.

B. VCA Framework

The application of the VCA framework to this case is described below.

Step 1: Analyzing Value Creation

The analysis established that the Brand:

- acts as a guarantee of highest quality and reliability;
- helps to attract and retain most skilled employees given its reputation and culture based on strong corporate values; and
- increases cross-selling opportunities due to a uniform appearance.

Therefore, it was concluded that the Brand was indeed a CSF of the Group. Other CSFs included: (i) the technology/technological knowledge; (ii) the global size of the Group; and (iii) the dense local sales network.

Step 2: Linking the Enterprise's Functions, Risks, and Assets (IP) with Value Creation

Functions related to the Brand (and related intangibles) are not only:

- Central Marketing functions, and
- Local Marketing functions,

but also:

- Central Operational Management functions.

As a matter of fact, the key Brand attribute relates to operational excellence and related processes and is, therefore, 'controlled' by central Operational Management functions.

Risks related to the Brand range from strategic risks (loss of reputation/trust in the event of severe product failure or accident) to financial risks (less cross-selling, reducing cash flow).

The related trademark legal rights are owned by the central group company.

Step 3: Mapping Roles, Responsibilities, and Control of the Individual Group Entities

Under the VCA framework, Step 3 determines the group entities that can be held responsible for the major risks related to a certain value driver. This evaluation is made relying on an understanding of the entities' functional capabilities. This analysis is accorded to the OECD new risk process involving the identification of 'control'.

Under both the VCA framework and the OECD new risk process, the aforementioned situation of the Company suggests that the Group's Central company should be held responsible for the upside and downside related to the Brand.

This analysis of 'control' under the VCA framework and the new OECD risk process can be supplemented by the OECD *DEMPE* process as described in the revised Chapter VI.

Table 2.2 illustrates that the central group entity virtually controls all of the key functions with respect to the Brand while the funding of related costs is provided by local group entities which are recharged as brand building costs as well as the costs of central functions involved in the Brand development:

Table 2.2 DEMPE Analysis for the Brand (Before Change of TP Policy)

Brand	*Functions (Perform/Control)*	*Funding (Provide)*	*Risks (Control/Bear)*
Development	C	L	?
Enhancement	C	L	?
Maintenance	C	L	?
Protection	C	L	?
Exploitation	L	L	L

where 'C' stands for Central group entity; 'L' stands for Local entities.

Following the new OECD guidance on DEMPE, it is uncertain which entities can be claimed to 'control/bear risks' related to the intangible when one entity controls/ performs the functions and other entities fund them. Such a situation may actually qualify as an illustration of mismatch between value creating functions and assumption of related risks under the new OECD risk process.

Step 4: Assessing Bargaining Positions in the Internal Pricing Process

Steps 1-3 of the VCA framework suggest that:

- The Brand is a valuable intangible asset.
- Functions involved in the development and maintenance of the Brand are hosted centrally; stated otherwise, control of the brand-related risks lies centrally.
- Consequently, the Central Group company should be held responsible for the upside/downside related to the Brand.

In terms of the transfer pricing design, this could signify that:

- The central group entity could stop re-invoicing to local entities those costs that are related to the Brand development.
- The local entities could be willing to pay a trademark fee if the trademark adds benefits and value to their local business.
- It is also worth noting that the local entities may possibly claim at arm's length that they had been funding brand building costs for years and that this would be taken into account in an arm's length negotiation with the Brand owner.

The above suggests that:

- A trademark license contract could be established between the group central entity and the local entities.
- The trademark royalty could be assessed in regard to the underlying profitability that the local entities using the trademark are in a position to make. In the absence of reliable comparable uncontrolled transactions (in a B2B industrial context), the Profit Split Method (PSM) could be appropriate to determine arm's length royalty between the group entity and each individual entity.
- Any transfer pricing method could take into account the past and history of the entities. Prior funding by the local entities should be accounted for at arm's length in the royalty determination.

If the above is achieved, an alignment between value creation and profit allocation will be achieved. This alignment is illustrated in Table 2.3:

Table 2.3 DEMPE Analysis for the Brand (After Change of TP Policy)

Brand	*Functions (Perform/Control)*	*Funding (Provide)*	*Risks (Control/Bear)*
Development	C	C	C
Enhancement	C	C	C
Maintenance	C	C	C
Protection	C	C	C
Exploitation	L	C, L	C, L

C. New Transfer Pricing System

The OECD Guidelines describe the 'PSM' as a method which 'seeks to eliminate the effect on profits of special conditions made or imposed in a controlled transaction (…) by determining the division of profits that independent enterprises would have expected to realize from engaging in the transaction or transactions'.[14]

The PSM could qualify as the appropriate method to determine the royalty fee to be agreed upon between the central group entity and the individual entities if the following conditions are met:

- the contributions of both the Central Group entity and local entities are both unique and valuable; and/or
- the economic circumstances under which the parties operate are unique; and/or

14. Paragraph 2.108.

- the sharing of costs/risks as reflected by the conduct of the parties is unique; and/or
- the Brand is unique.

In this case, as noted above:

- The Brand has been identified as a valuable intangible asset.
- Central functions are key contributors to the Brand value.
- The license contract is negotiated under unique circumstances where the local entities had been funding the Brand building costs in the past.

- No external relevant reference may provide insight into the royalty value considering the B2B industrial sector in which the Company operates.

Under these circumstances, the PSM is selected. It is worth noting that method selection depends upon the facts and circumstances of the case.

Under the PSM, different types of analyses may be conducted. Three are presented here – non-mutually exclusive – of the usually most promising types of PSM:

- The Contribution Profit Split Method (Contribution PSM): the combined profits (generally, the combined operating profits) are divided among the participants in the value chain based upon the relative value of the functions that are performed. In order to justify this division, the OECD Guidelines recommend the use of external market data. In practice, the determination may be based upon an analysis of the relative value of each participant's contribution. This analysis can either be based on external data (such as data from joint ventures, for example) or internal data (including financial data).
- The Comparable Profit Split Method (CPSM): the combined operating profits of participants are divided among the participants in the value chain based on data from observed comparable transactions between third parties. Comparable transactions should refer to a division of profits and should satisfy comparability criteria (similar activities and circumstances).
- The Residual Profit Split Method (RPSM): this relies on a categorization of functions, risks and assets according to which benchmarkable functions are distinguished from entrepreneurial functions. Once arm's length returns have been attributed to routine functions, residual profits are divided between the two affiliates based on an appropriate allocation principle.

In this case, the RPSM may prove superior in terms of methodology as benchmarkable returns can be identified for the benchmarkable activities, including technology, thus allowing a determination of the residual return and what intangible assets and entities contribute to this residual. It is worth noting that selecting the RPSM within the PSM depends upon the facts and circumstances of the case.

The Brand value and, within the brand value, the share attributable to the licensor lies within the residual as illustrated in the graph below:

Figure 2.4 Determination of Brand Value and Share Attributable to Licensor

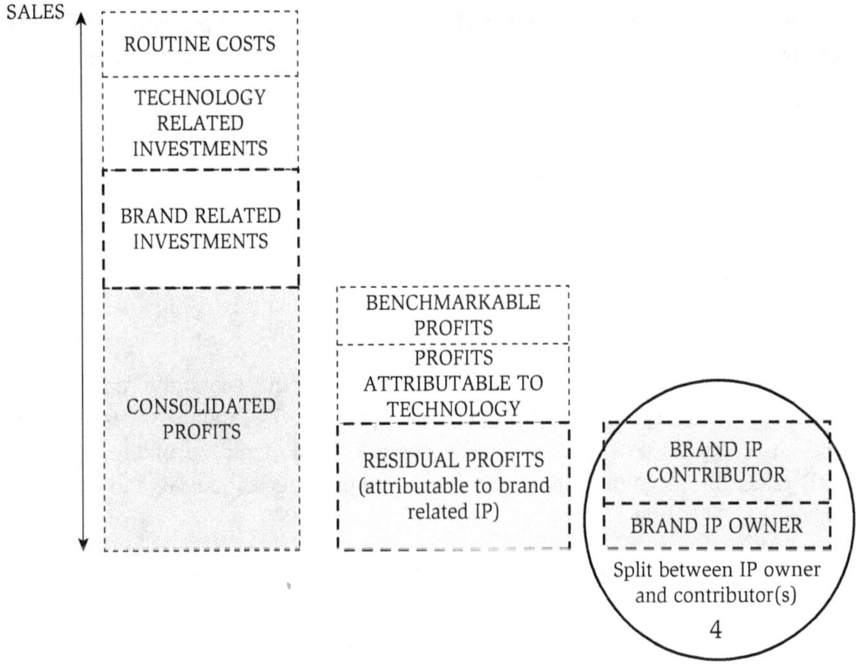

The residual profit acquired by the local entities represents the incremental value that they may possibly generate. Therefore, it reflects the returns that can be attributed to the company's competitive advantage and directly relates to the development of intangibles – in the case at hand – the Brand (provided that there has been remuneration for technology). How third parties would decide to split this incremental value relating to the development of intangibles depends upon their respective bargaining power; such bargaining power depending itself on their contribution to value creation and to the development of such intangibles.

The investments on brand development by local entities prior to the trademark license contract and by the group central company from the initiation of the license contract can be used as a proxy to arrive at an arm's length split of residual profits. The reasons for including historical brand development costs in the model is to recognize the contribution and intangibles development role of local entities prior to the creation of the licensing agreement.

It must be acknowledged, however, that not all costs have the same importance. Some of them are of a more strategic nature and have a longer lifetime while others have a shorter reach or investments need to be renewed frequently considering the nature of the costs or the cycles of the business.

Therefore, rather than looking at costs expensed on a yearly basis by the negotiating parties, the 'economic capital' developed by each of them should be examined. It is worth noting that the choice of method for determining the split factor depends on the facts and circumstances of the case.

This approach (use of capital instead of expenses) is supported by the OECD which tends to suggest approaches based on capital rather than yearly expenses:

> An allocation key based on expenses may be appropriate where it is possible to identify a strong correlation between relative expenses incurred and relative value added.[15]
>
> Cost-based allocation keys have the advantage of simplicity. It is however not always the case that a strong correlation exists between relative expenses and relative value.[16]
>
> 'Asset-based or capital- based allocation keys can be used where there is a strong correlation between tangible or intangible assets or capital employed and creation of value [...]'.[17]

By dividing the residual profit based on the respective economic capital of the transacting parties, the returns achieved by each party on the capitalized costs and not on the costs expensed is equalized. The capitalization (build-up of the economic capital) takes into account appropriate assumptions on gestation lag and economic lifetime:

- The gestation lag is the time between when the investment is made and the moment it generates the first revenues.
- The economic lifetime is the period of time during which the investments may generate revenues.

Each party's economic capital is calculated every year as following:

$$EC_n^L = EC_{n-1}^L - Depr_{n,n-1}^L + Inv_{n-x}^L$$

$$EC_n^C = EC_{n-1}^C - Depr_{n,n-1}^C + Inv_{n-x'}^C$$

where:

EC_n^i: Economic Capital of party i in year n

$Depr_{n,n-1}^i$: Economic Depreciation in year n of the Economic capital of party i in year $n-1$ based on the economic lifetime of the investments made

Inv_{n-x}^i : Investments made by party i in year $n-x$

$Inv_{n-x'}^i$: Investments made by party i in year $n-x'$

x and x' : Investments' gestation lags

15. Paragraph 2.138.
16. Paragraph 2.139.
17. Paragraph 2.136.

As seen in the previous equation, each party's economic capital does not equal the yearly costs incurred by each party (accounting approach) but includes the entrepreneurial investments capitalized by taking into account a gestation lag.

Comparing the economic capital of each party is then a beneficial proxy for assessing their respective contributions and for how these two parties would share profits at arm's length.

$$Share\ of\ Residual\ Profit_n^L = \frac{EC_n^L}{EC_n^L + EC_n^C}$$

$$Share\ of Residual\ Profit_n^C = \frac{EC_n^C}{EC_n^L + EC_n^C}$$

The model fulfills the objectives set out in regard to the very special circumstances of the case as it takes into account the prior investments and funding by local entities. Concretely and schematically, what the model does is that the royalty charged by the central entity includes a ramp-up of the rate to acknowledge that the central entity has full economic ownership of the brand's intangibles after the contribution of local entities has been extinguished in accordance with the intangibles' life duration – as can be illustrated in the figure below:

Figure 2.5 Determination of Brand Royalty Ramp-Up

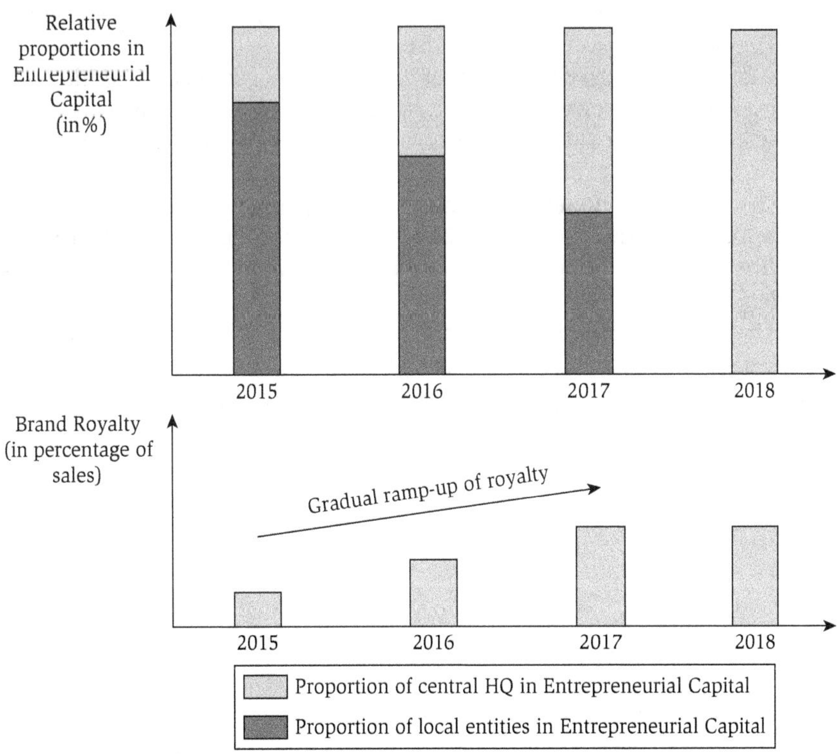

D. Case Study Summary

In the opinion of the author, the case study provides a beneficial illustration of how the VCA framework can help MNEs in navigating the post-BEPS requirements and, more specifically, the requirements related to the new OECD risk process.

This case study demonstrates that the VCA framework goes deeper than the OECD new risk process. Beginning with a holistic/top down approach, it helps qualify the bargaining power of transacting parties and is a useful tool for method selection and application.

While the OECD new risk process focuses only on human contribution made on a contemporaneous basis, the VCA framework brings the control/SPF/important functions aspect into a broader context where history, legal rights, and intangibles development are taken into account.

We can also note that rigorous economic analyses can be made to quantitatively interpret what the VCA has determined qualitatively. In the previous example, a cost capitalization model under RPSM helps to take into account the funding activities by the local entities of brand building costs in the past.

V. CONCLUSIONS

This chapter provides a comparative analysis of the OECD new risk process under revised Chapter I with (new) guidance from Chapter VI, (existing) guidance from Chapter IX, and PE-related concepts and definitions.

The new OECD risk process may prove to be useful for tax authorities when challenging extreme arrangements where risk follows neither the functions nor the financial capacity, with cash boxes being good examples of such situations. For the non-extreme situations, it still remains uncertain how, in practice, tax authorities will define risk and identify the entities performing risk management functions, having control, and the financial capacity. It is also not clear how tax authorities will reallocate risks in the event that they determine a discrepancy between control and risk assumption.

The new OECD process incites a number of questions as it creates an opportunity for consideration of control at a certain point in time only (ignoring the history, legal rights, and intangibles development of an entity). However, the arm's length principle itself refers to commercial and financial relationships between entities within a group which necessitates mapping the relative position of group entities involved in the process of jointly creating value. This relative position must be assessed through a full-scope VCA which should encompass functions (and people) as well as risks and assets.

The BEPS context calls for a comprehensive understanding of where value is created within MNEs. Guidance from revised Chapter I on risk, the new OECD risk process, is a tool primarily directed towards tax authorities to review extreme situations and, therefore, may appear to be unpractical to MNEs. The broader VCA framework is certainly more relevant for MNEs that would like to review the arm's length nature of their transfer pricing systems in the post-BEPS environment.

CHAPTER 3

Transfer Pricing Aspects of Intangibles: The License Model

*J. Scott Wilkie**

* I am grateful and wish to acknowledge regular continuing discussions with Ms Marta Pankiv, a talented and thoughtful PhD student at the Vienna University of Economics and Business with whom I have the good fortune to be helping in her work as one of her supervisors. Apart from our regular conversations in which each of us is an interlocutor for the other, Marta prepared a detailed summary of the OECD's work on 'intangibles' (Pankiv) which has been helpful to me in confirming or clarifying my own thinking, even though I acknowledge that the opinions – and errors – in this chapter are my responsibility.

I. INTRODUCTION

The 'license model' illuminates a fundamental concern of transfer pricing and Base Erosion and Profit Shifting (BEPS), specifically, the relationship between where income arises and the capacity of parties to transactions, particularly the 'licensor', to perform and be responsible for obligations and exploit rights that have been assigned contractually and are intrinsic to earning income. The ensuing income tax question corresponding to the dominant tendency of transfer pricing to focus on economic analysis is frequently expressed as whether any of them is entitled to the income assigned to them that they ostensibly earned. More pointedly, as Actions 8-10 reports reflect, the key question is whether they actually earned the income, or some particular amount of it.

Transfer pricing is commonly perceived as establishing the authority to tax based on the 'economic substance' of transactions and the parties to them. It is as if transfer pricing exists apart from the law – tax and private law. This perception can make it fairly easy for critics to marginalize the impact of Actions 8-10 recommendations on the basis that taxation is according to the law and not economics.

Transfer pricing exists within and can only function according to the legal systems for which it is relevant, that is, to which it is accessory like the rest of tax law. The legal system comprises not only tax law but, more fundamentally, the private law that defines and establishes the requirements and expectations for organizational forms and contracts on which tax law relies and to which the tax law is accessory. Transfer pricing concerns the nature, connotations of, and the consequences of legal relationships. It is not a parallel system that supplants the law; however, neither does it require a surrender to legal form or formalistic legal analysis. Legal concepts and legal analysis – in particular, the law of contracts – entail an evidence-based inquiry into when and to what extent and, accordingly, to what financial outcome it is reasonable for parties to rely on each other. This is a LEGAL and not an economic substance analysis even though economic analysis and transfer pricing guidance inform the law's evidentiary inquiry according to which contractual reliance is tested.

What is commonly described as an inquiry into the 'economic substance' of transactions is actually an evidence-based analysis of the 'reasonable expectations of the parties' in regard to transactions; it is fundamentally a legal analysis grounded in the law of contract and related law concerning damages consequential on the non-performance of contracts.[1] It is asking, as a matter of legal construction, whether the

1. See Fuller, Lon. L. and William R. Perdue, Jr., *The Reliance Interest in Contract Damages* (1936) 46:1 Yale Law Journal 52-96, at 1, and see also Fuller, Lon L., *Consideration and Form* (1941) 41 Column Law Review 799; Boyle, James, *Legal Realism and the Social Contract: Fuller's Public Jurisprudence of Form Private Jurisprudence of Substance* (March 1993) 78(3) Cornell Law Review particularly at 372, 374, 375, and 390, and Dworkin, Ronald, *Law's Empire* (Cambridge, Mass.: Harvard University Press, 1986); See also Wilkie, J. Scott, *'Master File', 'Local File' and 'Country-by-Country Reporting': A Canadian Perspective*, (2016) Vol. 23 No. 2 International Transfer Pricing Journal, International Bureau of Fiscal Documentation, 115, particularly notes 14 and 15, and Prebble, Zoë M. and John Prebble, *The Morality of Tax Avoidance*, Victoria University of Wellington Legal Research Papers, Paper No. 9/2012 (SSRN: http://ssrn.com/abstract=1650 363), [Vol. 43-2010] Creighton Law Review 693; Prebble, Rebecca and John Prebble, *Does the Use of General Anti-avoidance Rules to Combat Tax Avoidance Breach Principles of the Rule of Law? A*

parties' reliance on each other to commit to obligations, perform various functions, and exploit assigned rights is reasonable. Consequently, in the event of non-performance, could the parties, in full view of all of the relevant circumstances, justify recompense for a meaningful loss? This is the type of analysis that the law of contracts demands in all cases, not just taxation. Those expectations and that reliance may not be reasonable because, for example, the parties to those transactions (notably to the awareness of each other, as would be the case in a non-arm's length setting) lack the functional and financial capacity to do what their self-selected legal forms and written contracts otherwise would suggest they are or should be doing. An evidence-based legal analysis detects what are, in law, the terms of their transaction.

This chapter makes two primary, related points. First, not only in the context of Actions 8-10 concerning intangibles but also, more generally, transfer pricing is essentially concerned with the legal substance of associated parties' dealings. Taxation is according to law and legal principles even when transfer pricing is concerned. Second, in the absence of a world tax order or code that would affirmatively establish the 'source' of income – there is no 'natural law of source' – the Actions 8-10 recommendation together with the other BEPS recommendations effectively seek to establish the source of income by negative implication, i.e., carving out where it is not reasonable to consider income to have been earned leads by default – negative

---

Comparative Study [Vol. 55:21] Saint Louis University School of Law 21; and Bogenshneider, Bret N., *Manufactured Factual Indeterminacy and the Globalisation of Tax Jurisprudence* (23 Nov. 2015) 4:2 University College London Journal of Law and Jurisprudence 250; SSRN: Http://ssm.com/abstract=2694539; Lon Fuller's scholarship substantially informs recourse to notions of 'reliance' and 'expectation' (parallel in many respects to like notions found in the law of tort) for the interpretation of contracts, taking account not only the construction of their terms but also looking beyond, or perhaps into the significance of, the formal elements of contracts and their making to determine their ultimate or substantial implications and from those their essential terms and what they mean in a particular context. Important to this analysis are the consequences of non performance, and how, in light of reliance and expectations, a party should be compensated for that non-performance. By considering the nature of promises that may or are asserted to be cognizable under the law in this way, what has been referred to as a realist approach engaging what for its time may have been seen as 'modern' contract theory, the attempt is made to affirm or establish the terms of a bargain by looking at how parties could reasonably have been expected to perform and rely on others to perform it. This does not necessarily dispense with more typical and formalistic approaches to evaluating contracts, but it does take a view of form as kind of framework in which promises are made, recognizing the importance of the behavior and conduct of parties in relation to adopted form to discover whether the form fully discloses the terms and conditions of a contract. The thinking alluded to in this note informs and provides the building blocks for the 'legal substance' analysis which follows. Directionally Fuller's outlook on the law, encapsulated in his own words (Fuller 1 at 1), as what may be described as an agglomeration of self-defining and consequently self-fulfilling legal fictions or constructs, the purposes of which must be kept in view, is useful, indeed important to bear in mind and significantly influences the comments in this chapter:

> We are still too willing to embrace the conceit that it is possible to manipulate legal concepts without the orientation which comes from the simple inquiry: toward what end is this activity directed? Nietzsche's observation, that the most common stupidity consists in forgetting what one is trying to do, retains a discomforting relevance to legal science. ...It is, as a matter of fact, clear that the things which the law of damages purports to 'measure' and 'determine' – the 'injuries', 'items of damage', 'causal connections', etc. – are in considerable part its own creations, and the process of 'measuring' and 'determining' them is really a part of the process of creating them.

implication – to where it is (more) reasonable to consider it to have been earned. This is precisely the type of inquiry that the 'license model' invites. The significance and fate of the 'license model' is and, as can be argued under a thorough legal analysis, always has been associated with whether the licensor plays a meaningful, transformative role and, consequently, whether the arrangements to which it purports to be a party to are effective or, indeed, are all of the relevant arrangements. Once it is established where income is not considered to have been earned then, impliedly its 'source' may reasonably and more evidently be revealed in a manner visible to all potential taxing states. Consequently income may be taxed and overlapping tax claims resolved in a familiar way according to applicable law with the assistance of transfer pricing analysis according to Chapters I-III of the Transfer Pricing Guidelines as significantly enhanced and refined by the BEPS recommendations.

The OECD's adoption of economic concepts in transfer pricing, both generally and in its recommendations concerning Actions 8-10, offers an analytic framework or code for what fundamentally is a legal analysis.

II. THE SIGNIFICANCE OF INTANGIBLES: THE ARM'S LENGTH STANDARD

'Intangibles' are the fundament of the 'BEPS' project initiated by the Organisation for Economic Co-operation and Development (OECD) and, in many respects, were the catalyst for it. The OECD's review of its guidance in Chapter VI of the OECD Transfer Pricing Guidelines was well advanced before the BEPS project crystallized in its underlying February 2013 scoping paper and resulting July 2013 'Actions'. The 'Arm's Length Standard' (the 'ALS') supplies the context in which 'intangibles' become enormously significant when operating within and even navigating a variety of legal constructs for discerning how, where, and by whom income – profit – is earned and to whom and territorially to which jurisdictions it should consequently be attributed.

The title of this chapter is meant to be provocative. It is also meant to convey the perspective that the OECD clearly has 'the end' towards which the BEPS project is directed in mind and is notably cognizant of how 'legal concepts' can be 'manipulated' to allow circumstances to appear to be and to be perceived as other than what evidently, on closer examination, they may actually be in relationship to the objectives that serve that 'end'. Despite the continuing connection between transfer pricing and 'economics' of 'substance', the OECD's approach demonstrates a strong current of 'legal substance' analysis that is actionable not only according to transfer pricing guidance but also by the fundamental law that provides the framework for business organizations and contracts with which transfer pricing must contend.

This chapter investigates BEPS-related developments concerning intangibles with reference to the so-called license model[2] for concentrating and then deploying manifestations of intangible value in international business arrangements of

2. Verlinden, Isabelle, *Unpublished Slides Depicting a 'License Model'*, part of a presentation in 2015 and the Vienna University of Economics and Business.

Multinational Enterprises (MNEs). The objective of this chapter is to identify critical implications of the OECD's first stage conclusions for Actions 8-10[3] of the 'license model' and using that model as a point of reference for inferring those implications and commenting on their practical significance. The essence of this is that the OECD expects parties engaged in commercial activities within a commonly controlled group to have the functional capability and financial resources as, or at least acting as, autonomous parties to assume the obligations and to exploit the opportunities organizationally and contractually allotted to them.[4] While the transfer pricing outlook expressed in the BEPS reports speaks in terms of economic substance and commercial rationality,[5] there is reason to believe that actually it concerns and is focused on discovering and understanding the 'legal substance'[6] of relationships between MNE group members. Included would be contractual relations that are no less contractual because they are not written down but readily - even inevitably - can be inferred from parties' dealings. Consequently, what also takes shape is a more well-developed approach to discerning the 'source' - in both qualitative and territorial terms - of income earned within an MNE according to prevailing as well as the new transfer pricing guidance but firmly grounded in the law. The result may be that the 'model' as a descriptive construct is as fine as any model can be but that the diffusion of MNE income among constituents of the model will be quite different after taking a more explicit account of features and tendencies of the ALS that, until now, may have been merely latent in Article 9 of the OECD Model Tax convention.

3. OECD, OECD/G20 Base Erosion and Profit Shifting Project Aligning Transfer Pricing Outcomes with Value Creation Actions 8-10: Final Reports. It is expected that the OECD Transfer Pricing Guidelines (Transfer Pricing Guidelines for Multinational Enterprises and Tax Administrations (Paris: OECD 2010)) will be amended in accordance with the recommendations in the reports on Actions 8-10.
4. OECD, Actions 8-10, Executive Summary, pp. 9-11, and Revisions to Section D of Chapter I of the Transfer Pricing Guidelines, in particular paras. 1.33, 1.34, 1.42, 1.43, 1.45, 1.46, 1.47, 1.49 and 1.50, and Revisions to Chapter VI of the Transfer Pricing Guidelines, particularly the Summary, and paras. 6.3, 6.35, 6.36 and 6.42, as well as Revisions to Chapter VIII of the Transfer Pricing Guidelines, in particular para. 8.39 and, generally, the approach taken in Chapter IX of the Transfer Pricing Guidelines and in the OECD's 'Accepted OECD Approach' in its 2008 and 2010 Reports on The Attribution of Profits to Permanent Establishments, in particular their reliance on transfer pricing guidance to infer transactions within a single legal entity that would have independent legal significance between legally separate entities and, in that connection, a decided focus on observable contributions notably associated with 'people functions'. See also Hickman, Andrew, Melinda Brown and Mayra Lucas (head of unit, Transfer Pricing; adviser, Transfer Pricing; and adviser, Transfer Pricing, respectively), Actions 8-10: Aligning transfer pricing outcomes with value creation, International Tax Review OECD BEPS Project, December/January 2016 (www.internationaltaxreview.com) 35.
5. *Ibid.*, Actions 8-10, Executive Summary.
6. See *supra* note 1 and post, note 18; see Wilkie. J. Scott, *The Taxation of Cross-Border Corporate Profits,* presented in Santiago, Chile on 19-20 Nov. 2015 at the David R., Tillinghast Conference Sponsored by the International Fiscal Association and the University of Chile, entitled 'The New International Tax Cooperation Paradigm: Impact on Domestic Tax Regimes and the Cross-Border Allocation of Taxing Rights' (publication pending).

III. THE LICENSE MODEL

Generally, the license model presupposes that intangibles will have gravitated to 'ownership'[7] or relatively unlimited use by a central 'intangibles' MNE group member; it licenses the use of those intangibles to other MNE group members engaged in the production, sale, and delivery of products and services to third party customers of the MNE. The intangibles company is paid a fee or royalty for the use by other group members of the intangibles. The intangibles company may contract with other group members, even its parent, for ongoing services in order to maintain and develop the intangibles and to procure financing for its activities that would not be supported by its license fee or royalty income. Typically, the intangibles company depends, through outsourcing or other such arrangements or, even, the stewardship of superior MNE group members, on others within the MNE group for various services and overarching operational, creative, and other oversight for which it would pay various fees, though measurably more modest in amount than the royalties it receives. The outcome is commonly a concentration of group profit in the intangibles company even if it may only be the licensor and have few independent resources as well as limited independent functional and financial capacity to accomplish anything. In any event, its activities may be more closely associated with routine administration than entrepreneurial endeavors of any kind and corresponding responsibilities for them except in a purely legal sense according to governing contracts. Typically, an intangibles company of this type would be located in a low-tax jurisdiction and, depending on the nature and scope of its activities, a jurisdiction possibly offering targeted tax preferences either legislatively or by rulings.[8]

Of course, none of this needs to be the case. It is equally possible, tax and certain other considerations aside, that the intangibles company would be a robustly constituted entrepreneur able to orchestrate, take responsibility for, and exploit the intangibles in its charge as any entrepreneur would considering its expected profitability. Correspondingly, it would have its own resources or, at least, the executive and managerial competencies and capacity to engage, direct, evaluate, and apply the work of others to serve its objectives. In such a case, whether evaluated in terms of its situation in a preferential tax regime or more generally, its allocated profitability according with the expectations of an 'owner'/entrepreneur might well be reasonable.

7. Like many concepts addressed in Actions 8-10, 'ownership' is inextricably linked to discerning the contractual features of the organizational and contractual arrangements of MNE group parties. It is an inescapable fact that, despite the inevitable reliance by transfer pricing on industrial economic analysis, transactions occur within and are defined by the legal systems on which they and their parties depend for what law generally provides in any context, that is a predictable and hopefully well (enough) defined framework for honorable, 'civil' and enforceable dealings among parties taking account of their circumstances and interests. The force of – indeed, the need for – the law and its legal constructions (see *supra* note 1 and, in particular, the second epigram drawn from Fuller and Perdue) cannot be avoided but, nevertheless, as this chapter addresses, the law does not necessarily speak for itself and transactions that adopt legal formulations must still be evaluated, construed, and tested in order to determine their faithful (or not) alignment.
8. See OECD Action 5.

This would be different, however, than the possibly more stereotypical intangibles or 'IP' company that primarily merely exists as a legal personality and depends entirely upon others to do work intrinsic to the creation, care for, and deployment of intangibles in which it has no meaningful capability to organize or control. It is with the latter type of intangibles company that the OECD is concerned even though the 'pure' transfer pricing analytics apply to both, i.e., the 'P' and 'S' aspects of BEPS and the care that must be taken not to conflate them.

The 'license model' is generally contrasted with the 'cost contribution arrangement' model. However, except in formal including contractual terms, there appears to be little differences between the two, at least insofar as the application of the ALS and the attendant BEPS issues are concerned. Cost contribution arrangements can be understood conceptually as comporting with constellations of separate intangibles owners that, constructively through such arrangements, cross-license their 'owned' intangibles to other MNE group members for fees that are essentially recovered from market transactions rather than the other 'owners'. The effect, however, is and is meant to be similar to the license model, particularly insofar as the ALS is concerned. 'Owners' and 'users' of intangibles contribute to their Development, Enhancement, Maintenance, Protection, and Exploitation (in BEPS terms, in Actions 8-10, 'DEMPE' functions[9]) collaboratively in proportion to the benefits they expect to objectively realize from those intangibles. There is mutual dependency concerning the DEMPE functions, an acknowledgment of shares inputs and outcomes, and a market-based mechanism for each to realize the benefits of its share of the DEMPE functions and, particularly, their cost. Each approach, the licensing mode approach and the cost contribution approach, is meaningfully the same as the ALS means and the objectives it serves.

IV. TRANSFER PRICING AND BEPS

Both models, even according to this brief description, illustrate and indeed host the two primary concerns of the BEPS. The overarching directional significance (apart from associations with perceptions of colorable tax avoidance) of the 'P' and 'S' components of BEPS should not be disregarded. At the same time, BEPS is concerned with the 'correct' measurement of income according to where it is earned and, consequently, its 'source'. These are complementary objectives which should not be conflated. Both are prominent in how BEPS, and particularly Actions 8-10, address 'intangibles'.

On the one hand, it is and always has been the goal of transfer pricing analysis to assist this determination, affording an opportunity for tax jurisdictions to be able to otherwise assert sustainable tax claims to determine how and to what degree the allocated income to its taxpayers (or cognizable establishments – 'permanent establishments') should be taxed. This is the 'P' component of BEPS.[10]

9. See Actions 8-10, Part B, and in particular paras. 6.34 and 6.71, and Example 2 in Annex to Chapter VI – Examples to illustrate the guidance on intangibles.
10. Even with the most refined transfer pricing guidance, concerning intangibles in particular, intersecting and possibly conflicting inter-nation tax claims are inevitable. That was the case

A significant focus, even the catalyst, of BEPS is 'Shifting' income through the artful use of private legal constructions, the application of conflicts of laws, principles, and tax treaties. The result is to cause income to come to reside, that is seems to have been earned, where, according to the ALS, it should not be considered to have been - indeed, according to some measures, could not possibly have been - earned. The various government hearings held at the outset of and during the BEPS project to investigate the tax planning practices of MNEs, notably those whose 'stock in trade', is dominated by measures of 'reputation', market presence, and product offerings that are not 'tangible', focused on these outcomes as fiscal and tax policy concerns.[11] These concerns are not so much about transfer pricing and tax, in general, as they are about the legal environment in which transactions take place, notably concerning intangibles, which makes it difficult (or easy, depending on one's perception) to determine and alter the source of income. Tax regimes are accessory to private law regimes; private law regimes differ among countries. Conflicts of laws' principles reconcile characterization, qualification, and other differences among countries' laws so as to determine a common perception for all interested parties of the legal construction to which, then on its own terms, the tax laws apply. In the absence of significant international synchronicity - there is no world tax order, legislator, or administrator - the leaves may fall where they fall, too often it came to be thought in places where there are no trees.

A. The Realities of BEPS

In one way or another, all of the BEPS Actions and outcomes, although some more directly than others, concern three fundamental realities underlying how global business operations are conducted by MNEs and how those operations are envisaged by legal and tax systems. The ALS, in its former guise and as altered by the ongoing work on Actions 8-10, should be understood in this context. This has a dramatic effect on how the ALS is perceived, interpreted, and applied and whether even the Actions 8-10 outcomes should be considered as embellishing rather than changing the ALS by enhancing its underlying legal implications and analysis. This chapter proceeds accordingly, not as a 'deep dive' into transfer pricing techniques, although there is much of that, it is respectfully said, in the Actions 8-10, but to interpret and construe what the OECD has accomplished with its recommendations and consequently how, in that context, the 'license model' is or is not valid.

---

under the existing guidance, and it will be the case under the new. In some fashion, means to resolve disputes about those claims is intrinsic to the effectiveness and effect of transfer pricing guidance. See OECD Action 14.

11. General notice can be taken of the public hearings and of the continuing interest of legislators in the United Kingdom and the United States with considerable reference to transfer pricing, of the European Commission's interest in tax practices of MNEs and, in that regard, how countries have administered their tax systems.

B. Legal Considerations

First, these operations occur according to legal constructions whereby the features established by the countries' private law and differences which are resolved with the application of conflicts of laws principles. Organizational forms, legal entities, and contractual relationships between legally distinct 'persons' and the like are generally respected and indeed necessary for orchestrating orderly commercial relationships and other affiliations including those across borders.

C. 'Comparable'

Second, we are entitled to be skeptical that these legal considerations have the same significance when employed by and within MNE organizations as they do for engagements between genuine third parties, that is, individuals who have no connection to or interests in each other apart from their immediate commercial engagements.[12] This is because, in the absence of adverse interests between transacting parties, there are no meaningful or a limited possibility of constraints on how the legal constructions are used or, in fact, what they necessarily mean or foreshadow in any particular circumstances. The absence of adverse commercial interests coupled with the ability to 'control' the circumstances of transactions between legally distinct parties of common interest existing within the economic unity that is an MNE is the essence of the 'problem' addressed by the ALS. The ALS, given validity by Article 9 of the OECD Model Tax Convention, is not a prescription for setting transaction prices except when necessary, but not by inevitable implication. Rather, it exists to ensure a fair dispersion of profit among enterprises comprising an MNE. It attempts to do so by identifying and neutralizing the effects of conditions and circumstances that do not reflect commercial considerations consistent with the rhythm of business operations and that, consequently, amount to a chauvinistic exercise of corporate power notwithstanding the normal exigencies of commercial operations and behavior.

Despite the reliance on the Transfer Pricing Guidelines as if they had legal significance in the nature of statutory law, Article 9 is not prescriptive or transactional; it is directional. It identifies and then adjusts 'profits' for 'conditions ... 'made or imposed between the two enterprises in their commercial or financial relations which differ from those which would be made between independent enterprises ...'.[13]

---

12. See Wilkie, J. Scott, *Reflecting on the 'Arm's Length Principle': What is the 'Principle'? Where Next? Fundamentals of International Transfer Pricing in Law and Economics* (Wolfgang Schön and Kai A. Konrad eds.) (Berlin: Springer, 2012) 137-156, and Wilkie, Scott, *The Definition and Ownership of Intangibles: Inside the Box? Outside the Box? What is the Box?* (2012) 4:3 World Tax Journal 222-248, and in them references to Rosenbloom and Vann. See Vann, Richard, *Policy Forum: The Policy Underpinnings of the BEPS Project – Preserving the International Corporate Income Tax?* (2014) 62:2 Canadian Tax Journal 433-441 and Vann, Richard, *Taxing International Business Income: Hard-Boiled Wonderland and the End of the World* (2010) 2:3 World Tax Journal 291-346.
13. See OECD Model Tax Convention, Article 9(1).

Context matters. The focus is and always has been on profits - indeed, the combined profits - of enterprises in relationship to each other.[14] The evaluation of the profits of one enterprise, one legal constituent of a group, or at least one other is not meaningful in the context of Article 9 except in relationship to another group member. The combined results of both are always relevant; the ALS has no meaning otherwise. Implicitly, then, despite respect for legal formalism - indeed, essential legal formalism for the good order of commercial and personal relationships - the essential economic unity of commonly controlled enterprises, effectively as co-ventures or partnerships even if not so organized in legal terms, is not only recognized but establishes an underlying premise of the ALS. The ALS seeks to eliminate, for tax reporting and paying purposes, the effects of legal formalism undertaken essentially for its own sake from dealings between commonly controlled enterprises. Hence, it seeks to excise the effects of 'commercial or financial relations' that effectively are gratuitous when compared to and contrasted with those of 'independent' parties. In result, it intends to achieve a measure of enterprise profit akin to what would be earned without those distorting effects. Whether that profit would, necessarily, be the 'same' profit earned by independent enterprises according to a 'fair market value' standard or whether prices of goods and services would necessarily be the same as charged and paid by disinterested counterparties is not directly the issue even though there may be a resulting alignment.[15]

14. See Wilkie, J. Scott, *Reflecting on the 'Arm's Length Principle': What Is the 'Principle'? Where Next? Fundamentals of International Transfer Pricing in Law and Economics* (Wolfgang Schön and Kai A. Konrad eds.) (Berlin: Springer, 2012) 137-158 and Wilkie, Scott, *The Definition and Ownership of Intangibles: Inside the Box? Outside the Box? What is the Box?* (2012) 4:3 World Tax Journal 222-248; consideration is given to what might be described as factor-based profit splitting, i.e., an alignment of necessary business measures comporting with inputs and outputs without the adoption of a prescriptive or inelastic algorithmic framework that would amount to formulary apportionment. See, also, Michael Durst papers: Durst, Michael C., *Self-Help and Altruism: Exploring the Problem of Tax Base Erosion in Developing Countries,* Bloomberg BNA Transfer Pricing Report (29/5/2014), 23 Transfer Pricing Report 478; Durst, Michael C., *Developing Country Taxation, Part II: The Limitations of Corporate Income Taxation,* Bloomberg BNA Transfer Pricing Report (24/7/2014), 23 Transfer Pricing Report 228; Durst, Michael C., *Developing Country Taxation, Part III: Surmounting Transfer Pricing Problems of Distributors and Manufacturer,* Bloomberg BNA Transfer Pricing Report (16/10/2014), 23 Transfer Pricing Report 797; Durst, Michael C., *Designing a Hybrid Transfer Pricing Method,* BloombergBNA Transfer Pricing International Journal (30/3/2015), 16 TPTP 28; Durst, Michael C., *Can a 'Shared Net Margin Method' Provide a Global Transfer Pricing Standard,* Bloomberg BNA Transfer Pricing Report (30/4/2015), 23 Transfer Pricing Report 1639, 2/5/15; Durst, Michael C., *Can a 'Shared Net Margin Method' Provide a Global Transfer Pricing Standard,* Bloomberg BNA International Tax Monitor (30/5/2015), 23 Transfer Pricing Report 1238, 2/5/15; Durst, Michael C., *Developing Country Taxation, Part VII: Don't Lose Focus on Domestic Revenue Sources,* Bloomberg BNA Transfer Pricing Report 2015, 24 Transfer Pricing Report 713; Durst, Michael C., *Proposed Structure for a 'Value Creation' Method,* Bloomberg BNA Transfer Pricing Report 2015, 24 Transfer Pricing Report 972.
15. See Boadway, Robin, *Policy Forum: Piecemeal Tax Reform Ideas for Canada – Lessons from Principles and Practice* (2014) 62:4 The Canadian Tax Journal 1029-1059; Kane, Mitchell A., *Transfer Pricing, Integration and Synergy Intangibles: A Consensus Approach to the Arm's Length Standard,* (2014) (October) World Tax Journal 282; Schön, Wolfgang, *International Tax Coordination for a Second-Best World* (Part I) (2009) (October) World Tax Journal 67; Schön, Wolfgang, *International Tax Coordination for a Second-Best World* (Part II) (2010) (February) World Tax Journal 65; Schön, Wolfgang, *International Tax Coordination for a Second-Best World*

The 'comparables' analysis that has spawned and dominates even in the Transfer Pricing Guidelines has become a transfer pricing industry that does not capture the essence of the ALS. Seeking comparable analogues as an analytic expedient in order to effectively search for circumstances and terms of transactions that are attributable more to the unchecked enforcement of corporate power than the dictates of rational commercial dealing may certainly be beneficial within limits – as an analytical device. However, it is not the 'rule', and there are limits. Even the analogues may be imperfect if they closely search for comparable transactions when, as stipulated by Article 9, the ultimate comparator is a more expansive evaluation of all market and other circumstances within which particular transactions take place – all of the circumstances of transactions taking into account the features and objectives of the commonly controlled parties.[16] As a result, notwithstanding the cohesive association of the ALS with transaction-based separate entity dealings, it may be that what really is and always has been at stake at the heart of the ALS are comparable circumstances[17] and not comparable transactions, even though transactions remain a part, but possibly not the

(Part III) (2010) (October) World Tax Journal 227; and Wilkie, J. Scott, *Policy Forum: BEPS One Year In – Taking Stock* (2014) 62:2 Canadian Tax Journal 455-475; Wilkie, Scott, *Reflections on 'BEPS': Tax, Law and 'Law and Economics'* (31 Jul. 2014) University of Calgary School of Public Policy Blog (http://policyschool.ucalgary.ca; Wilkie, J. Scott, *Reflecting on the 'Arm's Length Principle': What is the 'Principle'? Where Next? Fundamentals of International Transfer Pricing in Law and Economics* (Wolfgang Schön and Kai A. Konrad eds.) (Berlin: Springer, 2012) 137-158; Wilkie, Scott, *The Definition and Ownership of Intangibles: Inside the Box? Outside the Box? What is the Box?* (2012) 4:3 World Tax Journal 222-248; Wilkie, J. Scott, *Intangibles and Location Benefits (Customer Base), June / July 2014 Bulletin for International Taxation: BEPS Special Issue* (International Bureau of Fiscal Documentation) 352 360; Wilkie, J. Scott, *Canada Waiting for 'BEPS' … Canada 'Appears' CCH* (2014) (September–October) International Tax Journal, CCH, 5-12; Wilkie, J. Scott, *The Taxation of Cross-Border Corporate Profits*, presented in Santiago, Chile on 19-20 Nov. 2015 at the David R. Tillinghast Conference sponsored by the International Fiscal Association and the University of Chile, entitled 'The New International Tax Cooperation Paradigm: Impact on Domestic Tax Regimes and the Cross-Border Allocation of Taxing Rights' (publication pending); Wilkie, J. Scott, *'Master File', 'Local File' and 'Country-by-Country Reporting': A Canadian Perspective*, (2016) Vol. 23 No. 2 International Transfer Pricing Journal, International Bureau of Fiscal Documentation, 115.

16. See the practical insight of Fris, Pieter (Pim), and Sebastian Gonnet, NERA Economic Consulting, *How Analysis Can Define the Nature, Use and Pricing of Intangibles, in Intellectual Property* (4th ed.) International Tax Review, Tax Reference Library No. 24 (www.internationaltaxreview-.com), published in association with: The Ballentine Barbera Group, Ernst & Young, FTI Consulting, NERA Economic Consulting, and applications of transfer pricing analysis along these lines discussed by de Homont, Philip and Alexander Voegele, *Brand Management Centres in the Age of BEPS*, International Tax Review, 29 Oct. 2015; de Homont, Philip and Alexander Voegele, *License Fees Determined by the 'Willingness-to-Pay'*, NERA Economic Consulting, http://www.nera.com/content/dam/nera/publications/2015/ITR%20Ot%202015%20sp%20feat%20intangible%20nera.pdf; de Homont, Philip and Alexander Voegele, *Intangible Contributions in the Automotive Industry under BEPS*, International Tax Review, 15 Dec. 2015. See also Vann, Richard, *Policy Forum: The Policy Underpinnings of the BEPS Project – Preserving the International Corporate Income Tax?* (2014) 62:2 Canadian Tax Journal 433-441; Vann, Richard, *Taxing International Business Income: Hard-Boiled Wonderland and the End of the World* (2010) 2:3 World Tax Journal 291-346 and Wilkie (footnote 16).
17. See the approach taken by Fris, Pieter (Pim) and Sebastian Gonnet, NERA Economic Consulting, *How Analysis Can Define the Nature, Use and Pricing of Intangibles, in Intellectual Property* Tax Reference Library No. 24 (4th ed.) International Tax Review (www.internationaltaxreview-.com), published in association with: The Ballentine Barbera Group, Ernst & Young, FTI Consulting, NERA Economic Consulting.

controlling part, of the analysis. Such an opinion of the ALS does not require the abandonment of either its focus or the legal constructions that divide MNEs as unitary economic 'firms' into constituent pieces for various commercial and legal reasons. It requires only that the ALS be understood for what it actually is and that the fiscal significance of those legal constructions not be accepted uncritically and that their 'legal substance', not just 'economic substance', is understood according to plausible legal interpretations on which the ALS would fairly build.[18]

18. See *supra* note 1. This concept of 'legal substance' draws on the private law scholarship of Lon Fuller, a distinguished legal scholar who is credited with what has been described as a 'realist' approach to private and particularly contract law that, as earlier noted, is also influenced by the law or torts. An overarching theme is what is, despite selected formalism, the reasonable expectation of the parties to an arrangement – a contract – as disclosed not only by a doctrinaire reading of their contracts but also an attempt to understand them considering their capacities to contract, that is, to commit to obligations and generate and exploit rights. Partly, this legal interpretive or constructionist exercise would be necessarily informed by an evaluation of what would happen, what 'damages' would be due, in the event of non-performance not merely as a type of prescriptive entitlement according to formal terms but also as a reasonable construction of those terms in light of how the parties to a contract behaved, and possibly could only have behaved, in relationship to each other as disclosed by evidence of their transactions. This approach was developed as a normative method to generally understand contracts. It has added significance where, as in any transfer pricing analysis, there may be reasonable doubt about relying on contracts that are written without a more thorough inquiry because of the absence in the case of non-arm's dealings of the sort of independence and adversity of interest between contracting parties that it may fairly be stated underlies the law of contract and judgments about their construction and the reasonable limits of their performance. At least in his private law scholarship, he has been described as a legal 'realist'; that is, he is concerned with the actual relationships between parties and what that implies for their enforceable legal arrangements. In that sense, he adopts a purposive approach that examines whether reliance of one on the other is justified and, in a like manner, whether the expectations of one on the other are justified taking into account the circumstances of their transaction. In private law, Fuller offered a resolutely contextual account of the relationship of form to substance. Boyle says of Fuller: 'The need for investing a particular transaction with some legal formality will depend upon the extent to which the guaranties that the formality would afford are rendered superfluous by forces native to the situation out of which the transaction arises ...'[footnote 82, Fuller, Consideration and Form, p. 804]. Fuller further provides the example of formalities designed to make the parties think about what they are doing. As usual, he takes a purposive view of such general requirements, saying that the need for them depends on whether 'the factual situation, innocent of any legal remolding, tends to bring about the desired circumspective frame of mind' [footnote 83, Fuller, Consideration and Form, p. 804]. Thus, this is the criterion for the utility of form: is the purpose that a formal requirement is already accomplished by the context? This is a jurisprudential way of saying precisely what constitutes the OECD's work in Actions 8-10 when, in pursuit of rational economic outcomes, it acknowledges the significance or parties conduct – evidence – to inform the nature as well as the terms and conditions of contracts, to affirm that those written are capable of being what they purport to be, and to illuminate those that exist through parties' activities even if not written including, in this regard, to modify or displace, as a law-based change, those that are. Distinctly, this is not an economic substance, tax avoidance, or recharacterization exercise or analysis; it is normative contract law according to what may be described as the 'modern contract theory' credited to Fuller. This is a significant influence in this chapter on what variously, in the chapter, may be referred to as 'legal substance' and the 'reasonable expectation of the parties'. A similarly directed influence in this chapter is derived from and is attributed to the jurisprudential scholarship of Ronald Dworkin whose theory of 'legal integrity' broadly requests the interpretation and construction of law with reference to the purposes that it is discerned through legal and not political analysis; it exists to serve that is, context – evidence of actions, circumstances, and 'environment'; and influence, as they must, any rational conception of the law, why it exists, and how particular patterns of activity and

behavior fit within it. The influences of Fuller and Dworkin affect the comments in this chapter from time to time even without a direct or repeated reference every time; this is noted and acknowledged at the outset. Effects that may be considered to be aligned with this approach can be seen in actual judicial decision making. For example, in the influential transfer pricing decision of the Supreme Court of Canada in *The Queen v. GlaxoSmithKline*, 2012 SCC 52 (Supreme Court of Canada), the Court effectively noted that unwritten contracts could exist with respect to intangibles even if the counterparty would not necessarily be the owner of the intangibles: [57] Although it is stated above that the purchase price appeared to be linked to some of the rights and benefits conferred under the License Agreement [with a different group member], I make no determination in these reasons as to whether the rights under the ranitidine patent granted to Glaxo Canada to manufacture and sell Zantac and the exclusive right to use the Zantac trademark are linked to the purchase price paid by Glaxo Canada to Adescha. However, arguably, if the purchase price [of an active pharmaceutical ingredient] includes compensation for intellectual property rights granted to Glaxo Canada, there would have to be consistency between that and Glaxo Canada's position with respect to Part XIII withholding tax. More broadly in two other cases, Canadian courts have, even in one case in the face of competing contracts principles, taken an elastic and expansive - purposive - approach to considering all relevant circumstances to comprehend what parties did and what their bargains actually and legally were. Another significant Canadian case concerning the construction of contractual arrangements, in this situation involving an investigation of the intention of the parties to determine the relationship between them, is *The Royal Winnipeg Ballet v. The Minister of National Revenue*, 2006 FCA 87 (Canada, Federal Court of Appeal). See also *Sattva Capital Corporation v. Creston Moly Corporation et al.*, 2014 SCC 53 (Supreme Court of Canada), particularly paras. 46-50 and 56-61 and in that regard, the Court's approach to understanding the meaning of words relative to 'contextual factors' in para. 48. It is notable in that case that the Court does struggle with the difference between construing or interpreting contracts and supplanting them with terms that the parties would not have intended and to which they did not agree; still, this line of analysis occurs as an element of interpreting contracts with the benefit of evidence as to their surrounding circumstances notwithstanding more form driven approaches associated with a classical application of the 'parol evidence rule' that would, or perhaps would have, limited recourse to extrinsic means of interpretation if the words of the contract were perceived to be clear on their own. In other words, clarity is not merely determined by using words that, in some linguistic sense, are thought to disclose their own meaning. An example of an evidence-based inquiry into the legal significance of contracts is the approach taken by the UK Court of Appeal *in Eclipse Film Partners No 35 LLP v. The Commissioners for Her Majesty's Revenue and Customs* [2015] EWCA Civ 95 (CA). That case was concerned with whether a partnership was carrying on a 'trade' as required by UK tax legislation in order to support the deduction by partners of financing expenses. The Court closely examined evidence about the significance of contracts in light of the capacities of relevant parties to perform certain undertakings and, in context, the significance of those undertakings. In short, it engaged in the exercise of construing the contracts and understanding the roles and responsibilities of the parties considering relevant factual evidence of an exercise in legal analysis. Paragraphs 111, 117, 120-123 and, notably (for a close analysis of the pertinent contracts) 130-141, encapsulate the Court's attention (and, as referred to by the Court of Appeal, that of the First-tier Tribunal from which the appeal was taken) as a matter of legal analysis to 'the commercial reality of the arrangements provided for in the network of contractual documents' (para. 137) and 'the reality of the transaction' (para. 141), all without considering the arrangements to be a 'sham' or otherwise disregarding the existence of the arrangements (contracts and parties) being scrutinized. Also see the approach taken by the Tax Court of Canada in its decision ultimately affirmed on appeal by the Supreme Court of Canada, in *Continental Bank of Canada and Continental Bank Leasing Corporation v. The Queen*, 94 DTC 1858 (Tax Court of Canada; its decision was subsequently and ultimately after an intervening appeal to the Federal Court of Appeal of Canada affirmed by the Supreme Court of Canada, [1988] 2 S.C.R. 298 (Supreme Court of Canada); the Tax Court's inquiry concerned whether the terms of the parties' arrangement aligned with their conduct, and, if not, their conduct reflected their arrangement (notable, in particular, is the Tax Court's reasons on pages 1868-1871 of its reported reasons; in order to determine the effect of contracts, the Court needed to inquire into their consistency with the

D. 'Intangibles', 'Profit', and the 'Source' of Income

Third, by attributing measurable and significant 'value' to 'intangibles' in or constituting a 'supply chain',[19] according to doctrinaire[20] constructions of the legal arrangements that orchestrate 'supply chains', it seemingly is possible and is or has been commonly thought to direct profit to entities, political jurisdictions, and geographies despite the absence in those entities or places of observable commercial activities let alone those that would comport and be commensurate with reasonable expectations generated by the terms and apparent obligations and rights associated with contracts. In effect, the 'source' of income for which, in any event, there is no 'normative' standard[21] could become whatever the parties to the arrangements determined it to be

---

nature of the parties' reliance on each other – their relative rights and obligations and their capacities to enjoy and perform them as the case may be). The reference to the Canadian cases is not meant to reflect a comprehensive canvas of possibly relevant law but merely to show the willingness of adjudicators to engage in more far-reaching contact analysis that would be limited simply by particular contracts (and the parties to them) and their terms. An inquiry into parties' terms of dealing, according to this way of looking at 'legal substance', seems to invite an inquiry into the fiscal significance of entities to which the law gives their life, for example corporations, in the sense discussed in this chapter. That is, whatever the reason for the respect accorded to corporations for various other legal purposes, it is not unfair to question what their fiscal or tax significance is, notably when they are self-selected elements of the deconstruction of an economic enterprise – the dealings of an MNE which lack the hallmarks of independence, autonomy, and adversarial self-interest which are foundational expectations of contracts. The doubt about the fiscal significance of entities and their contracts is compounded with the lack of observable features that would typically be identified with the capacity to act independently and in a self-interested way (an underlying tenet of the ALS). This subsequently affects the construction and significance of their contracts. As this chapter discusses, this seems to animate the OECD's approach to Actions 8-10 even if not specifically stated in this manner. It is suggested, however, that those directly affected by this would be well-advised to approach their 'planning' and reporting on it (including documentation) with this mind set. See Wilkie, J. Scott, *The Taxation of Cross-Border Corporate Profits,* presented in Santiago, Chile on 19-20 Nov. 2015 at the David R. Tillinghast, Conference sponsored by the International Fiscal Association and the University of Chile, entitled 'The new International Tax Cooperation Paradigm: Impact on Domestic Tax Regimes and the Cross-Border Allocation of Taxing Rights' (publication pending). See also, for a recent commentary on the interaction of contract law and transfer pricing: Pichhadze, Amir, *Exposing Unaddressed Issues in the OECD's BEPS Project: What About the Roles and Implications of Contract Interpretation Law and Private International Law in the Transfer Pricing Arm's Length Comparability Analysis?,* February 2015 World Tax Journal 99.

19. This, with various ways of expressing contributions to value, is a recurrent notion in Actions 8-10 and will receive additional attention in the second stage of the OECD's work on building the first phase work on Actions 8-10.
20. That is, formalistic, including in the sense of classical contract principles contrasted with the 'realistic' and 'purposive' approach taken by Fuller; see *supra* notes 1 and 18. The purposive approach which, nevertheless, reflects established contract law principles, seems to be reflected in the approach taken by the OECD to use an evidence-based inquiry to establish the terms of parties' transactions and, more pointedly, whether the evidence of those dealings aligns with the expressed terms in their contracts or whether their contracts are or should be construed to be somewhat different than a more limited perspective would suggest. See the discussion of *Eclipse Film Partners No 35 LLP v. The Commissioners for Her Majesty's Revenue and Customs, supra* note 18.
21. See Wilkie, J. Scott, *Policy Forum: BEPS One Year In – Taking Stock* (2014) (2014) 62:2 Canadian Tax Journal 455-475 and Wilkie, J. Scott, *The Taxation of Cross-Border Corporate Profits,* presented in Santiago, Chile on 19-20 Nov. 2015 at the David R. Tillinghast Conference sponsored by the International Fiscal Association and the University of Chile, entitled 'The New

with few limits that are, in principle, infinitely malleable according to the formulation of transactions in reliance on private law constructs. In effect, seemingly turned upside down are long-standing jurisdictional norms the purpose of which, from the earliest days of work on 'transfer pricing' by the League of Nations, had been to align the 'source' of income with the circumstances undertaken to earn it in relation to an objectively determinable place at which that income and an appropriate amount of the income would be considered to have been earned. The latter were generally understood if for no other reason than because of the simplicity of industrial circumstances that naturally aligned the features of business and the interests of tax jurisdictions in terms of observable manifestations of business.[22] These formed an indisputable number of possibilities for determining what factor inputs and market circumstances were intrinsic to the income earning process; a further, separate question was whether an economic actor being present at a location was sufficient, in relationship to that income, to sustain a tax claim by the place, the 'source state', where the observable activities occurred and a market was located.

Bluntly, in large part because of the absence of adversity among contracting parties and the facility afforded by typical interpretations and applications of relevant law, the 'source' of income could be said to be, almost by the forces of fiscal and legal alchemy, wherever it was booked. This outcome would be thought to be sustainable as long as there was a legal connection that carried the income to that place. The often ephemeral – even diaphanous – nature of 'intangibles', said nevertheless to account for so much MNE profitability, played into formalistic planning of this nature and the outcomes sought to be justified by it. Less attention, except in purely legal terms, was

---

International Tax Cooperation Paradigm: Impact on Domestic Tax Regimes and the Cross-Border Allocation of Taxing Rights' (publication pending), referring to observations made by Professor Hugh Ault. See Ault, Hugh J. and David F, Bradford, *Taxing International Income: An Analysis of the U.S. System and Its Economic Premises, in Taxation in the Global Economy* (Assaf Razin and Joel Slemrod eds.) (Chicago: University of Chicago Press, 1990), http://www.nber.org/chapters/c7203; and for a recent examination the significance of territorial source, see Kane, Mitchell A., *A Defense of Source Rules in International Taxation* (2015) 32 Yale Journal on Regulation 311; see also Shay, Stephen E., J. Clifton Fleming, Jr., and Robert J. Peroni, *The David R. Tillinghast Lecture 'What's Source Got to Do With It?' Source Rules and U.S. International Taxation* (2002-2003) 56 Tax Law Review 81.

22. See Wilkie, J. Scott, *Reflecting on the 'Arm's Length Principle': What is the 'Principle'? Where Next? Fundamentals of International Transfer Pricing in Law and Economics* (Wolfgang Schön and Kai A. Konrad eds.) (Berlin: Springer, 2012) 137-158 and Wilkie, Scott, *The Definition and Ownership of Intangibles: Inside the Box? Outside the Box? What is the Box?* (2012) 4:3 World Tax Journal 222-248. See also: Carroll, Mitchell. B., *Taxation of Foreign and National Enterprises (Volume IV)* (Geneva: League of Nations, 1933), and Carroll, Mitchell B., *Prevention of International Double Taxation and Fiscal Evasion, Two Decades of Progress Under The League of Nations* (Geneva: The League of Nations, 1939); it is interesting that as the League's development of international income allocation principles developed according to a residence – source jurisdictional dichotomy with an evident interest in establishing a suitable presence in a source country to which source country profits could and should be attributed, still a great deal of attention was paid to the functional connection of income earning activities to places where conceivably, even only conceivably, they could be considered to have been earned although it still remained to be determined how much of an enterprises profits then should be so attributed. See also Bird, Richard M. and J. Scott Wilkie, *Source v. Residence Based Taxation in the European Union; the Wrong Question?, Taxing Capital Income in the European Union Issues for Reform Ed. Sjbren Cnossen* (Oxford U.K.: Oxford University Press, 2000) Ch. 4.

paid to the autonomous functional capacity of parties to earn and to be accountable for earning income judged with reference to the productive, creative, and financial activities typically required by independent parties engaged in the same undertaking.

Yet, it is the autonomous capability of enterprises – the legal personalities that populate MNEs – that is at the core of the ALS. However, according to the ALS, it has seemingly been that transfer pricing practices and outcomes affecting the concentration of income in unproductive locations have been said to be defensible and justifiable as natural outcomes of the ALS and its legal foundations. However, the ALS intrinsically is, and always has been, concerned with the circumstances of an enterprise in relation to another enterprise within a commonly controlled group to determine where the profits to the earning of which each (necessarily) made a contribution should be considered to be earned. Even among those who venerate the Transfer Pricing Guidelines as the 'rule' rather than the 'tool' would have to acknowledge that their infrastructure foundationally concerns transactional activities of and accounted for by separate parties.

V. 'INTANGIBLES'

It is important when evaluating the implications of Actions 8-10 for the license model to have a clear perspective on the concept of 'intangibles' adopted for transfer pricing. Notably, there are primarily three questions to ask. In the 'pure' transfer pricing context, does 'intangibles' mean something different in Chapter VI of the 'old' Transfer Pricing Guidelines than it means taking into account, in particular, the Action 8 recalibration of Chapter VI and related changes to other sections of the Transfer Pricing Guidelines? Next, is the application of the Transfer Pricing Guidelines to consider 'intangibles' as meaningfully different under the 'new' approach compared to the 'old'? Finally, what elements of the analysis appear to be different, and, in fact, are they different and, just as important, whether different in kind or emphasis, are they compatible with the ALS and grounded in the legal constructions on which the license model and other transfer pricing planning would be said to be grounded?

A. What Does 'Intangibles' Mean? How Do the Guidelines Apply?

The former guidance in Chapter VI of the Transfer Pricing Guidelines specifically addresses 'commercial intangibles' comprising 'trade intangibles' and 'marketing intangibles'.[23] Insofar as they describe various manifestations of legally protectable as well as legally less well-defined 'value', for example, pertaining to 'know how' (and its more contemporary equivalent of 'show how'), these categories may overlap.[24] That

23. OECD Transfer Pricing Guidelines, paras. 6.2-6.5. This chapter resists the urge to conclude that there is an entirely new transfer pricing regime, particularly insofar as 'intangibles' are concerned, or that the ALS is somehow being regenerated rather than refining its application within well- and long-established expectations. However, others may not share that opinion. See Wittendorff, Jens, *BEPS Actions 8-10: Birth of a New Arm's Length Principle*, Tax Notes International (25 Jan. 2016) 331.
24. *Ibid.*, paras. 6.4 and 6.5.

said, in one way or another, both categories describe features regarding the distinctiveness of an MNE as an organization and of its products and services that, no matter how defined by law, accounting, or other principles and practices, are not tangible. Because of their uniqueness, they presumably are or are capable of being transferred in a manner that the law would recognize if only by offering some type of a remedy for breach of confidentiality.[25] Implicitly, Chapter VI recognizes 'synergistic value' though not in terms that express an MNE's composition and uniqueness. It does this through recognizing that excess profits that defy easy measurement according to a typical comparable analysis may exist and need to be apportioned using a profit split methodology.[26] Chapter VI also recognizes that contributions may be made by individuals other than the 'owner' of the value of intangibles. In order to be considered in a transfer pricing analysis of compensable contributions, those contributions are expected to be active and deliberate and to be delivered in a commercial way; in other words, they do not arise passively as a mere consequence of being within an MNE group.[27] In effect, the chapter is concerned with distinctive features of MNEs and their products and services, therefore, focuses on profits that arise from MNEs being commercial ecosystems in the nature of unitary economic firms and, to some degree, exist only because of this.

Intangibles that are difficult to value[28] for various possible reasons are also acknowledged, as are the possibility that *ex post* as well as *ex ante* valuation techniques may need to be applied. Intangibles are not considered as a parallel transfer pricing universe although certain well-defined intangibles in the nature of legally protected intellectual property (i.e., 'property') or confidential knowledge may be capable of being transferred on their own and accordingly subjected to a narrow transactional transfer pricing analysis for which comparables may be particularly relevant. Here, though, and more broadly, the transfer pricing analysis of and pertaining to intangibles is according to Chapters I-III of the Transfer Pricing Guidelines.[29] Chapter VI, to use a phrase that recurs in the Actions 8-10 Report, is supplemental guidance concerning the application of Chapters I-III or, otherwise stated, the way to conduct an analysis with reference to comparable transactional and market circumstances in order to test the freedom from gratuitous distortions of a taxpayer's income.

The distinctive nature of a taxpayer - its defining characteristics - is, in fact, foundational in commencing a comparison to ostensibly comparable circumstances and transactions. Intangibles affect the commercial character of an MNE and its members, their commercial personalities, as the MNE would be understood for purposes, then, of applying tax law. This is as much an influence of intangibles in a tax analysis as determinations associated with whether and to what extent they may constitute

25. *Ibid.*, paras. 6.36. and 6.26.
26. *Ibid.*, paras. 6.26 and by implication Part D, a much less developed expression of what underlies the OECE's focus on contributions and their effect, taking into account parties' 'reliance' on each other and their 'capacities'. In both cases, those terms are considered in this chapter on their entitlement to share in an MNE's profits.
27. OECD Transfer Pricing Guidelines, para. 7.13.
28. OECD Transfer Pricing Guidelines, paras. 6.24-6.31.
29. *Ibid.*, paras. 6.13-6.15.

cognizable assets (generally but at least when applying tax law), even property, the value of which may be realized through equally cognizable tax realization events – transfers within or outside an MNE group. Effectively, intangibles, as any other business input (or output) are enfolded in a typical transfer pricing analysis relying on the various analytical methodologies to detect whether the resulting income of MNE group members is undistorted by the exercise of MNE governance and control to effect uncommercial outcomes simply because, through that means, those outcomes would be possible.

The Actions 8-10 Report recalibrates and more descriptively explains the nature and testing of the value of 'intangibles' but does not change their predominant nature or substantively how they should be analyzed in the context of the Transfer Pricing Guidelines. Much more clearly than the former Chapter VI, the new guidance indicates that intangibles are manifestations of value that are not tangible or financial but can be. They are controlled and are implicitly transferable absolutely or in a more limited way through letting, i.e., a license or royalty arrangement.[30] The hallmarks of intangibles, various examples of which are identified and explained, are that control may be exercised over them and are, in some aspect, distinctive in ways that are or may be valuable to an MNE. Additionally, their definition is not controlled or limited by legal or accounting notions; they are transferable in one way or another.

The demarcation of intangibles treated as such by the transfer pricing guidance and other intangibles that are not is generally revealing for transfer pricing analysis and testing the license model. For the most part, intangibles in the 'new' context which comprise what the former guidance would categorize as trade or marketing intangibles, address a mélange of intellectual property, 'know how', 'show how', and confidential processes and product features that are cognizable under private and tax law and often accounted for according to the dictates of financial accounting even if the contemporary exposition of this notion in the new guidance abjures these features as limitations.[31] In other words, patents, trademarks, confidential information, and the other categories of itemized intangibles all, in one manner or another, contribute to MNE distinctiveness but are also capable of being transferred with or without the business in which they are used even though their use in an MNE's business may offer the capacity to generate 'excess profits' and accordingly make a typical comparables analysis more difficult or even not particularly meaningful. These intangibles, therefore, have a dual implication for MNE profitability – as potential transaction objects in themselves and as determinants of an MNE's commercial personality and identity that distinguishes it from, i.e., makes it less comparable to, others including those that ostensibly might seem to be of the same genus if not the same species.

Not included among intangibles are value and 'goodwill'; 'workforce', even though transfers of 'workforce' or significant members may be the medium for an intangibles transfer; and market characteristics including locational factors and group

30. Actions 8-10, notably paras. 6.2, 6.3, 6.6, 6.7, 6.8 and 6.9.
31. Actions 8-10, Revisions to Chapter VI of the Transfer Pricing Guidelines, Part A.3.

'synergies'.[32] These are aspects of MNE 'togetherness' that affect the nature and character of an MNE despite seeming comparability with other enterprises selling similar products and providing similar services and may, accordingly, account for an MNE's excess profits[33] that other purveyors of similar goods and services might not be able to realize because they lack the intrinsic, though invisible, features of the putative comparator. Even so, these 'non-intangible' intangibles still affect and form an element of the transfer pricing analysis but more as an adjunct to explicit other transfers of value commonly addressed by Chapters I-III of the Transfer Pricing Guidelines.

In all cases, explicitly or by implication and, in one way or another, intangibles (including 'non-intangibles' intangibles) are elements of a typical transfer pricing analysis (to be) conducted according to Chapters I-III of the Transfer Pricing Guidelines.[34] This is required for cognizable assets that may be, even if they are not, transferred in stand-alone transactions or elements of distinctive MNE value that may be commercialized and monetized through multiple contributions of group members because of the protective 'togetherness' that defines an MNE. These are reflective of an MNE's unique features that subsequently define unique characteristics and functionality with respect to products and services or, at least, customers' perceptions of them or that allow for and capitalize on various production, processes, and other efficiencies that are valuable even if only by making the MNE a relatively lower cost producer.[35] Carrying forward is the same recognition that benefits of passive association generally are not compensable; however, activating value inherent in reputation and other resources in a deliberate, systematic, and calculated manner is or at least may be compensable and, therefore, factors into a transfer pricing analysis via Chapters I-III.[36]

When it began its study of intangibles and revisions to Chapter VI before the commencement of BEPS, the OECD resisted an initial inclination to create what amounts to a parallel transfer pricing universe by hypothesizing intangibles to be in the nature of property and in turn applying the transfer pricing guidance by hypothesizing 'transactions' in those hypothesized intangibles that could be unsuitably incorporated into the typical ALS paradigm.[37] It may be that this was never the intention of the

32. *Ibid.*, in particular, Parts A.4.6, A.4.7, A.4.8 (distinguished from 'marketing intangibles' (para. 6.16 and addition to the Glossary redefining 'marketing intangible) and Part D.7. See also paras. 6.133 and 6.140 which reflect, at least with respect to 'intangibles', the need to consider the uniqueness of MNEs as part of that of analysis that Chapters I – III of the Transfer Pricing Guidelines contemplate.
33. See Kane, Mitchell A., *Transfer Pricing, Integration and Synergy Intangibles: A Consensus Approach to the Arm's Length Standard, 2014* (October) World Tax Journal 282.
34. Actions 8-10; it is clear that the OECD's work on intangibles is seen as complementary to Chapters I – III, offering an analytical framework to take 'intangibles' into account such as Chapter VI conceives them as elements of the transfer pricing analysis that would otherwise take place, in the way that it otherwise would take place. There are recurring references to Chapter VI being 'supplementary guidance': for example, paras. 6.3, 6.48f and 6.109.
35. See *supra* notes 32 and 34, and Boadway, Robin, *Policy Forum: Piecemeal Tax Reform Ideas for Canada – Lessons from Principles and Practice* (2014) 62:4 The Canadian Tax Journal 1029-1059 and Kane, Mitchell A., *Transfer Pricing, Integration and Synergy Intangibles: A Consensus Approach to the Arm's Length Standard* (2014) (October) World Tax Journal 282.
36. Actions 8-10, Revisions to Chapter VII of the Transfer Pricing Guidelines, para. 7.13.
37. See Wilkie, J. Scott, *Reflecting on the 'Arm's Length Principle': What is the 'Principle'? Where Next? Fundamentals of International Transfer Pricing in Law and Economics* (Wolfgang Schön

original conception of the revised intangibles guidance, however that intent was detectable. In fact, as long as the controlling factor is to treat intangibles and 'non-intangibles' intangibles (goodwill, market characteristics (distinguished from 'marketing intangibles'), location savings, and synergies) under the same umbrella as inputs in order to form part of a typical transfer pricing analysis organized and conducted according to Chapters I-III of the Transfer Pricing Guidelines, it may not actually matter which rubric encompasses 'intangibles'.

The new Chapter VI and its accessories, as with the old complement Chapters I-III, allow for the particular identification of property or like property interests and other features of MNEs that affect the comparability of the transactions in which they engage by affecting their very commercial nature and the implications of otherwise similar markets and other circumstances for how the MNE capitalizes on its resources, including those that are intrinsic to its nature. Partly, though, this conclusion will be affected by the third dimension of intangibles material for the present analysis and perhaps the defining unique contribution of Actions 8-10 which bridges the 'P' and 'S' aspects of BEPS in the transfer pricing arena.

B. What Is Different?

One aspect of the transfer pricing analysis is singularly different. Again with respect to the OECD, the courage and perspicacity of which is almost boundless in the work it has done and the artistry it has implemented (about which more will come later), this element of the analysis has been latent but obscured by 'legal lore' that found justification and solace in the unbridled adherence to legal constructions as dispositive determinants of fiscal consequences grounded in transfer pricing. Fundamentally, a fair question could be asked, particularly regarding MNEs as 'economic unities' and acknowledging the absence of adverse interests among their legally separated constituents, as to why 'corporations' and 'contracts' have determinative fiscal significance even though they supply the means by which economic units organize themselves and conduct global business.[38] This is not the same thing as 'looking through the corporate

and Kai A. Konrad eds.) (Berlin: Springer, 2012) 137-158; and Wilkie, Scott, *The Definition and Ownership of Intangibles: Inside the Box? Outside the Box? What is the Box?* (2012) 4:3 World Tax Journal 222-248.

38. This is, it is suggested, an underlying influence on how the OECD has sought to address the 'source' of income though not in so many words. As this chapter contends, the OECD is essentially, at the same time, able to respect and does not need to change as much as explain and possibly recalibrate the ALS, respect for private law legal constructions, and the nuances of 'legal substance' informed by evidence-based inquiries in the nature of 'economic substance'. See Wilkie, J. Scott, *The Taxation of Cross-Border Corporate Profits*, presented in Santiago, Chile on 19-20 Nov. 2015 at the David R. Tillinghast Conference sponsored by the International Fiscal Association and the University of Chile, entitled 'The new International Tax Cooperation Paradigm: Impact on Domestic Tax Regimes and the Cross-Border Allocation of Taxing Rights' (publication pending), LaBrie, F.E., *The Principles of Canadian Income Taxation, Income Tax and the Corporate Entity* (Don Mills, Ontario Canada: CCH Canadian, 1965); and McMahon, Martin, *Comparing the Application of Judicial Interpretative Doctrines to Revenue Statutes on Opposite Sides of the Pond in Comparative Perspectives On Revenue Law Essays in Honour of John Tiley* (John Avery Jones, Peter Harris and David Oliver eds.) (Cambridge U.K.: Cambridge University Press, 2008) Ch. 3, 40-74.

veil', 'recharacterizing', or applying anti-tax avoidance doctrines and rules to ignore the existence of legal constructions and contracts.

It is something quite different. It is much more closely associated with a thorough, penetrating and, in legal theory terms, enlightened inquiry into the 'legal substance' of internal MNE arrangements despite how they are configured even though it is too frequently mislabeled as an economic substance or recharacterization analysis.[39] It does this fully within the typically understood parameters of the ALs. It neither disavows nor ignores the legal constructions to which so much transfer pricing significance has historically been attributed. It intends, in the first instance, to identifying all, and not just the written, contractual relationships of the parties involved, it being understood that contracts between parties establish the platform on which Chapters I-III apply. It also intends, again in the first instance, to determine how and in what ways the law contemplates, in regard to the written contracts between parties, their genuine contractual relationships, the character of those relationships, and even more importantly, their terms.[40]

This is not an extra-legal, recharacterization exercise. Rather, it involves evaluating the capacity of parties to commit to obligations, conduct activities, supervise the performance of activities by others, and exploit entrepreneurial rights with reference to their actual characteristics, resources, competencies, and functional and financial capacities. The OECD's approach to risk, disregarding the economic and game theory analyses that could be used to measure or quantify risk, is similarly directed, and the transfer pricing tools are and remain in place to address it. Risk typically arises from someone not doing something that is required according to objective competence standards or someone doing something that, according to similar standards and limitations on authority, should not to be done – at least by that individual. Risk may also be endogenous – in a product or service, because of inherent volatility, instability, or danger for some other reasons associated with possibilities of abuse or misuse. Risk is, nevertheless, controllable in some manner if only by controlling the circumstances in which it would arise and those in which it would not otherwise be recognized including the performance (or the failure to perform) of those functions that generate the risk in the first place and who would be the responsible actors in respect to the type of risk involved. It is worth recalling that the ALS is grounded in the independence of enterprises, i.e., separate entities engaged in transactions; their autonomous capacity to assume the transactions is, in a manner of speaking, a hallmark of the ALS, the beginning point for determining if the affected circumstances entail distortions compared to those of arm's length parties. If, to adopt the adage, reward follows risk and

39. See Actions 8-10, Executive Summary, paras. 1.42-1.49 of the Revisions to Section D of Chapter I of the Transfer Pricing Guidelines, the Summary to the Revisions to Chapter VI of the Transfer Pricing Guidelines which reflect the pervasive attention in the revisions to 'both the capability to perform relevant decision-making functions together the actual performance of such functions', and paras. 6.36, 6.42, 6.48, 6.50, 6.51, 6.52, 6.133 and 6.140. While addressing different aspects of the transfer pricing of intangibles, their direction and themes are clear and oriented within the framework provided by legal analysis and the legal constructions that host the transactions (value transfers) taking place contractually if not memorialized in a written contract but pursuant to a contract no less.

40. *Ibid.*

risk follows reward, it is hardly surprising that evidence as to who influences the risk impinges on, if not determines, who is responsible for it and who subsequently benefits from assuming that responsibility.

Applying normative contract theory is evidence as to the conduct and resources of parties to a relationship that informs their reasonable expectations of each other; it is their reasonable expectations that informs the terms of their contract and contributes to resolving a conflict between the apparent, i.e., written and actual terms. This is all about 'intangibles' – those that are definable and well enough defined by the OECD in Actions 8-10 – as well as the 'non-intangible' intangibles that reflect synergistic effects and the circumstances in which cognizable transactions in or affected by intangibles take place. This mode of contract analysis does not offend even classical notions of a contract and the role of extrinsic evidence in contract interpretation. Whether parties to contractual arrangements have the capacities to sustain reasonable expectations about the performance of those contracts necessarily affects even outside a tax-based transfer pricing analysis how much regard, from an organizational perspective, should be paid to them and, consequently, whatever other significance they may have or what their fiscal significance should be. All of this is normative legal analysis.

Others might dismiss this line of thinking as recharacterization, as substance over form, or as business purposes analysis and the like; however, it is none of those although the hint of tax avoidance seeming to fit those descriptors might be the initial source of curiosity from a transfer pricing (and profit shifting) point of view. The OECD variously describes this way of thinking as detecting the economic substance of transactions and events, reconditioning or recalibrating them according to the expectations for rational economic actors and actions. That way of speaking is compatible with typical transfer pricing analysis even though it might create the impression that the analysis is extra-legal and, therefore, collides with private law legal conventions that are defensible according to conflicts of laws principles and that necessarily must be respected for what they purport to be. In fact, the substance that the OECD seeks in Actions 8-10 and particularly reinforced by the recommendations in the Action 5 Report and continuing work of the Forum on Harmful Tax Practices, is the *legal substance* of the legal arrangements determined, as would be any legal analysis, by taking systematic account of evidence of parties' conduct and consequently legal inferences drawn bout their reliance on each other which necessarily bears on their relative expectations of entitlements in relation to each and the extent to which the law, not just the tax law, should recognize them.

The OECD guidance effectively searches for the substance of legal arrangements among MNE constituents by attempting to discover evidence of their transactions and comparing that evidence to how they have configured their activities. It merely inquires whether that evidence accords with the reasonable expectations that parties would have of each other with reference to the obligations they purport to have assumed and the rights they purport to enjoy and are able to exploit. Once these have been carefully determined, a normative transfer pricing analysis with the functional and valuation analytical assistance that comprises much of the Actions 8-10 Reports takes over, as indicated by the Actions 8-10 Reports themselves, applicable in a fashion that is similar if not the same as familiar transfer pricing analysis – which might, in any event, have been applied by those skeptical of structural planning without observable 'substance'.

It is worth repeating that this is a legal and not an economic analysis. Even though facts and circumstances – the fodder of transfer pricing analysis – inevitably dominate in more typical legal fora, empirically proven facts and circumstances constitute evidence of conduct and situations in relationship to the legal implications of those circumstances. This analysis nurtures the comparables-based analysis typically employed according to Chapters I-III of the Transfer Pricing Guidelines without supplanting it. It is entirely consistent with the overarching objections of Article 9 of the OECD Model Convention. It adopts the nature and significance of transfer pricing analysis more or less on their commonly understood terms, leaving open whether intangibles should be treated as comparability factors or transaction objects in their own right while nevertheless recognizing that 'intangibles', as Chapter VI will define them, will often, if not always, have a hybrid role contributing to the comparability (or not) of economic actors – taxpayers – and their circumstances as much as to the comparability of transactions as they might be more narrowly understood.

VI. WHAT HAS THE OECD DONE, AND WHAT ARE THE IMPLICATIONS? A 'DEFINITION' OF 'SOURCE'

Fundamentally, transfer pricing attempts to illuminate the organizational and qualitative source of income. Other principles and conventions determine the jurisdictional entitlement to sustain a claim to tax income; examples which, of course, are also objects of the BEPS project include how treaties allocate inter-nation taxing rights and how a 'permanent establishment' is defined.

Source is an elusive concept. It is not, as earlier observed, normative in tax terms.[41] There is no controlling principle. The source of income is very much affected by the many types of private law legal conventions and by how inter-nation collisions among them may be resolved according to the conflicts of laws principles. It is unlikely and, in any event, likely imprudent to assume sufficient homogeneity among countries' general and tax laws that would all see the same apparent circumstances in the same way with the same legal effects. It would be an even greater challenge to align tax systems both in terms of base and rates, i.e., the measurement of income and the intensity of taxation. The OECD's work on Actions 2, 3, and 4 are clearly directed to the

41. Again, see Wilkie, J. Scott, *Policy Forum: BEPS One Year In – Taking Stock* (2014) (2014) 62:2 Canadian Tax Journal 455-475 and Wilkie, J. Scott, *The Taxation of Cross-Border Corporate Profits*, presented in Santiago, Chile on 19-20 Nov. 2015 at the David R. Tillinghast Conference sponsored by the International Fiscal Association and the University of Chile, entitled 'The new International Tax Cooperation Paradigm: Impact on Domestic Tax Regimes and the Cross-Border Allocation of Taxing Rights' (publication pending), referring to Professor Hugh Ault's observation in this regard, and see also Bird, Richard M. and J. Scott Wilkie, *Source- v. Residence-Based Taxation in the European Union: The Wrong Question? in Taxing Capital Income in the European Union Issues and Options for Reform* (Sijbren Cnossen ed.) (Oxford UK: Oxford University Press, 2000) Ch. 4, 78-109; and Wilkie.

possible, even likely, absence of factual and legal homogeneity. To a lesser extent, Actions 1, 6, and 7 are similarly directed although, for now, not quite fashioning constructive business presences in 'source' countries to more readily permit typical source taxation of taxpayers on a primary, not a withholding, basis.

Countries have different social welfare objectives and constraints and, consequently, different fiscal and policy interests which they are entitled to pursue unimpeded but within limits. Yet, the task that transfer pricing – the 'P' part of BEPS – has always confronted is to identify where income is earned in the absence of common standards with an awareness that countries' tax and legal systems cannot be relied upon to be the same or recast for purpose. The OECD has effectively defined source by negative implication, through legal insight and considerable transfer pricing art much more clearly than former Chapter VI of the Transfer Pricing Guidelines.[42] Doing so required approaching the transfer pricing 'problem' – both the 'P' and 'S' aspects of it – in the manner or at least with an awareness of the sensitivities previously outlined but also the latent characteristics of transfer pricing analysis in a legal environment. The possibilities that the 'source' of income – its qualitative and geographic 'sources' – would not be evident or could be *self-selected* because of the predominant value to an MNE of intangibles and the facility to enter into private arrangements by contract without facing contractual adversity are what distinguish transfer pricing's 'next generation' framed by Actions 8-10.

The source of income is determined by what the source of income is not. At the risk of being too poetic, 'You don't do what you can't do.' The effect of the law-based analysis and the articulation of how to analyze 'intangibles' of any kind is to identify where income is more than likely not earned – in other words, with the OECD's predominant focus on 'value creation' and 'supply chains' to excise the significance, but not the fact, of gratuitous intermediation for the allocation and attribution of MNE income. It does this without necessarily requiring the application of a profit split analysis. Intermediaries and contracts are not neglected; the corporate veil is not pierced; arrangements are construed to detect their legal features which, not surprisingly, should align with their economic characteristics and implications. Effectively, the emphasis of the 'P' and 'S' analyses shifts with the benefit of a more thoroughgoing analysis of facts and circumstances on the 'S' component. Any 'source' convention is exactly that, a convention. Other methods could be adopted, and the OECD recommends this one. By detecting where observable functions are not performed and observable financial capacity is not present, the OECD effectively identifies where contracts and organizational presence are marginal, deserving not of disregard but only a 'risk adjusted' or risk free reward.[43] The structures are not disregarded, however,

42. See Wilkie, J. Scott, *The Taxation of Cross-Border Corporate Profits*, presented in Santiago, Chile on 19-20 Nov. 2015 at the David R. Tillinghast Conference sponsored by the International Fiscal Association and the University of Chile, entitled 'The new International Tax Cooperation Paradigm: Impact on Domestic Tax Regimes and the Cross-Border Allocation of Taxing Rights' (publication pending).
43. That is, the legal superstructure is not discarded, but its fiscal significance is measured in line with how income is, and possibly only can be, 'earned'. While the possibility of 'excess' or super profits or rents has always existed and remains, there is a closer alignment between economic

their fiscal effects are moderated or even neutralized to conform to what a normative legal analysis would consider defensible. All of this depends on being able to detect 'substance' - not evaluated solely in terms of 'people functions', though these are important for controlling risk, but also organizational capacity which includes the ability to finance operations other than as a dependency that receives and disburses capital infusions from others or cannot face independent financial markets alone.

What is subsequently left is an identification of income with entities within an MNE family in particular locations that corresponds to notable, measurable, observable activities, and related resources of various types[44] on which others - even the counterparties which are cast as the 'gratuitous intermediaries' and whose fiscal significance has just been neutralized - depend. The revised transfer pricing guidance affords the possibility to infer or it implies contracts that carry an entitlement to 'intangibles' with them in some manner even if none of the parties necessarily directly originated the intangibles or, if a party did, there is no written contract establishing salient terms.[45]

This is also not an economic analysis even though it is informed by relevant evidence of facts and circumstances which inevitably reveal the economic characteristic and fortunes of parties; nor is this analysis or, more broadly, the approach it reflects in any sense fanciful as a matter of transfer pricing *simpliciter* or the law that hosts it. Indeed, in celebrated and well-known transfer pricing cases, a Court of some distinction instructed that a singular contract for the supply of a good - a raw material - be tested to determine if, implicitly, there were other relationships in the nature of contracts for intangibles and services. Again, this is a legal analysis. The result is not just a determination of the responsible parties in a supply chain but also a consequential measurement of their income by applying typical transfer pricing analysis. While

---

analysis that explains those notions and legal analysis that directs where they may come to rest without, as Kane observes and is reflected similarly but expressed differently in Wilkie, J. Scott, *Reflecting on the 'Arm's Length Principle': What is the 'Principle'? Where Next? Fundamentals of International Transfer Pricing in Law and Economics* (Wolfgang Schön and Kai A. Konrad eds.) (Berlin: Springer, 2012) 137-158; and Wilkie, Scott, *The Definition and Ownership of Intangibles: Inside the Box? Outside the Box? What is the Box?* (2012) 4:3 World Tax Journal 222-248, the need to create a 'synergistic intangible'. All of this operates according to what Article 9 of the OECD Model Tax Convention actually states, notwithstanding the sometimes slavish treatment of the Transfer Pricing Guidelines as the statement of the principle. This approach, as observed earlier, is consistent with how the OECD recommends profits be attributed to 'permanent establishments'.

44. It is noteworthy that Actions 8-10 do not deny the business reality of 'outsourcing' without relinquishing the benefits of the outsourced activities; however, the transfer pricing analysis presumes that the outsourcer has the capacities and resources necessary to engage contractors, evaluate their work, direct projects or operations to which contractors are engaged to contribute, and all the while direct those operations with a controlling mind that is not merely the representation of others in an MNE group. This has a direct bearing, of course, on how the 'licensor model' fares in regard to Actions 8-10. See the G Revisions to Section D of Chapter I of the Transfer Pricing Guidelines, paras. 1.63, 1.65, 1.69, Revisions to Chapter VI of the Transfer Pricing Guidelines in relation to outsourcing, in particular in the Summary, and paras. 6.34, 6.51, 6.53, 6.54, 6.56, 6.57, and 6.63 and (for comparative purposes, paras. Revisions to Chapter VIII of the Transfer Pricing Guidelines, paras. 8.17 and 8.18).
45. See *supra* note 18, and the reference to and discussion of *The Queen v. GlaxoSmithKline*, a decision of the Supreme Court of Canada.

consistent with treating MNEs as economic entities, this way of thinking is not an application of nor does it depend on unitary or formulary tax principles. The results of this approach may, as the OECD anticipates, be readily or almost readily revealed through an enhanced profit split methodology; profits splits already being within the OECD stable of devices considered to be consistent with and, therefore, able to be used to apply the ALS. Work on profit splits to analyze the significance of 'highly integrated operations', 'unique and valuable contributions', and 'synergistic benefits' is yet to come with guidance on how to attribute profits. However, the approach offered by the OECD to address 'hard to value intangibles' as an income measurement matter indicates a tendency to be both practical and skeptical of results being dictated by legal formalism as if parties were genuinely adverse in interest when they are not, in effect by pretending, justified by a particularly strained outlook on the ALS, that bargains among MNE group members are commercially immutable and, therefore, should be immune from periodic adjustments.

VII. BACK TO THE LICENSE MODEL

A. Seen through New Eyes

The license model and, more specifically, its more controversial formulations, involve an MNE group member with substantially insufficient independent resources and commercial autonomy being the holder of title to 'intangibles' of various types and, therefore, the putative legal owner. It purports to license them to others within the MNE group in order to earn royalties that, after the payment of relatively modest contract charges for research and development, management, and the like, leave it with substantial profits that are possibly not meaningfully taxed anywhere. Among other things, this model depends fundamentally on legal formalism. It also depends on the notion of 'permanent establishment' continuing to be too restricted and still too dominated by arcane limitations to permit the taxation of the licensor's profits by the countries where substantial activities occur and are performed by others on its behalf and on which it depends for any meaningful commercial significance. Moreover, it is potentially very important to this model that countries' 'CFC'[46] rules not reach the licensor's income to subject it to immediate (or possibly any) taxation even if distributed; indeed, countries may, even as responsible sovereign international citizens, have very 'personal' economic, fiscal, and tax policy interests to defend in not adopting more expansive CFC rules.

B. The OECD's Reaction

What is the OECD to do? What are countries to do that require the fewest reactions to the greatest number of actions but adequately deal with both the 'P' and 'S' aspects of

46. 'Controlled foreign corporation'.

BEPS in a fashion that fundamentally conforms to existing OECD guidance and is capable of according with relevant private law? What, then, *has* the OECD done?

The OECD recalibrates the transfer pricing rules[47] to align more closely with what Article 9 states is to be done rather than with voluminous analytical guidance about how to do it. In doing so, it causes income to come to rest where an evidence-based analysis regarding both inputs and production processes, on the one hand, and markets on the other suggests it is and can only be considered to be earned taking due account of applicable legal conventions and what they mean and not merely what they are commonly thought to permit. Stated differently, it establishes the source of income according to what is *not* the source of the income and subsequently leaves it to the jurisdictions that may be entitled according to standards continuing to reflect prevailing standards of and for applying the ALS in order to tax it in the first instance by applying the Transfer Pricing Guidelines which, at least directionally, continue much as they have been understood. This may not, according to comparable transactions or comparable market circumstances or even in other ways, be grounded in overt comparability in order to allocate profits including, by default, excess or synergistic profits where they reasonably may be considered to have been earned. Effectively, this is likely to reflect the fact that despite 'legal ownership' of intangibles, all within an MNE contribute in some manner to their generation and, therefore, whether through service fees, product prices royalties, or in other ways, should benefit from group profitability. This is not formulary. It is, however, factor based[48] without prescribing the weights to be attached to components of the algorithm comprising the factors.[49] Even so, those factors must be addressed and, in relative terms, rewarded through what is relative. What is the suitable reward may be different among MNEs that appear to be similar.

C. A 'New View' of the License Model

The outcome of applying the license model will depend on what the licensor actually does and, in legal terms, may reasonably be expected to and be relied upon to do directly by its own hand and with its own resources or as a contractor of others in its group and, most notably, those to which it may have outsourced functions on which it depends for creative, strategic, and managerial direction and by which it is financed. In other words, the reward to which the licensor will be entitled when applying the advanced transfer pricing analysis that Actions 8-10 Report frames and consequential

47. See Wittendorff, Jens, *BEPS Actions 8-10: Birth of a New Arm's Length Principle* (25 Jan. 2016) Tax Notes International 331 for his perspective on what this means for the ALS as we know (have known) it.
48. See Wilkie, J. Scott, *Reflecting on the 'Arm's Length Principle': What is the 'Principle'? Where Next? Fundamentals of International Transfer Pricing in Law and Economics* (Wolfgang Schön and Kai A. Konrad eds.) (Berlin: Springer, 2012) 137-158; and Wilkie, Scott, *The Definition and Ownership of Intangibles: Inside the Box? Outside the Box? What is the Box?* (2012) 4:3 World Tax Journal 222-248.
49. See Kane, Mitchell A., *Transfer Pricing, Integration and Synergy Intangibles: A Consensus Approach to the Arm's Length Standard* (2014) (October) World Tax Journal 282.

changes to Chapters I-III, VI, and VII of the Transfer Pricing Guidelines will host will depend on what the licensor does and, more pointedly, even as a competent overseer, it has commissioned others to do on its behalf. If it lacks functional and financial competence and capability to do what an entrepreneurial reward would suggest it does or if its direct functions and responsibilities are limited, for example, to administrative functions within the array of potential DEMPE functions, then it should be so rewarded, and the profit to which it would otherwise lay claim does not belong to it. In effect, that excess profit is held by the licensor in what amounts to a custodial capacity for others. Whether this is an appropriate result will depend on the absolute capacity and observable resources of the licensor relative to others with which it directly or indirectly interacts as a member of its MNE. It will not depend on judgments about suitable degrees of taxation or whether tax systems are suitably comparable; by default, this way of thinking about and applying the transfer pricing rules affords the possibility of arresting legal and tax system arbitrage without trenching on the sovereignty of states to make fiscal and tax policy determinations that accord with their economic and other circumstances, albeit in line with international standards of 'fiscal good taste'.

The result is achieving what may be the primary objective of the OECD and the G20, specifically, to purge supply chains of gratuitous intermediaries while doing as little damage as possible to established conventions for measuring profit and applying tax claims. Stated more positively, perhaps, an underlying premise of transfer pricing is to follow the rhythm of a business, identify its relevant factor inputs and who supplies them, identify key organizational and governance forces that shape the strategic and entrepreneurial resources of and possibilities for the business, and to ensure that, as both transacting parties and group members, the legally separate constituents of MNEs are rewarded in a manner that is sympathetic to being members of an economic whole. Once positioned, employing this inverted concept of 'source', countries will be free to apply their tax (transfer pricing) law to the organizational and contractual arrangements they discover existed in the first place and were latent in but obscured by uncritical adherence to legal form essentially for its own sake.

VIII. THE PRACTICAL REALITY

There is one material constraint on construing and applying transfer pricing guidance, both generally and in a way that is specifically attuned to intangibles as this chapter examines them. It is a particular version of the 'triangular problem' of international tax. Most commonly encountered in treaty situations, it broadly reflects situations in which outcomes are only fair and rational with regard to the allocation and activation of taxing rights if the interests of all pertinent jurisdictions are addressed. However, sometimes, there are treaty gaps.[50] Using the licensor model as a point of reference, a

50. The OECD proposes to address a particular aspect of triangular situations, in OECD Action 6, Section A.1.b.vii 'Anti-abuse rule for permanent establishments situated in third States'. More generally, there is a strong transfer pricing focus among a number of the actions, all in one manner or another relating to the identification of the 'source' of income and its connection in

determination that profits are not allocable or attributable to a licensor in the licensor model may be unsatisfying if the countries to which, applying this way of thinking, the profits would be assigned do not know about them. In a manner of speaking, this is what is in play in a perverse way (to the sensibilities of BEPS) concerning the Belgian 'excess profits regime' according to legislation that seems to be a carefully crafted parsing of Article 9 and appearing to emphasize the disentitlement of a Belgian taxpayer to profits that 'should have been included in the profits of another company'.[51] Examined as objectively as possible (and also possibly 'innocently'), the proposition forming the basis of this feature of Belgian tax effectively seems to be that wherever 'excess profits' - no doubt attributable to 'intangibles' of some kind - were earned, according to the Belgian authorities, it was not in Belgium. The Belgian entity is perceived by those tax authorities as lacking the resources, essentially, the functional and financial capacity, to be responsible for those 'intangibles' and accordingly to be entitled to profits associated with them even as a 'central entrepreneur', in fact, and applying the type of legal analysis developed here thus did not earn them. They were considered as belonging to some other taxing state.[52]

The problem is, of course, that other taxing states are not involved in the discussion and, therefore, there is a present and persistent risk that those profits become what has been described as 'stateless'. This outcome essentially seems to utilize the basic principles of BEPS and particularly its transfer pricing aspects in a way that was not intended.[53]

---

a taxable manner to that 'source' and by the State that hosts that 'source', or at least material elements of it, in a way somehow or other cognizable by (or at least not defeated) tax treaties and principles underlying their distributive rules. This is particularly relevant, that is, the OECD's work on Actions 6 and 7 for the license model and how it should persist as an organizational arrangement within MNEs. It might be approached differently with the OECD's observations in mind.

51. See European Commission, State-aid, and see International Tax Review, Belgian excess profits tax scheme illegal says Vestager. See European Commission, Press release. See, for Belgium's views and those of the European Commission, European Commission on 3 Feb. 2015, C(2015) 563 (final), notably at paras. 20, 25, 27, 31,37, 40, 41, 70, 71, 75, and 76. But now also see the final decision of the European Commission on 11 Jan. 2016 confirming and elaborating on the Commission's view of impermissible 'state aid' in this case, C(2015) 9837 final.
52. Curiously, perceived this way, this sounds like a determination that the recommendations flowing from Actions 8-10 might, in fact, be argued to support if not require. Interestingly, generally and for purposes of this discussion, the types of 'intangibles' evidently in play include 'knowhow, procurement advantages, client lists etc.' (para. 31, European Commission, European Commission, C(2015) 563 (final)), 'synergies and economies of scale' (para. 71, European Commission, European Commission, C(2015) 563 (final)), and in reference to para. 1.10 of the OECD Transfer Pricing Guidelines 'synergies, economies of scales or of other efficiencies' which, according to the contested tax rulings (Advance Pricing Arrangements) were not considered by Belgium (or, it must be assumed, the affected taxpayers) to originate or otherwise have their 'home' in Belgium. But now also see the final decision of the European Commission on 11 Jan. 2016 confirming and elaborating on the analysis concerning the Commission's view of impermissible 'state aid' in this case, C(2015) 9837 final; that analysis examines the issues.
53. There are other interesting implications, though beyond the immediate scope of this chapter, that are noteworthy. There is a general sense in the OECD's and the G20's work that all income should be taxable somewhere, though whether and to what degree it follows that it should also be 'subject to tax' and by whose standards that should be determined persist as difficult questions that, implicitly, the OECD's very careful and insightful Action 11 Report not only reflects but, in a manner of speaking, concedes. One of the key implications of the Action 11

report is how difficult it is to establish what BEPS is and then to measure it. This is no doubt significant in part because constituting the obvious features and excesses of BEPS are intersections and even collisions of countries' economic and social welfare aspirations as well as resulting public choices activated and funded with the assistance of and, in some cases, through their tax systems. In this respect, countries are effectively in the roles, among themselves, of economic actors using their fiscal resources as if they were commercial parties to 'buy' resources necessary to advance their public choices; see Kingson, Charles I., *The Coherence of International Taxation* (1981) 81:6 Columbia Law Review 1151-1289 in this regard. There is also, as there always has been for 'international tax rules', an inextricable link to international trade even as trade regulations would apply and, following that course, countries' use of their fiscal resources including their tax citizens – their taxpayers – to 'invest' in economic pursuits to fund deliveries according to their national economic and social welfare choices and, more broadly, to enrich their economic prospects. In doing so, each country will inevitably evaluate its key trading interests, economic vulnerability, risks attendant on incompatible private law, and tax regimes with trading partners, etc. and, as a result, calibrate or recalibrate its regulatory regimes including its tax systems to serve its interests with due sensitivity to 'competing' but qualitatively like the interests of other countries. Disregarding whether the tax policy interests and choices of other countries are or should be a factor in devising their tax policy (the Canadian legal scholar Allison Christians thinks about international tax problems with this kind of awareness: see Christians, Allison, *Networks, Norms and National Tax Policy* (2010) 9:1 Wash UI Global Studies Law Review 1; Christians, Allison, *Sovereignty, Taxation, and Social Contract* (2009) 18:1 Minnesota Journal of International Law 99), from the individual perspective, makes the sorts of questions dominating the parallel (to BEPS) 'state aid' discussion more complex and nuanced. For example, all of the focus, regardless of the 'technical' features of business organizations of the affected MNEs and the merits of the European Commission's legal analysis, is on the tax jurisdictions, the tax systems which underlie the direct outcomes alleged to constitute the deliberate preferential use of tax rules and administration, in this case Belgium, but more generally in Ireland, the Netherlands, and Luxembourg. Accordingly, the preferential opportunities alleged to be engendered by the 'excess profits tax' regime arise from Belgian law and are judged to be out of sync with global standards, at least as they are evolving. However, as a 'thought experiment', consider whether it could be stated that Belgium is just following the new guidance; it should only tax income that is 'sourced' to Belgium, according to the resources, responsibilities and competency of Belgian enterprises The focus then shifts a bit to the roles and responsibilities of others, assuming either perfect or imperfect information flows. In the latter case, countries, through the a priori design of, for example, their CFC regimes could simply sweep foreign affiliate income into their domestic tax bases relying on the usual self-enforcing nature of tax law regardless of how much information, in an affirmative sense, they have gathered. A countries 'deliberate' decision not to tax income earned by foreign affiliates effectively subsidizes them relative to their domestic contemporaries even in the same industries; see Shay. Is that 'aid' by a 'state'? Is it a 'subsidy' in any possible sense that would interest the WTO (World Trade Organization) via the GATT (General Agreement on Tariffs and Trade), the GATS (General Agreement on Trade in Services), and the SCM (Subsidies and Countervailing Measures) Agreement? Does a country that designs its tax regime for foreign income with territorial features have a national interest for which it pays – invests – by deferring or exempting taxation – that it prosecutes through the 'agency' of its taxpayers? By what normative standard would this be judged, and is it possible that it is the 'offending' 'state aid' and not the renunciation by a country of the tax base that, according to contemporary objective and normative standards, it has concluded should not claim? These are enormously difficult questions. The authors of a recent paper considering recent state decisions in the context of United States taxation are evidently affected by questions such as these, which are endemic in any tax policy analysis that takes into account the economic, fiscal and other interests of that country in an international context.: see Tavares, Romero J.S. Tavares, Bret N. Bogenschneider and Marta Pankiv, *The Intersection of EU State Aid and U.S. Tax Deferral: A Spectacle of Fireworks, Smoke and Mirrors* (2016) 19:3 Florida Tax Review 121. Two immediate reactions are observed in this chapter. First, it is difficult, in the absence of a 'global tax system' and the nature of 'source' as a tax concept, to affirmatively define and apply a common 'source' concept. It is easier, considering the OECD's and the G20's BEPS objectives, to apply business-oriented

What is the remedy? What allows the construction in this chapter of Actions 8-10, notably Action 8, to apply in the manner not only argued here but, in fact, reflected in the approach taken in reaction to those Actions? The answers seem to lie in possibly the most unlikely of places – in the realm of process rather than substantive law. Action 13, and to a possibly slightly lesser degree Action 14, appear to be of great importance.

Disagreements about the 'source' of income according to the distributive rules of tax treaties and, therefore, about the allocation of taxing rights are, and always have been, the fodder of international dispute resolution, for the most part, now under the 'Mutual Agreement Procedure' on a consequential basis and according to 'Advance Pricing Arrangements/Agreements' and their like on an anticipatory basis. Transfer pricing, under both the 'old' and 'new' approaches, essentially concerns determining the entitlement, and possibly conflicting entitlements, of countries to tax income based on the source of that income and the proximity to the putative taxing jurisdiction of activities and the expenditure of other resources to earn it. Therefore, Action 14 is important.

However, Action 13, the 'see all, know all' recommendation, is critical. Its importance and, in particular, the significance of the achievement, at least in principle, of an international commitment to Country-by-Country (CbC) reporting, has been heralded, though it and the timing of its implementation by countries continue to draw critical comments.[54] It may possibly have more far-reaching substantive significance that has been obscured by jousting over substantive aspects of transfer pricing, possibly expecting that everything that needs to be known will be.[55] Consideration of

---

analysis that follows the rhythm a business to identify where, relying on respectable private law legal analysis, the source is not. From there, countries can then decide whether, how, and with what they assert potentially legitimate tax claims that reflect the evolved approach to analyzing where income is considered to be earned, not according to any absolute or exclusive standard but, as with any source conception, according to the selected standard. Influencing this analysis, also, may be 'subject to tax' considerations that figure in other Actions The second response is to again emphasize the importance of general awareness of how an MNE conducts its business and, hence, even for the effectiveness and selection of the standards for analysis envisaged by the Actions 8-10 Report, information recording and exchange contemplated by the Acton 13 Report.

54. See Wilkie, J. Scott, *'Master File,' 'Local File' and 'Country-by-Country Reporting': A Canadian Perspective*, (2016) Vol. 23 No. 2 International Transfer Pricing Journal, International Bureau of Fiscal Documentation, 115. As has been generally reported, a number of countries seemed uncertain about the application of country-by-country reporting before 2017.

55. One notable commentator who has, in his own way, realized this is Michael Durst. Through a continually unfolding analysis that is sensitive to political as well as analytical implications of 'formulary apportionment', he has devised a modified TNMM approach that would broadly allow known and knowable (with sensitivity to the tax administration constraints faced by tax regulators particularly in the developing world) financial and business measures of an MNE group member's operations in relationship to a compatible consolidated or group measure with an allocation of sorts based on a more or less prescriptive choice. Apart from emphasizing the need to be realistic and practical not only with reference to the resources of MNEs but also tax regulators, his work reinforces the importance of information exchange for any of this to 'work', the possible limitations, and resulting accommodations that might flow from imperfect information including that the information would not be universally known as would be necessary to reliably apply what appears to be the (negative) source approach constituting the OECD's transfer pricing work; see Durst, Michael C., *Self-Help and Altruism: Exploring the Problem of Tax Base Erosion in Developing Countries*, Bloomberg BNA Transfer Pricing Report (29/5/2014),

'intangibles' during the BEPS project (and before) has been dominated by transfer pricing techniques and substantive law considerations following the usual form-driven models.[56] The uneasy realization percolates, multilateral treaty or not, that it will not be easy to align countries' tax (and legal) systems in ways envisaged by recommendations or best practices advanced in reply to other BEPS Actions. In any event, for political or other reasons, it may be only a fond and faint hope that accommodating and supportive law changes should necessarily be expected. Changes in law take time, even in the best of times; they also invoke countries' re-examination of various priorities served in one way or another by their tax systems and that, even with the best of international intentions, still might not completely accord with developing international aspirations.

Yet all of the Actions, in one way or another, are connected, with emphasis on the 'S' of BEPS. In one manner or another, they are concerned with setting standards for determining the 'source' of income by negative implication. Even if this might be considered to be a second best effect, it is achievable compared to the inevitably elusive

23 Transfer Pricing Report 478; Durst, Michael C., *Developing Country Taxation, Part II: The Limitations of Corporate Income Taxation*, Bloomberg BNA Transfer Pricing Report (24/7/2014), 23 Transfer Pricing Report 228; Durst, Michael C., *Developing Country Taxation, Part III: Surmounting Transfer Pricing Problems of Distributors and Manufacturer*, Bloomberg BNA Transfer Pricing Report (16/10/2014), 23 Transfer Pricing Report 797; Durst, Michael C., *Designing a Hybrid Transfer Pricing Method*, Bloomberg BNA Transfer Pricing International Journal (30/3/2015), 16 TPTP 28; Durst, Michael C., *Can a 'Shared Net Margin Method' Provide a Global Transfer Pricing Standard*, Bloomberg BNA Transfer Pricing Report (30/4/2015), 23 Transfer Pricing Report 1639, 2/5/15; Durst, Michael C., *Can a 'Shared Net Margin Method' Provide a Global Transfer Pricing Standard*, Bloomberg BNA International Tax Monitor (30/5/2015), 23 Transfer Pricing Report 1238, 2/5/15; Durst, Michael C., *Developing Country Taxation, Part VII: Don't Lose Focus on Domestic Revenue Sources*, Bloomberg BNA Transfer Pricing Report 2015, 24 Transfer Pricing Report 713; Durst, Michael C., *Proposed Structure for a 'Value Creation' Method*, Bloomberg BNA Transfer Pricing Report 2015, 24 Transfer Pricing Report 972; See also Vann, Richard, *Policy Forum: The Policy Underpinnings of the BEPS Project – Preserving the International Corporate Income Tax?* (2014) 62:2 Canadian Tax Journal 433-441; Vann, Richard, *Taxing International Business Income: Hard-Boiled Wonderland and the End of the World* (2010) 2:3 World Tax Journal 291-346; and Wilkie, J. Scott, *Policy Forum: BEPS One Year In – Taking Stock* (2014) (2014) 62:2 Canadian Tax Journal 455-475; Wilkie, Scott, *Reflections on 'BEPS': Tax, Law and 'Law and Economics'* (31 Jul. 2014) University of Calgary School of Public Policy Blog (http://policyschool.ucalgary.fca; Wilkie, J. Scott, *Reflecting on the 'Arm's Length Principle': What is the 'Principle'? Where Next? Fundamentals of International Transfer Pricing in Law and Economics* (Wolfgang Schön and Kai A. Konrad eds.) (Berlin: Springer, 2012) 137-158; Wilkie, Scott, *The Definition and Ownership of Intangibles: Inside the Box? Outside the Box? What is the Box?* (2012) 4:3 World Tax Journal 222-248; Wilkie, J. Scott, *Intangibles and Location Benefits* (Customer Base) (June–July 2014) Bulletin for International Taxation: BEPS Special Issue (International Bureau of Fiscal Documentation) 352-360; Wilkie, J. Scott, *Canada Waiting for 'BEPS' ... Canada 'Appears'* September–October (2014) CCH International Tax Journal, CCH, 5-12; Wilkie, J. Scott, *The Taxation of Cross-Border Corporate Profits*, presented in Santiago, Chile on 19-20 Nov. 2015 at the David R. Tillinghast Conference sponsored by the International Fiscal Association and the University of Chile, entitled 'The New International Tax Cooperation Paradigm: Impact on Domestic Tax Regimes and the Cross-Border Allocation of Taxing Rights' (publication pending); Wilkie, J. Scott, *'Master File,' 'Local File' and 'Country-by-Country Reporting': A Canadian Perspective*, (2016) Vol. 23 No. 2 International Transfer Pricing Journal, International Bureau of Fiscal Documentation, 115.

56. See Wittendorff, Jens, *BEPS Actions 8-10: Birth of a New Arm's Length Principle*, Tax Notes International (25 Jan. 2016) 331, who prospectively examines transfer pricing analysis.

alternative of a universal affirmative notion of source. The effect of the OECD's work, not only respecting Actions 8-10 but more generally, is to excise from value chains gratuitous intermediaries – parties that are materially insignificant in legal as well as economic terms. Giving effect to this depends on those who might have legitimate claims to tax (or not, as the case may be) the resulting displaced income of, for example, licensing intermediaries, knowing enough about MNE group circumstances to know that they may have a claim to tax that income. Observable transfers of goods and services are readily discernable and easily identified with bilateral transactions. Transfers of intangibles are less obvious even though they account for much of the concern that underlies BEPS in both its 'P' and 'S' aspects.

Action 13 discreetly focuses mostly on this. It is likely that MNEs and their constituents already report much of the information contemplated for the 'local file' and even the 'master file'.[57] The sort of information contemplated by CbC reporting is also, which is not unreasonable to expect, readily obtainable if not already reported even if not as part of income tax reporting and 'packaged' in the way envisaged by Action 13. A key aspect of Article 13 reporting is the focus in the 'master file' on an MNE's generation and deployment of 'intangibles' on a group wide basis to complement the more overtly transaction-based reporting that will populate a 'local file'. The 'master file' is, in effect, an extension or the context for what the CbC report will necessarily disclose about the commercial, the business rhythm, and ostensible 'presence' of an MNE. Action 13 forces MNEs to direct their institutional minds and to address catalysts for and measures of profitability that are not tangible and that, adopting the framework of one commentator,[58] in one way or another reflect 'unilateral integration', 'bilateral integration', and 'common control' value. The latter is most closely identified with the 'synergy intangible' that the OECD has not attempted to fashion by leaving that value, among others, to be encapsulated by the application of Chapters I-III that are enlightened by a more thorough analytical framework for 'intangibles'.

Without the general adoption of reporting that accords with the Action 13 report, however, it is less clear how the expectations of the transfer pricing guidance can be achieved effectively and in a timely manner. While the negative source concept may explain whether and to what extent a licensor in the licensor model has earned the income recorded by it, that may be a meaningless outcome – in terms of the focus on

57. See Wilkie, J. Scott, *'Master File,' 'Local File' and 'Country-by-Country Reporting': A Canadian Perspective,* (2016) Vol. 23 No. 2 International Transfer Pricing Journal, International Bureau of Fiscal Documentation, 115.
58. See Kane, Mitchell A., *Transfer Pricing, Integration and Synergy Intangibles: A Consensus Approach to the Arm's Length Standard* (2014) (October) World Tax Journal 282, whose opinions articulate concepts expressed differently in Wilkie, J. Scott, *Reflecting on the 'Arm's Length Principle': What is the 'Principle'? Where Next? Fundamentals of International Transfer Pricing in Law and Economics* (Wolfgang Schön and Kai A. Konrad eds.) (Berlin: Springer, 2012) 137-158; Wilkie, Scott, *The Definition and Ownership of Intangibles: Inside the Box? Outside the Box? What is the Box?* (2012) 4:3 World Tax Journal 222-248; and Wilkie, J. Scott, *Intangibles and Location Benefits* (Customer Base), (June–July 2014) Bulletin for International Taxation: BEPS Special Issue (International Bureau of Fiscal Documentation) 352-360.; See also Wilkie, J. Scott, *Policy Forum: BEPS One Year In – Taking Stock* (2014) (2014) 62:2 Canadian Tax Journal 455-475.

'double non-taxation' that characterizes BEPS – if, as the Belgian example illustrates, other contending tax jurisdictions are unaware of the latent tax potential and without collaborative tools among them to determine 'source' by first eliminating where, as they might commonly agree, income or substantial amounts of it is not earned.

IX. A CONCLUDING COMMENT

It is evident from a more expansive and less 'technical' or methodological perspective that the impetus and effect of the Actions 8-10 recommendations addressed to 'intangibles' is to eliminate the significance for 'value' or 'supply' chains of what this chapter refers to as 'gratuitous intermediaries' and 'gratuitous intermediation.[59] These are legal constructions ('persons' according to the law) with ostensible legal and commercial significance according to legal formalism but that lack the necessary capacity, as autonomous economic and business actors even with an MNE to be responsible for the obligations they purport to have undertaken or to cultivate and exploit rights formally assigned to them, as contributing as productive operators or at least informed directing minds. However, it is equally evident that, as fastidious and thorough as the OECD's work is, it is a fair interpretation that, for the most part, it builds concepts, tendencies, analytical foundations, and expectations not only of the transfer pricing guidance it supersedes but of countries' tax laws that adopt, incorporate, or are otherwise influenced by and attempt to bring about that guidance.

For taxpayers and tax authorities, this has an important implication. Changes in law may be unnecessary to provide significance to the new guidance on intangibles in situations like or illustrated by the license model. A combination of an application of the transfer pricing guidance that has always supported the activation of Article 9 and a constructive interpretation of countries' private law and conflicts of laws principles as they apply to organizational forms and contractual relations that connect them, both with their full potential as elements of the interpretation and application of legal systems, may be sufficient. There is no doubt that the OECD's work elucidates and illuminates what may be regarded as the 'true' transfer pricing analysis – considering the demands of Article 9, in fact, the only transfer pricing analysis that could ever be. However, the outcomes that the OECD seeks, which amount to aligning tax outcomes with the rhythm and intrinsic demands and features of global business conducted by MNEs, are not mysterious or unreasonable.

For taxpayers alone, the implications are equally clear – even if transfer pricing analysis may be more involved. Certainly, the legal forms and fictions so essential for the organized conduct of business operations anywhere, let alone globally, are not under attack. However, taxpayers are expected to at least respect and organize themselves in a manner consistent with and to operate in accordance with the inherent

59. See Wilkie, J. Scott, *The Taxation of Cross-Border Corporate Profits*, presented in Santiago, Chile on 19-20 Nov. 2015 at the David R. Tillinghast Conference sponsored by the International Fiscal Association and the University of Chile, entitled 'The New International Tax Cooperation Paradigm: Impact on Domestic Tax Regimes and the Cross-Border Allocation of Taxing Rights' (publication pending).

legal expectations of those forms and not expect those forms to be self-explanatory simply as legal constructions depicted on an organization chart. This means that MNE members connected in a 'supply' or 'value' chain must have a reason for being there and to have the resources to fulfill that reason within the expectations of the ALS which compares their circumstances and the transactions they initiate to those of independent actors to be able to function as the separate entities that the ALS fundamentally expects them to be and, in fact, assumes that they are. All relevant circumstances must be considered under the 'old' and 'new' guidance in order to establish the significance and value of their contributions. In other words, there must be contributions, otherwise their involvement in the chain is to be marginalized – but no more than the business planning itself will by design have marginalized that participation. The rest, once roles and responsibilities that are functionally significant have been identified, engages that type of transfer pricing analysis better constructed tools which, together with healthy measures of self-consciousness about defending formal arrangements bereft of functional significance, has become the essence of contemporary transfer pricing.

After all of this, it is evident that the OECD's objective was not to introduce a new transfer pricing regime – not to displace the ALS as it was known and replace it with something different, even antithetical to its key tenets.[60] Placing suitable weight on both the 'P' and 'S' aspects of BEPS and paying due regard to the direction and conclusions of BEPS work on a number, if not most, of the other BEPS Actions, the target of the OECD are companies in the nature of 'cash box companies' or, more generally stated, non-functional intermediaries that because of that lack of function fairly can be said, too, to lack legal substance as such and in their purported dealings. Their fiscal marginalization and substantial elimination from a transfer pricing matrix leaves transfer pricing analysis to proceed as it otherwise would. Inevitably some fundamental, even imponderable questions still remain though other BEPS Actions may in one way or another address them. For example, some, concerning hybrid and deductible charges, may despite their specific focus be seen as directed to achieving a measure of equivalence in how corporate distributions are treated consistently despite their form. In any event, these are questions that can be expected to persist despite attempts to make the allocation of taxing rights among countries more prescriptive even where facts and circumstances dominate, as in transfer pricing, to give life and meaning to the legal forms and constructions that host transactions and the parties to them.[61] For example, a modified unitary perspective of MNEs might consider an intermediary, even if it is a 'cash box', as simply a component of another more robust group member and its non-taxation as a design feature of the other group member's CFC or other tax rules. In effect, it is perceived as a means to deliver 'support' or, in the current European environment, subsidy or aid that might or might not transgress limitations and regulation in this regard. As noted, license models are closely identified with formalistic planning of this nature even though it is equally possible that they

60. See Wittendorff, Jens, *BEPS Actions 8-10: Birth of a New Arm's Length Principle*, Tax Notes International (25 Jan. 2016) 331; there is significant play concerning the meaning and application of the ALS, and there is no doubt it may seem as if a new regime has been presented.
61. See the second epigram at the outset of this chapter.

could be robust commercial focus entities within an MNE for developing and deploying intangibles of any commercial kind. From this vantage, it is plausible to contend that too much adverse significance would be attached to a preferential intermediary if it was not seen as an emissary of an MNE's home jurisdiction.

That context invokes consideration of other BEPS Actions and simply reiterates a continuing undercurrent of transfer pricing. However, perceiving the transfer pricing analysis as this, this chapter also effectively acknowledges that point of view and even an analytical perspective. The 'negative source' concept that this chapter argues, though not in terms of the OECD, appears to have embraced even as a latent influence and essentially 'combines' entities that 'should' be combined without, however, affirmatively stipulating what 'source' means or where income necessarily 'belongs'. In so doing, it offers a principled way grounded in legal principles and underlying most tax systems to indicate where it is not. The ALS persists, and legal arrangements are not disregarded.

The rest, at that stage, is transfer pricing as commonly understood for putative tax jurisdiction claimants and for taxpayers to work out as they would in any case in the context of Chapters I-III of the Transfer Pricing Guidelines.

The OECD does not intend to interfere in this process. The degree of ensuing taxation and how, if at all, taxation is imposed by countries having established legitimate tax claims or had the claims established for them is for the countries to determine. Among others, this is evident in the assessment of BEPS found in the Report on Action 11 which amounts to an analytically thorough and honest assessment that BEPS is very difficult to determine in any absolute sense and, in many respects, is relative to facts and circumstances that include the underlying motivation for taxpayer behavior. Certainly, avoided tax is not enough; what is enough and on what principled or empirical basis the determination would be made is difficult to ascertain. Equally, as the commentary on Action 5 notes, a regime is not preferential simply because it engages less intense taxation, i.e., has low rates, as long as it does not discriminate in their application. The next stage of the OECD's work on intangibles, with the perspective of this chapter in mind, will likely be very important. The OECD looks forward to scrutinizing transactional profit split methods with particular regard to the types of factors that serve to distinguish MNEs correspondingly, the emphasis in the OECD's work to date has been on adding value and contributions. This is reflected in the evident focus in its work to explain the source of income, even by negative implication, which in relation to 'intangibles' is quite directly on inputs, i.e., factors of production in economic terms, as well as to what end and by whom they are mobilized to create and deliver saleable products and services As noted earlier, this is certainly not formulary; however, considering businesses actually operate and MNEs are organized, it is hardly surprising, particularly in a transfer pricing analysis, that the OECD and tax administrations correspondingly would need to be and choose to be guided by the same type of business analysis in which MNEs must be engaged.

Ultimately, though, all of this depends on a collective awareness by tax authorities and taxpayers of the circumstances addressed by all of them at the same time. Action 13 reporting is of significance; Action 13 reporting is even more significant if, as this chapter contends, the necessary guidance and law are already established.

CHAPTER 4

Transfer Pricing Aspects of Intangibles: The Cost Contribution Arrangement Model

Yariv Brauner

I. INTRODUCTION

Admittedly, a better title for this chapter might be Plus ça change, plus c'est la même chose.[1] The chapter argues that the Base Erosion and Profit Shifting (BEPS) project has made only minimal progress in its work on the transfer pricing for intangibles despite the prominence of the issue. More specifically, it achieved nothing but increased confusion and incoherence in the context of the specific rules for Cost Contribution Agreements (CCAs).

The failure of the current transfer pricing rules for intangibles was the primary trigger of the BEPS project in the first place. We all remember the public outrage over the low effective tax rates of the likes of Apple, Google, Microsoft, etc.[2] These and other Multinational Enterprises (MNE) achieved such low rates based on the combination of the unsuccessful norms that comprise the international tax regime. Yet, transfer pricing for intangibles, and particularly the United States' idiosyncratic cost sharing rules, carried most of the weight in permitting such tax planning.[3]

It all comes down to the arm's length based transfer pricing rules that dominate the international tax regimes. This essentially universal norm has become the dear child of tax authorities and the Organisation for Economic Co-operation and Development (OECD) over the last almost eighty years.[4] Taxpayers adjusted and, to a large extent, also generally accepted it as the devil you know. Globalization has also elevated it to being the most important issue for MNEs,[5] yet, as proven by BEPS, the arm's length notion that is often used as a legal standard, if portrayed as a principle, has proven not to be up to the task.[6]

1. Alphonse Karr, *Les Guêpes* (1849).
2. See, e.g., Charles Duhigg & David Kocieniewski, *How Apple Sidesteps Billions in Taxes*, New York Times (accessed 28 Apr. 2012), http://www.nytimes.com/2012/04/29/business/apples-tax-strategy-aims-at-low-tax-states-and-nations.html?_r=0; Jesse Drucker, *Google Revenues Sheltered in No-Tax Bermuda Soar to $10 Billion*, Bloomberg (accessed 10 Dec. 2012, 12:01 AM), http://www.bloomberg.com/news/2012-12-10/google-revenues-sheltered-in-no-tax-bermuda-soar-to-10-billion.html; Richard Waters, *Microsoft's Foreign Tax Planning under Scrutiny*, Financial Times (accessed 7 Jun. 2011, 2:38 AM), http://www.ft.com/cms/s/2/0880cd54-90a1-11e0-9531-00144feab49a.html#axzz2sl7hvIaz; and Edward D. Kleinbard, *Through a Latte, Darkly: Starbucks's Stateless Income Planning*, Tax Notes, accessed 24 Jun. 2013), at 1515.
3. See, e.g., Edward D. Kleinbard, *Stateless Income*, 11 Florida Tax Review 699, 706 (2011). For more details on the mechanics of cost sharing based planning, see, e.g., Yariv Brauner, *Cost Sharing and the Acrobatics of Arm's Length Taxation*, 38 Intertax 554 (2010), and Harry Grubert, *Foreign Taxes, Domestic Income, and the Jump in the Share of Multinational Company Income Abroad: Sales Aren't Being Globalized, Only Profits*, 65 National Tax Journal 247 (2012).
4. For an excellent exposition of the origins and history of arm's length, see Jens Wittendorff, *Transfer Pricing and the Arm's Length Principle*, International Tax Law (Kluwer Law International, 2010).
5. See, e.g., EY, *2010 Global Transfer Pricing Survey*, available at http://www.ey.com/GL/en/Services/Tax/International-Tax/2010-Global-Transfer-Pricing-Survey---1--Transfer-pricing-as--absolutely-critical-.
6. See, OECD, *Addressing Base Erosion and Profit Shifting* (12 Feb. 2013), available at http://www.keepeek.com/Digital-Asset-Management/oecd/taxation/addressing-base-erosion-and-profit-shifting_9789264192744-en#page1.

Real changes, however, are difficult to accept and more difficult to implement. This chapter tells the story of the resistance of governments and the OECD to reform arm's length in the context of BEPS despite the obvious necessity acknowledged, for the first time, by the BEPS project itself. It concludes that it does not matter how many times arm's length proponents repeat the mantra that it is the best and only way to tax MNEs, the difficulties of the BEPS variety are here to stay.

Arm's length, a uniquely important norm for taxation of (border crossing) MNEs provides them with a tax benefit that is not available to other firms that are not subject to the transfer pricing rules.[7] The consequence is inefficiency that is amplified by the costly compliance and enforcement of these rules. This is particularly true for transactions involving intangibles. Intangibles justify the MNE business model and define it and, hence, are central to transfer pricing, yet they are notoriously difficult to value.[8] Market based valuation, which is the basis of the arm's length design, is obviously problematic since legally protected intangibles (IP) cannot have comparable property legally transacted on the same market, and non-legally protected intangibles rely on secrecy or unique capabilities - non-comparable - for value creation and preservation.[9]

Such difficulties have been exacerbated by the particular application of arm's length that has gained dominance in the practice, which I call here literal arm's length. The literal version of arm's length applies its logic transaction by transaction (hence, sometimes called transactional arm's length), ignoring the surrounding circumstances and the context of the application of the rules. It is appealing because of its instrumental ease; the application is narrowed to a limited study of comparability. For taxpayers, this version provides some clarity and opportunities for planning that they had obviously taken. For the courts, it is appealing to be amenable to a relatively common legal application rather than complex economic valuation exercises. Moreover, the same approach has been promoted by governments pressed to produce rules that can be complied with and enforced. Now that governments understand their mistake, it is very difficult to reverse. The problem is not just in the manipulability of literal arm's length but also in its incompatibility with the very purpose of transfer pricing - the prevention of abuse by related parties engaged in non-market transactions. In the treaty context that is most relevant here, it violates the charge to interpret the treaty, including Article 9 that introduces arm's length according to its object and context.[10] If

7. See, e.g., my critique in Yariv Brauner, *Formula Based Transfer Pricing*, 42 Intertax 615 (2014).
8. For a more detailed study of the valuation difficulties presented by intangibles and the insufficiency of the permissible transfer pricing methods in this regard, see Yariv Brauner, *Value in the Eye of the Beholder: The Valuation of Intangibles for Transfer Pricing Purposes*, 28 Virginia Tax Review 79 (Summer, 2008).
9. Alternative methods of valuation do not fare much better: cost-based valuation is challenged by the systemic disconnection between the costs and the value of intangibles, and income-based valuation suffers from the inherent volatility of earning from intangibles. *Ibid.*
10. Article 31 of the Vienna Convention on the Law of Treaties (1969).

the OECD has been trying to do anything in BEPS, it is to shift from a literal to a substantive arm's length.[11] The push back demonstrates the difficulty of achieving this.[12]

Nonetheless, these structural problems were exploited by MNEs to minimize their effective tax rates. Tax authorities' unwillingness to reform to the arm's length based transfer pricing regime created a time bomb that exploded with the financial crisis and BEPS, leaving governments starving for revenue.[13] The G20[14] demanded action and charged the OECD with finding solutions to BEPS.[15] The OECD - the reluctant caretaker of the international tax regime - was required to solve the very problems it had faced for a long time.[16] Next, the chapter briefly reviews the first BEPS steps toward reform of the transfer pricing rules for intangibles before it focuses on the work on CCAs.

II. BEPS: THE PROMISE

The OECD was not only charged by the G20 to lead the BEPS project with no supervision beyond the highest political levels but also succeeded in positioning itself as an independent partner to the G20, taking ownership of the project rather than acting in a subordinate role.[17]

A. The BEPS Report

First, on 12 February 2013, the OECD issued the original BEPS report declaring that BEPS is indeed a problem that requires response.[18] Aggressive tax planning by MNEs was declared the primary target, yet, for the first time, the OECD also acknowledged the structural deficiencies of the competition based international tax regime.[19] It realized that only a more collaborative approach to norm standardization could save the regime. The report further denounced the ad hoc approach to tax reform, stating that only a comprehensive, principled reform could stabilize the regime. Finally, the report

---

11. See Jens Wittendorff, *BEPS Actions 8-10: Birth of a New Arm's Length Principle,* Tax Notes Internationl 331 (25 Jan. 2016) .
12. I have elsewhere argued that it is perhaps impossible to refocus the rule and the alternative reforms, therefore, are preferable. See, *supra* note 9.
13. See, e.g., *The Great Corporate Tax Dodge*, Bloomberg, http://topics.bloomberg.com/the-great-corporate-tax-dodge/ (accessed 8 Feb. 2014).
14. As well as the more exclusive G8 organization that gave way to the G20 on this matter. See, e.g., Prime Minister's Office & Cabinet Office, *G8 factsheet: tax*, Gov.UK (7 Jun. 2013), https://www.gov.uk/government/publications/g8-factsheet-tax/g8-factsheet-tax (accessed 8 Feb. 2014).
15. G20, *G20 Leaders Declaration*, at 48, G20 at Los Cabos, Mexico (18-19 Jun 2012), https://g20.org.tr/wp-content/uploads/2014/12/G20_Leaders_Declaration_Final_Los_Cabos_0.pdf (accessed 27 Jun. 2016).
16. Since none of the matters raised by BEPS had been new; they have all been subject to tax policy debate and work (albeit with different intensity) prior to BEPS.
17. See, e.g., the language used in the forward to the September 2014 deliverables: OECD and G20 countries, working together on an equal footing.
18. See, OECD, *Addressing Base Erosion and Profit Shifting, supra* note 6.
19. See, e.g., Yariv Brauner, *BEPS: An Interim Evaluation*, 6 World Tax Journal 10 (2014).

acknowledged that reform means change, including the replacement of some traditional norms with new ones. These three basic insights of BEPS, i.e., collaboration, a holistic approach, and innovation were supposed to guide the project.[20]

The report identified transfer pricing for intangibles as a key pressure area: Transfer pricing, in particular in relationship to the shifting of risks and intangibles; the artificial splitting of ownership of assets between legal entities within a group; and transactions between such entities that would rarely take place between independents.[21] It asserted an intention to revise the transfer pricing rules that produce undesirable results from a policy perspective and mentioned the already on-going project on intangibles that the OECD had started years before.[22]

Such policy statement projected two potentially dramatic consequences. First, the OECD expressed an intent to shift transfer pricing practice away from the legal and economic pseudo-reality to a more pragmatic, business focused approach relying on the principle that profits should follow action or value creation. Such an approach, interestingly, resembles the traditional approach of the United Nations to transfer pricing, an approach rejected until then by the OECD.[23] The second, even more dramatic consequence, was the willingness of the OECD to divert from the exclusive application of arm's length for the first time. Such stubborn exclusivity to arm's length had been the hallmark of OECD policy in the past[24] and, hence, the dramatic effect of its willingness to abandon it even if only in rare and difficult cases.

B. The BEPS Action Plan

The 9 September 2013, Action Plan devised the actual contour of the BEPS project.[25] Although aggressive transfer pricing was the beating heart of BEPS planning, it was not so obviously featured as such by the action plan. The plan included a set of fifteen items in no particular order or priority that were chosen by the OECD with no obvious organizing principle behind it. It seemed to be a compromise between a minimalist approach seeking to counter BEPS planning by the exposed MNEs and a more maximalist approach seeking fundamental reform of the international tax regime. The complexity presented by transfer pricing required, however, that four out of the fifteen items be devoted to it. Several other items relate, more or less indirectly, to the work on transfer pricing as well.

In the transfer pricing context, the action plan distanced itself from the core BEPS tax planning schemes and the concrete criticism of the existing rules by ignoring the

20. See, e.g., Yariv Brauner, *What the BEPS?* 16 Florida Tax Review 55 (2014).
21. OECD, *Addressing Base Erosion and Profit Shifting*, *supra* note 6, at 48.
22. *Ibid.*, at 52.
23. See United Nations, *Practical Manual on Transfer Pricing for Developing Countries* (2012).
24. See the work on Article 7 and the AOA. Final report available at: http://www.oecd.org/ctp/transfer-pricing/45689524.pdf.
25. OECD, *Action Plan on Base Erosion and Profit Shifting* (19 Sep. 2013), available at http://www.oecd.org/ctp/BEPSActionPlan.pdf. For an analysis of the transfer pricing components of the action plan, see, e.g., Georg Kofler, *The BEPS Action Plan and Transfer Pricing: The Arm's Length Standard Under Pressure?*, 5 British Tax Review 646 (2013).

contribution of the unique United States rules and particularly of the cost sharing regulations to the troubling outcomes. Instead, the OECD chose to merely fold the work that it had already started to do on transfer pricing and particularly its intangibles project into the BEPS project.[26] On the one hand, it was sensible not to abandon all of the work done and insight acquired,[27] yet, on the other hand, very little was done to adapt such work to the new goals, perspective, and insight of BEPS.

Action Item 8 (Intangibles) is, appropriately, the first transfer pricing action item: Develop rules to prevent BEPS by moving intangibles among group members. This will involve: (i) adopting a broad and clearly delineated definition of intangibles; (ii) ensuring that profits associated with the transfer and use of intangibles are appropriately allocated in accordance with (rather than divorced from) value creation; (iii) developing transfer pricing rules or special measures for transfers of hard-to-value intangibles; and (iv) updating the guidance on CCAs.[28]

The tension between the different, unsettled goals of the BEPS project was apparent. On the one hand, it promised to deliver reform by establishing the principle that profits should follow value creation[29] and by expressing a willingness to divert from the arm's length standard as necessary (for hard-to-value intangibles). On the other hand, the narrow view of the project aiming at prominent BEPS schemes creeps in as well: the specific and misguided mention of CCAs, the focus on the definition of intangibles, and the unwillingness to explicitly seek alternatives to the arm's length standard all represent a more conservative side of the project.

The next action item introduced two specific intangible elements that were difficult to use within the current paradigm. Action Item 9 addressed risks and capital.[30] Both are very difficult to deal with in the arm's length context yet are critical for BEPS. Most important is the fundamental case of what is commonly called a cash-box, i.e., a legal owner of an intangible that merely finances its creation and manages its exploitation. Under the current OECD approach, mere financing may be viewed as risk taking and, as such, deserves a significant profit margin and, perhaps, even a residual profit margin. An alternative approach that seems to conform to the value creation principle advocated by the BEPS action plan would be to assign a

26. The OECD published a discussion draft first in June 2012, and a revised draft in July 2013. See, OECD, *Discussion Draft on Transfer Pricing Aspects of Intangibles*, June 2012; and OECD, *Revised Discussion Draft on Transfer Pricing Aspects of Intangibles*, July 2013.
27. Note that the OECD did choose to abandon (or shelve) a similar project on permanent establishments. See, e.g., Stephanie Soong Johnston, *OECD's Final Work on Permanent Establishments on Hold for BEPS, Official Says*, 2013 WTD 108-3 (3 Jun. 2013).
28. OECD, *Action Plan on Base Erosion and Profit Shifting, supra* note 21, ACTION 8.
29. A concrete articulation of this principle and basic derivative standards are not available. The final BEPS report obviously signal that no consensus has been achieved over the details where all sorts of devils lie.
30. OECD, *Action Plan on Base Erosion and Profit Shifting, supra* note 22, ACTION 9: *Develop rules to prevent BEPS by transferring risks among, or allocating excessive capital to, group members. This will involve adopting transfer pricing rules or special measures to ensure that inappropriate returns will not accrue to an entity solely because it has contractually assumed risks or has provided capital. The rules to be developed will also require alignment of returns with value creation. This work will be co-ordinated with the work on interest expense deductions and other financial payments.*

minimal profit margin to financing that is equivalent to any other similar financing (market interest rate). In some ways, this was the key test for BEPS: if it cannot condemn it, it would not be taken seriously, yet essentially no country had been able to effectively do so before (on its own).

Action Item 10 takes the above action items a step forward by explicitly acknowledging that certain related party transactions can never take place on the market between unrelated parties and thus do not conveniently fit the arm's length paradigm: Develop rules to prevent BEPS by engaging in transactions which would not or only very rarely occur between third parties. This will involve adopting transfer pricing rules or special measures to: (i) clarify the circumstances in which transactions can be recharacterized; (ii) clarify the application of transfer pricing methods, in particular profit splits, in the context of global value chains; and (iii) provide protection against common types of base eroding payments such as management fees and head office expenses.[31]

It is not difficult to see that this is where the most dramatic impact of BEPS could have been experienced, and this is where it would eventually (at least most likely) disappoint.

The de facto most important contribution of the action plan was, interestingly, in the administrative part where it presented a comprehensive scheme for standardization of transfer pricing reporting including the introduction of the innovative CbC report. Action Item 13 is beyond the scope of this chapter, yet I will mention it when relevant to the issues presented by the chapter and to emphasize my argument that BEPS resulted in very little in terms of substantive law reform, yet it opened the door to dramatic changes via the administrative innovations spearheaded by Action Item 13. Moreover, Action 13 may prove to go beyond procedure as it – especially via the Country-by-Country (CbC) reporting requirement – may shift the substance of the regime in the direction of more explicit deviation from arm's length.[32]

III. PROMISES UNDELIVERED

A. The September 2014 Action Item 8 Deliverable

In line with the action plan, the OECD delivered a draft report in September 2014 on Action Item 8.[33] The draft reflects a consensus over a few issues related to the transfer pricing of intangibles, yet it was primarily in a draft form since several issues did not achieve consensus and since the most difficult issues such as the treatment of risk, capital, and hard-to-measure intangibles awaited the September 2015 deadline.

31. OECD, *Action Plan on Base Erosion and Profit Shifting*, *supra* note 22, ACTION 10.
32. It is not realistic, in my opinion, to expect all countries to limit the use of these reports to only risk assessment. The confidentiality aspect of the report should also, most probably, be viewed as unrealistic.
33. See, OECD, *Guidance on Transfer pricing of Intangibles (Action 8: 2014 Deliverable)*, available at: http://www.oecd.org/tax/beps-2014-deliverables.htm.

The September 2014 draft includes three basic substantive norm changes: (I) in the definition of intangibles under the TPG; (II) in the guidance on identifying transactions involving intangibles; and (III) in the guidance for determining arm's length conditions for transactions involving intangibles. Specific issues covered are taking locational features into account, the accounting of group synergies, and assembled workforce. These basic changes resulted in amendments to the TPG, Chapters I, II, and VI, including multiple examples demonstrating the changes.

The 2014 report was an interim step, a status that was acknowledged by the OECD,[34] since very little progress was actually made by it in terms of the practice of transfer pricing for intangibles and the battle against BEPS. Essentially, all of the hard decisions and all of the difficult cases were left unresolved.

The first part of the report discussed location specific properties resulting in savings or conditions that may affect prices depending also on whether they are transferred to customers, etc. The two basic rules provided on the matter were, first, that location specific properties may matter and should be assessed based on all facts and circumstances and, second, that comparable transactions in the same market are superior to comparable transactions in different markets. Cynicism aside, these are quite obvious rules that do not advance the practice much, however, in most cases, they are followed anyway. The most difficult questions in this context include the following: What do we do when there are no local comparables but only so-so comparables in a variety of different markets? Do we use them? How much weight should we give to market differences? How should we combine comparability levels with market differences? At what point of difference would it be better to consider a transaction as not having appropriate comparables and deserving of special measures (beyond arm's length)? These questions were left unresolved.

The second issue discussed was the effect of an assembled workforce on the transfer pricing analysis. The OECD continues to reject it being designated a separate intangible, yet it accepted that, at times, seconded employee(s) may carry unique know how with them that may be viewed as a separate intangible that deserves separate compensation. This leaves taxpayers in perhaps a worse position in terms of clarity than they were before this amendment. It is also connected to the very limiting approach of the OECD to intangibles including in it, in effect, only intangibles that fit an arm's length analysis. This ostrich strategy is very short sighted and confuses the end with the means. This confusion is very typical of arm's length apologists,[35] yet it should be unacceptable in a project where the primary goal was to fix the ailments of this very policy.

The same tactics were used in the discussion of the third issue of group synergies. Addressing synergies must be a positive since they are the only reason for MNEs to organize as such, yet, to date, the OECD had been ignoring them by adhering to the

34. See the speech of Marlies de Ruiter, *Head of the Tax Treaty, Transfer Pricing and Financial Transactions Division*, OECD in the 16 Sep. 2014, webcast presenting the deliverables. Available at: http://www.oecd.org/tax/beps-webcasts.htm.

35. See, e.g., the United States' Ninth Circuit second opinion in the case of *Xilinx*, explained in Brauner, *Cost Sharing*, *supra* note 3, at 562.

literal arm's length standard. By equating non-market transactions to market transactions, the rules have minimized the significance of synergies. The OECD now accepts special allocations of them but only to those that are important, easily identifiable, and a consequence of a deliberate, concerted group action.[36] In these circumstances, the benefits (or burdens) of the synergy should be allocated among the group members based on their relative contribution to the creation of the synergy.[37] This means that benefits resulting from the mere membership in a group do not require arm's length adjustments. The report adds that comparability analysis is appropriate here. The framework that ignores synergies does not change, therefore, but rather views them as additional properties of the non-market-equated-to-market players. Note that this approach actually advocates apportionment, although it is based on completely invented (and, in fact, nonsensical) properties, i.e., relative contribution to the creation of the synergy. The faults of this artificial approach are elaborated below.

The report then turns to situations where arm's length methodology is not helpful. It provides that other methods may be used if an explanation of why the prescribed methods do not work, however, the report notes that there has yet to be established consensus over this permission of other methods. Further, the report clarifies that rules of thumb are not acceptable.[38]

The intangibles specific part of the report begins with the discussion of the definition of intangibles, which is, in fact, a discussion of scope. The OECD views transfer pricing through the arm's length lenses rather than through their actual anti-abuse purposes. Therefore, it simply excludes from the analysis (and hence from the definition of intangibles) those value generators that are not capable of being owned and transacted between independent parties. The report does not require separate transferability, however, and acknowledges that some intangibles may only be transferred in a bundle. Finally, the report clarifies that transfer pricing definitional determinations should be completely independent from economic, accounting, legal, or other tax determinations even if they are related to intangibles. It particularly clarifies that the same concepts apply even to goodwill and going concern. This goes beyond the ostrich strategy. Realistically, one cannot avoid the conclusion that the part related to the definition of intangibles must have been devised for the pre-BEPS OECD project on intangibles. It seems clear that the change of framework has not affected this part at all.

36. Action 8 Deliverable, *supra* note 29, at 18-20.
37. *Ibid.* The report gives a simple example of a group wide purchasing decision that results in a discount to be shared, first, by the group member managing the action and then by the rest of the group based on their relative purchasing volumes. Note that, despite its seemed plausibility, perhaps, in this simple example, the use of an allocative rule for synergies is awkward if not non sensible. Synergies cannot be meaningfully allocated among members of a group since they arise out of the unique complexity of the group, its membership, and its mode of operations not out of distinct, separable contributions. Only an insistence of viewing everything in terms of transactions fitting of the literal or the transactional arm's length methodology could lead one to this mistake.
38. But, this goes against a rather consistent response by the courts to the challenges that transfer pricing cases present to them. See Brauner, *Valuation, supra* note 8.

Then, the draft reaches what is perhaps the most critical question of what to do with a taxpayer that divides important functions from ownership (and risk). This is the fundamental difficult case (referred to above as cash-box planning) where a firm develops intangibles and then parks them in a low tax jurisdiction with little activity (what used to be called substance not so many years ago). The basic tax planning scheme is to assign the significant upside or residual profits to such tax jurisdictions based on legal ownership and risk or the nominal financing of the development of the intangible. The draft delivers the expected message quite clearly: the OECD wishes profits to follow substantive functions which should mean that the upside should be attributable away from the low tax jurisdiction legal owner of the intangible to the (typically high tax) entity or entities that perform the meaningful functions of development and commercialization of intangibles. Again, similar to the definition discussion, the draft seems to imply that tax law should conduct an independent attribution study, essentially ignoring legal or economic (whatever that means) ownership. The intention and policy are clear and laudable as they follow the principles and purpose of the BEPS project. The challenges are revealed once implementation is discussed. At this time, implementation is only vaguely discussed by the report partly because the report has yet to propose a specific alternative(s) to current practice that is reliant on legal ownership and directly rejected by the BEPS project. I think it is equally clear that, under the new approach, the OECD should permit attribution of profits to mere legal owners financing companies at levels no higher than market financiers, i.e., arm's length (market) interest. The draft also promotes profit split as an acceptable method in cases where comparables would not be sufficient to determine the division of profits according to these principles. One should note that it is likely the case that profit split would now become the rule rather than the exception for transactions involving intangibles.

The report does not elaborate on the actual implementation of the OECD's new approach, yet the latter support of profit split has been anticipated for a long time and is somewhat widely accepted as the best way for the OECD to abandon arm's length in the transfer pricing for intangibles without losing too much face. Further, the analysis process described by the OECD is very similar to the so-called investor model that the United States attempted to implement and had to back away from in the face of industry opposition. The interim report resonates about the importance of implementation aspects yet contributes little in operative terms.

B. The Final Report

The final BEPS report on Actions 8-10 follows the footprint of the September 2014 deliverable; however, it more forcefully projects a reluctance of the OECD to reform the transfer pricing rules and practice. Arm's Length is still king, and no dramatic norm changes are recommended by the report. Some commentators viewed it as establishing a new arm's length principle[39] – one that emphasizes anti-abuse beyond the comparability exercise – yet, as already mentioned, I disagree with the view that arm's length is a legal principle and that comparability between market and non-market transactions carry any normative meaning. In fact, anti-abuse is at the core and origin of arm's length; the only new aspect of it here is the explicit application of it to the most extreme of abuse cases – the cash-box example. Moreover, the report includes new guidance on a variety of points discussed in the context of BEPS (and elaborated on below), yet it is clearly presented as work-in-progress. Many issues that have been raised have not been fully analyzed and concluded on. Some require further public comments while others were left to the future as part of the on-going work of the OECD on transfer pricing and the transfer pricing guidelines.

This chapter argues that the success declared by the OECD on transfer pricing matters is indeed success – political success of the OECD in maintaining its dominant position as well as that of arm's length and the transfer pricing guidelines. Such success, however, may be fairly viewed as a failure of the BEPS project as a whole and particularly of the non-OECD factors within the BEPS community of states. The final report does not deliver on the original promises of enhanced collaboration, holistic reform, and innovation. The report on Action Items 8-10 definitely does not deliver for the more developing countries, although I do believe that these countries would eventually benefit from the administrative changes effected by BEPS led by the Action 13 consequences that are beyond the scope of this chapter. This next section will briefly demonstrate the above claims following the order of delivery by the final report to be then followed by the more specific focus of this chapter: the part on CCAs.

1. *Applying the Arm's Length Principle*

The first part of the report revises Section D of Chapter I of the TPG in response to the mandate under Actions 8-10 of the BEPS Action Plan requiring the development of transfer pricing rules which create transfer pricing outcomes in line with value creation.[40] Arm's length proponents consistently declare it a principle which it clearly is not. The transfer pricing rules ensure that tax systems operate according to desired legal principles such as fairness, ability-to-pay, etc. One may view them also as anti-abuse rules to the same effect. BEPS introduced a new principle: profits must follow value creation. This, however, is merely a different articulation of the above basic principles of taxation and international taxation. In anti-abuse terms, the OECD iterates that profits are to be taxed only by jurisdictions in which the value generating such profits is created and not elsewhere, specifically not in jurisdictions where no value is created (see the cash-box case).

Many pages have been written on principles, standards, and rules, and the differences among them, yet, for our purpose, a simple view of the legal principle

39. See Jens Wittendorff, *BEPS Actions 8-10: Birth of a New Arm's Length Principle*, Tax Notes International (25 Jan. 2016), 331.
40. OECD, *Aligning Transfer Pricing Outcomes with Value Creation*, Actions 8-10 – 2015 Final Reports (15 Oct. 2015), at 13.

suffices: it is deeper and more general than rules or standards, and it refers to the moral or other normative justification for them. There is no inherent justification for treating related and unrelated transactions alike beyond simplistic symmetry. One could have perhaps made an efficiency-based justification for such symmetry in some circumstances; however, such a case has not been made, and the arm's length transfer pricing rules hardly follow efficiency goals.

Arm's length, therefore, is not a principle; it is a standard. It serves as a basis for the specific rules that implement it and is justified by other principles. In the case of arm's length, it is justified as a method for allocation of profits. Even we know that, historically, it was one of several standards that could be used for achieving the goals that underlie our tax systems. It is perhaps the most desirable standard, yet it is not a principle. This is important because the installation of Arm's Length as king – in its literal form, narrowly following comparables and not general economic terms of transactions – blocks important criticism and a serious evaluation of its shortcomings. As already mentioned, it does not matter how many times the OECD will repeat that there is an international consensus that arm's length is the best and only way to apply transfer pricing, when it does not work, it simply does not work. A more open, critical approach to the difficulties presented must be superior to the current approach of the OECD. Indeed, for a short while, the OECD itself realized it and aspired to it (see the original BEPS report), yet it seems that the traditionalist guard has taken over and propelled the project back into oblivion. The OECD can congratulate itself, yet taxpayers and countries would still find themselves struggling with the arm's length rules for intangibles and, as argued by this chapter, would likely find themselves struggling even more than in the pre-BEPS era.

Moreover, there is a more sinister, bigger picture aspect to the refusal to re-evaluate arm's length and its application. The core difference between arm's length and its alternatives is not so much in accuracy or cost. The deeper problem with arm's length is in its pretense of having a normative justification. The pseudo-economical façade of arm's length generates a perception of not only accuracy but also of desert: when profits are allocated to be taxable in a jurisdiction (via an entity taxpaying in such jurisdiction) based on the knowing-all markets, such a country is perceived as deserving tax jurisdiction as if it were fruits of some natural law. This is very similar to the residence and source dichotomy but much less obvious and transparent. Thus, developed countries argue against changes in the rules that result in their receipt of a reduced piece of the pie (see the discussion of locational savings). After all, the end game is who gets to tax what. Arm's length permits this result by being both inherently tilted in favor of developed countries where most MNEs reside and headquarter by being complex and costly, which disadvantages developing countries, and also by framing the transfer pricing discussion in terms of economics, markets, and desert rather than political division of revenue.

It is not surprising, therefore, that developing countries are not happy with the outcome of BEPS despite the fact that some of them had voice in the decision-making process for the first time. As demonstrated in this chapter and others, they have actually benefitted little from this.

2. *Key Issues in the Final Report*

Others in this collection elaborated on the non-CCA extents of the final report. However, a few words are important nonetheless.

As already mentioned, the final report strongly affirms the commitment to the arm's length principle. The report does not really go beyond arm's length; it frames the valuation of hard-to-measure intangibles with arm's length terminology. It permits tax authorities to impute agreements, adjustment clauses, and contingent payments based on what unrelated parties would have agreed. This, of course, reminds us of the new Article 7 work and the famous AOA. The strong resistance to this approach and the immense difficulties to implement it did not affect the OECD. However, even beyond that, it is not difficult to observe that intangibles are difficult to valuate because there are no reasonable comparables. So, the tax authorities are now required to invent comparable conditions. Note that arm's length is based on market theories which stated that it is unlikely that an opportunity for a comparable transaction would arise without somebody taking advantage of it and, in the meanwhile, presenting a comparable transaction. This nonsense solution for hard-to-measure intangibles is that the OECD refuses to accept that it is truly possible to have a transaction in an intangible that does not have an acceptable comparable. As they stand, these recommendations would undoubtedly lead to much controversy, and it is difficult to see how even more detailed guidance could improve the situation.

Another example for the arm's length myopia is the treatment of group synergies. These, by definition, cannot be compared to market transactions and, therefore, had simply been ignored and adjusted for based on comparables found while ignoring these synergies. Yet, this was difficult to do in many cases and pressure had been applied about the logic of this exercise. The final report reached what looks like a compromise (i.e., very difficult to logically explain) materializing certain synergies – those described as arising from deliberate concerted group action – and assigning them or their allocated profits to the parties contributing to them. Other synergies continue to be ignored and are then adjusted for in the regular analysis. The problem is that synergies cannot really be contributed to – they occur because of the affiliation of the parties involved. It is nonsense, therefore, to seriously attempt to allocate them to particular parties. This is just the latest symptom of the irresponsible use of multiple legal fictions or metaphors in transfer pricing without a rigid analysis of the outcomes. It is simply left for taxpayers and their advisors to figure out. Again, there is no doubt that plenty of litigation will result from this guidance.

Interestingly, the final report does not pick up on the locational savings point which rejects the demand of developing countries such as China and India for profit allocations to market economies. This decision demonstrates the failure of the developing countries in BEPS, the importance of agenda setting, where changes require consensus and are otherwise rejected to the benefit of those enjoying the status quo (see also the lack of action on Action 1, or 7, as a matter of fact), and the success of the OECD in the deferral of the discussion of the demands of source countries for more taxation with its pseudo economic agenda of arm's length tweaking.

The final report follows the discussion draft in defining intangibles as essentially all that may be owned or controlled in a commercial setting. This means that intangibles do not fit the arm's length method since it is simply not an intangible if it cannot be transacted by unrelated parties. Goodwill is included but, again, it ties to the transactional setting rather than to a true value based profit allocation. In the operative context, the final report follows the cash-box company case by stating that mere legal ownership would not typically deserve profit allocation. The report goes on to describe a long list of functions including new terminology such as important functions that would deserve profit allocation.

The cash-box example is also used in the risk or Action 9 recommendations that provide that risk taking cannot enjoy profit allocation if the party is not capable of controlling the risk and does not actually do so. Controlling the risks is interpreted as making decisions about management and mitigation of risks, financial capability of absorbing the risk, paying for it, etc. Even though the cash-box is targeted by these rules, they state that the taxpayer does not have to perform the functions of controlling the risk itself; paying for them suffices. This is quite vague and would likely result in many interpretation conflicts and litigation but perhaps would eliminate the most egregious cases where one party is a true cash-box or an empty shell solely owning the intangible. Where the line is between a pure cash-box and a company that is kosher but truly has just a bit more than that pure cash-box may be a difficult and perhaps somewhat discouraging question for tax authorities. Much of the confusion results from the final report's new emphasis which departs from the discussion draft's analysis on the contractual terms rather than the functions performed. Many have interpreted the direction taken by the OECD to mean that risks are less important or perhaps only minimally important post-BEPS for transfer pricing analysis, yet the final report cannot be clearly interpreted to mean that.

The final report added guidance on low value-adding services to bring the TPG closer to the United States rules. It provides some unfinished work on commodities, simplifying their transfer pricing by potentially using publicly quoted prices rather than specific transactional data.

Finally, the anticipated empowerment of profit split, or really the transactional methods that already dominate the practice of transfer pricing anyway, was not completed by the final report and is left for the foreseen future. It seems that the opposition to these methods due to their inconvenient compatibility with the literal arm's length has weakened but not sufficiently enough to install them as the primary caretakers of the principle.

In conclusion, the final report introduced a lot of new uncertainty into an already uncertain body of norm with little concrete progress on matters unsettled prior to the BEPS work. Concretely, the report introduced the issues of potentially allocable synergies, hard-to-measure intangibles, and pure cash boxes yet supported them with very little immediately executable rules; it rejected locational savings and perhaps reduced the importance of (financial) risk taking in transfer pricing. This is clearly not dramatic progress. In any event, the cloud of legal uncertainty it left seems to overwhelm any progress it may claim to have achieved.

IV. CCA

The primary focus of this chapter is Chapter VIII of the TPG which concerns CCAs. The fate of this part of the final report is not much different from the others as described above. It was tweaked by BEPS primarily with an intent to make it coherent with the other changes to the TPG, yet it was not reformed. It became even less-focused than it had been pre-BEPS.

Perhaps the least intellectually defensible part of the TPG was that this chapter had not enjoyed much analysis or any other attention pre-BEPS; however, the importance of cost sharing, the idiosyncratic United States rule that had inspired the discussion of CCAs, forced the OECD to try and pour some content into this formerly essentially empty bucket. It did not do that. It merely recruited the chapter to support the other changes to the TPG and attempted to make it compatible to them. No serious thought was put into the sensibility of the regime or even to its mere necessity in the TPG. This next section begins with the intellectual (too generous a term, I admit) predecessor of CCAs and a major current influence over their evolution, i.e., the United States cost sharing regime.

A. Cost Sharing

Cost sharing is a regime prescribed by the United States transfer pricing regulations dating back to 1968.[41] It is a safe harbor regime that protects research joint ventures from regular transfer pricing scrutiny and some potentially cumbersome partnership taxation rules.[42]

Being such, the difference between cost sharing and CCA should be apparent.[43] While cost sharing serves as a safe harbor regime, the purpose of Chapter VIII is to provide some general guidance for determining whether the conditions established by associated enterprises for a CCA are consistent with the arm's length principle,[44] namely, to enforce and not to except from arm's length – the exact opposite purpose. This general purpose has not changed post-BEPS. This chapter wishes to clarify that CCAs and cost sharing are different creatures, and their analysis in combination is likely to, at best, confuse a coherent discourse and, worse, prevent it. This is not a merely academic assertion. Beyond the extensive discussion, direct or indirect, of cost sharing in the context of the reform of Chapter VIII, the confusion between the two and their interchangeable use are rampant.[45]

41. Prescribed by Treas. Reg. 1.482-7, pursuant to IRC Section 482.
42. Treas. Reg. 1.482-7(a)(1).
43. See also, e.g., G. Garner Prillaman & Barbara Mantegani, *OECD Guidelines Governing Cost Contribution Arrangements: A Comparison with the United States sec. 482 Cost Sharing Regulations*, BNA, 6 Transfer pricing report 389 (15 Oct. 1997).
44. 2010 TPG, 219.
45. See, e.g., Jens Wittendorff, *A Look at Cost Sharing in the OECD Discussion Draft*, 78 Tax Notes International 1121 (22 Jun. 2015); or David D. Stewart, *OECD Cost-Sharing Draft Doesn't Reflect Third-Party Arrangements* 2015 TNT 129-3.

Even beyond functions, cost sharing and CCA differ in scope as the former is limited to the development of intangibles and, perhaps most importantly, in their effect. Beyond the protection from regular transfer pricing scrutiny and partnership rules, cost sharing permits ex-post readjustments of the venture arrangements based on *ex ante* (dollar) contributions. These extraordinary benefits were provided in the 1960s with no background explanations. An attempt to track such regulative history resulted in no official material in their support. Yet, it is likely that the regulations were encouraged by lobbying efforts, that I could not track, that convinced the Treasury department that they would be helpful to American MNEs engaged in Research & Development, a goal that is favorable to essentially all governments.[46] CCAs are much less clear about these adjustments; however, at least according to the new examples provided by the BEPS report, these adjustments must be based on value, albeit not clearly *ex post* value.[47] There are various other differences between the regimes that are less relevant to the substantive focus I take in this chapter and, therefore, I will mention them only in a passing, if at all.

The golden age of cost sharing came only about three decades later, yet, as we have learned from BEPS, cost sharing is the single most important contributor to the transactions that had triggered the BEPS project. Without cost sharing, it would be very difficult, and usually very expensive, to export American created intangibles with little to no United States taxation. United States tax law has many rules that try to stop exactly this type of tax planning which are all essentially annihilated by cost sharing. Moreover, rules such as IRC Section 367(d) and the regulations promulgated pursuant to its authority have been constantly tightened, even currently, with the clear policy of preventing the very profit shifting that cost sharing evolved to enable.[48]

The United States Government had tried over the years to rationalize the cost sharing regime, yet all of these attempts had either faced political resistance that forced the IRS to back off and refrain from reform or, when regulatory reform had been attempted, it faced courts that bought into the notion that Arm's Length is king and hence cost sharing, a safe harbor regime (from arm's length), must apply the arm's length standard in the same manner – literal arm's length – otherwise accepted and practiced in the market. Combined with failures to properly litigate these cases, the United States would not scrap the cost sharing regulations perhaps due to the general reluctance to admit failure but more likely because they simply could not take away this extraordinary benefit endowed to the MNEs.

The original cost sharing rule appeared in the first set of comprehensive transfer pricing regulations.[49] Treas. Reg. sec. 1.482-2(d)(4) applied to a bona fide cost sharing

46. There is limited support for this general goal in Stanley Surrey, *Treasury's Need to Curb Tax Avoidance in Foreign Business through Use of 482*, 28 Jouranl Taxation 75 (1968), Surrey being a government official in addition to his academic stature during the 1960s.
47. See OECD, *BEPS Action 8: Revisions to Chapter VIII of the Transfer Pricing Guidelines on Cost Contribution Arrangements (CCAs)*, Public Discussion Draft (29 Apr. 2015 – 29 May 2015), Annex, 15.
48. See the proposed Section 367(d) regulations. See, e.g., the PWC alert on the finalization of these regulations, available at: http://www.pwc.com/us/en/tax-services-multinationals/newsletters/us-outbound-tax/final-section-367-1248-regulations.html.
49. T.D. 6952, 1968-1 C.B. 218.

arrangement. It was quite similar in form and language to the current regulations. These regulations, although not completely out of use, had not featured prominently in visible cross border tax planning or in any significant tax policy discourse prior to the 1980s when it was simply part of the debate over the proper transfer pricing treatment of transactions in intangibles.

The lengthy and controversial debate over the matter resulted in the Tax Reform Act of 1986 that introduced the one and only important amendment to Section 482 since its enactment. It provided that allocation of income generated by a transferred intangible should be Commensurate With Income (CWI) actually earned by the transferee from the transferred intangible.[50] The Conference Committee Report stated explicitly that, in enacting this amendment, Congress did not wish to preclude the use of legitimate cost sharing arrangements.[51] Interestingly, this Report specified that, in order to be compatible with CWI, a cost sharing arrangement should be one in which: (1) a participant bears its share of costs associated with development on both successful and unsuccessful projects; (2) the allocation of such costs should be proportionate to profits (as determined before any R&E deductions); and (3) if one party joins a cost sharing arrangement after research has already commenced, then the joining party must compensate the party that has already performed research; compensation was later termed a buy-in payment. The Report recommended that the government further study the need to modify the regulations accordingly.

The government followed up with the study that resulted in the publication of a policy White Paper in 1988.[52] Among other things, the White Paper suggested that participants in cost sharing arrangements be assigned specific geographical areas and that clear rationalization of the business terms would be reflected in the arrangements. Eventually, the IRS issued proposed regulations concerning cost sharing in 1992.[53] The proposed regulations were generally more flexible and pro-taxpayer than the ideas promoted in the White Paper. They relied on anti-abuse tests instead of restrictive cost sharing terms. The focus shifted from substantive reform of the cost sharing rules to instrumental changes, abandoning the impact of the 1986 legislations much in the same way that the CWI device had been effectively abandoned by the government. The inconvenient (in)compatibility of CWI and literal arm's length may explain this fate.

In any event, the proposed regulations provided that only controlled taxpayers that would use the developed intangibles in their active conduct of a trade or business would be eligible participants in cost sharing arrangements. Note the stark similarity to the BEPS project proposals. The intention was to prevent profit shifting. Yet, again, after an extensive commentary period, the regulations that were finalized in 1995 allowed even more flexibility for taxpayers in designing these arrangements.[54] A quick later revision of the regulations in 1996 eliminated active business as a requirement for bona fide participation.[55] It was sufficient that participants reasonably anticipate that

50. Tax Reform Act of 1986, Pub. L. No. 99-514, 100 Stat. 2085 (1986).
51. H.R. Rep. 99-281, 99th Cong., 2nd Sess. (1986).
52. Study of Intercompany Pricing, Notice 88-123, 1988-2 CB 458.
53. 57 FR 3571.
54. T.D. 8632, 1996-1 C.B. 85.
55. T.D. 8670, 1996-1 C.B. 99.

they will derive benefits from the use of the relevant intangibles. Again, the similarity to the reforms on the BEPS agenda is not surprising. Naturally, the following decade permitted a very convenient use of cost sharing structures.

It is apparent that the vulnerability of the cost sharing regime had not escaped the minds of United States government officials. In 2005, the IRS again issued proposed regulations that were supposed to constitute a radical departure from the current regulations.[56] The IRS had warned against the avoidance potential that cost sharing provided to MNEs. It proposed to view cost sharing arrangements under what became known as the investor model that allowed above-normal financial profits only to participants that contribute something beyond money to the arrangement (again, note the parallel to BEPS and particularly to the cash-box scenario). The thought was that the party with existing intangibles and research capacity would not permit a third party to invest in future development of crown jewel intangibles and receive profits beyond normal financial profits.[57]

In addition, the proposed regulations provided permissible methods to valuate buy-in payments. They required that the contribution of the actual research team earn part of the residual profits (beyond their costs). They required exclusive geographical division of interests, and they permitted periodic adjustment only to the IRS, not taxpayers.

The regulations were heavily criticized since they were designed to significantly limit the ability of United States MNE to shift profits to low tax jurisdictions. The primary argument used against the proposed regulations had been the familiar competitiveness argument despite the fact that competing jurisdictions had not employed similar rules at all. The anti-regulations campaign had been partly successful, resulting in temporary regulations issued in 2009. These regulations did not include many of the above proposals of the recommended regulations.[58] The focus of the temporary regulations shifted from the investor model to proper valuation of buy-ins, now called Platform Contributions (PCT). Their valuation was separated from the cost sharing arrangement itself. This meant that foreign subsidiaries, the sole contribution of which was money, could still not be compensated beyond normal financial profits. However, no clear contrast was drawn between those who brought something to the table and those who did not. In effect, it is just the price for the use of cost sharing that increased or was supposed to increase. This shift opened the door to ever more sophisticated and complex, yet costly, tax planning of the BEPS variety.[59]

The focus shift to buy-in regulation has not fared well. The basic rule for buy-ins is as old as the regulations, i.e., that buy-in payments should be made at arm's length

56. REG-144615-02 published at 70 Fed. Reg. 51116 (29 Aug. 2005), See also Robert S. Kirschenbaum et al., *Proposed Cost Sharing Regulations Introduce 'New' Standards*, 16 Journal International Taxation 12 (2005).
57. Preamble, 2005 proposed cost sharing regulations, *Ibid.*
58. TD 9441, published at 74 Fed. Reg. 340 (5 Jan. 2009). The temporary regulations further relieved other substantive and administrative requirements of the proposed regulations, generally to the benefit of taxpayers.
59. See, e.g., Neal M. Kochman & Stafford Smiley, *The Temporary Cost Sharing Regulations*, 36 Corporate Taxation 44 (2009).

in proportion to the participants' share of reasonably anticipated benefits and similarly to the rest of the shared costs.[60] In the tradition of literal arm's length, the buy-in payment was viewed technically as not being different than any other related party transfer of intangibles. This view is consistent with the IRS' insistence over the years to apply the literal arm's length standard in the context of cost sharing. Yet, once regulation of the cost sharing arrangements themselves became ineffective, the stakes became higher at this point of access to the safe harbor regime. Both taxpayers and the IRS struggled with the implementation of the buy-in rules which led to the writing and publication of the above-mentioned proposed and later temporary regulations. The investor model would have been particularly important for cost sharing where, ubiquitously, the partner of the United States MNE was its wholly owned, typically Irish, United States financed subsidiary. The regulations required the arrangement to make business sense consistently with a substantive, but not a literal arm's length. The regulations prescribed methods for valuation of buy-in payments that are similar to those featured in the intangibles transfer regulations.[61] Three new specified methods were introduced: the income method, the acquisition price method, and the market capitalization method.[62] In addition, Comparable Uncontrolled Transaction (CUT), residual profit split, and unspecified methods are also permitted.[63] CUT is the most straightforward articulation of the arm's length standard. It evaluates whether the amount charged for a controlled transfer of intangible property was at arm's length with reference to a sufficiently similar (comparable) uncontrolled transaction. The income method evaluates whether an amount charged in a PCT (buy-in) is at arm's length by reference to realistic alternatives available to the controlled participant.[64] This method assumes that the best reasonable alternative is developing the intangible on its own and then exploiting it. This is seemingly the preferred method in cases when only one party contributes 'non-routine' contributions (i.e., development) to the arrangement. The acquisition price method is most appropriate for determining the arm's length result where all of the non-routine resources and capabilities of a recently acquired target's business constitute external contributions,[65] i.e., when both participants contribute meaningfully to the arrangement. This method seeks to isolate the acquisition price of a target based on the value attributable to the external contributions. The arm's length determination is compared with reference to the amount charged for the stock or asset purchase of an entire organization in an uncontrolled transaction.[66] Simply put, when the cost sharing arrangement develops version 2.0 based on version 1.0, it effectively replaces version 1.0 and, therefore, the new participants should buy into its relevant part of the version 1.0 business. Again, this is

60. Section 1.482-7(f)(3).
61. Section 1.482-4(c)(1).
62. Section 1.482-7(g)(1) of the Regulation provides that the methods must be applied in accordance with the best method rule, the comparability analysis, and the arm's length range; Section 1.482-7(g)(1) of the Proposed Regulation.
63. Section 1.482-7(g)(1)(i)-(vi) of the Proposed Regulation.
64. Section 1.482-7(g)(4)(i) of the Proposed Regulation.
65. Section 1.482-7(g)(4)(iv) of the Proposed Regulation.
66. Section 1.482-7(g)(5)(i) of the Proposed Regulation.

a substantive arm's length approach rather than literal arm's length, a shift not dissimilar to the one BEPS purports to make. This was also the government's (losing) position in the *Veritas* case. The market capitalization method is used where substantially all of the non-routine contributions are covered by a PCT or a group of PCTs, again, a very common circumstance.[67] Here, the arm's length charge is equal to the adjusted average market capitalization divided among the participants based on their reasonably anticipated benefits shares. The residual profit split method looks at the combined operating profit or loss attributable to one or more external contributions and determines whether it is arm's length by reference to the value of the participant's contribution to the profit or loss. This method is designed for a situation where more than one controlled participant makes significant non-routine contributions to the cost shared intangibles.[68] The regulation also permitted the use of other 'unspecified' methods as appropriate. An interesting development in that regime was the use of projections, usually information closely associated with income type valuation that does not typically sit naturally with the market valuation flavor of the arm's length standard.

The temporary regulations allow taxpayer's flexibility in choosing the scope of projections used (group or single entity, for example); however, they must choose the most reliable projections based on all facts and circumstances in light of the completeness and the accuracy of the underlying data. The regulations further allow the use of probability weighted averages of possible outcomes. Generally, such probabilities were to be determined by top management. This may be ideal in terms of representation to investors; for purposes of calculating a buy-in (PCT) payment, it may result in overinflated payments since they often understate the risk (and overstate future benefit) of the endeavor. One can easily see that this is an anti-abuse type solution rather than a literal application of the arm's length standard as the IRS developed it over the years. A comprehensive exposure of the new buy-in rules is beyond the scope of this chapter, yet one should realize the complexity of these rules and their general anti-avoidance rather than a principle-based regime.

The IRS went beyond the regulations in its focus on buy-ins. In 2007, it had identified them as a Tier I issue and one of the most significant compliance challenges facing its then Large and Midsize Business Division (LMSB).[69] The IRS acknowledged that cost sharing arrangements 'are often used by taxpayers inappropriately to transfer intangible assets and associated profits offshore to related foreign affiliates for inadequate consideration. . .[the IRS] estimates that inadequate consideration has resulted in material underreporting of taxable income by U.S. Corporations'.[70]

Later that year, the IRS issued a Coordinated Issue Paper (CIP) with guidance on methods for evaluating buy-in payments.[71] The CIP acknowledges the above. Consistent with the investor model, the CIP gives preference to the income method of

67. Section 1.482-7(g)(6)(i) of the Proposed Regulation.
68. Section 1.482-7(g)(7)(i) of the Proposed Regulation.
69. LMSB-04-0307-027 (5 Apr. 2007).
70. *Ibid.*
71. LMSB-04-0907-62 (27 Sep. 2007).

valuation according to which the buy-in payment should be the present value of all projected income of the controlled foreign corporation (the newly established foreign subsidiary) reduced by all substantive contributions made by such controlled foreign corporation. Note that this is the 'akin to a sale' approach of the regulations.

This approach, however, was rejected by the court in *Veritas Software Corp. v. Commissioner.*[72] Veritas Software Corp. (Veritas), a United States corporation, and its newly established Irish subsidiary, Veritas Software International Ltd ('Veritas International'), entered into an agreement in 1999 for sharing R&D costs and into an agreement assigning Veritas' European sales agreements to Veritas International. The new (co-developed) software was based on the then existing product owned by Veritas. Pursuant to the cost sharing agreement, Veritas granted Veritas International a license to use these products. In exchange, it received a buy-in payment that was eventually adjusted to USD 118 million. Veritas calculated this amount using the CUT method. In 2006, the IRS challenged the buy-in valuation and came up with a competing number of USD 2.5 billion based on a mix of methods including the forgone profits method and the market capitalization method. In pre-trial, the government submitted a new analysis that reduced this amount to USD 1.675 billion, based on a discounted cash flow analysis, perpetual life, actual profits, and future projections. The government's position was that the buy-in payment must also take into account Veritas International's access to Veritas' R&D and marketing teams and distribution channels, customer lists, trademarks, trade names, brand names, and sales agreements.

The tax court held that the government's position was arbitrary, capricious, and unreasonable because it conceded USD 825 million of the buy in amount and failed to offer even a token defense of its original position. Further, the court rejected the government's revised position both on its merits and because the analysis of the government's expert did not support it. The court understood that the revised valuation was consistent with the IRS' 2007 CIP but did not accept the positions contained therein. The most important disagreement was over the character of the transaction subject to the buy-in payments. In the CIP and the revised position in Veritas, the government essentially viewed the transaction as a sale of the relevant business. From that perspective, the income method was appropriate because it evaluated the business as a whole including the synergistic value of the various properties transferred under the agreement. The tax court rejected this view of the underlined transaction, limiting the buy-in requirement to the isolated pre-existing rights in the intangibles required to be transferred in order to develop the cost shared intangibles since this had been the transaction structured by the taxpayer.[73] Further, the court rejected the use of an income method to valuate existing intangibles based on perpetual life because such valuation could not isolate the value of the pre-existing intangibles from, for instance, future improvements and development including the developments funded by the cost sharing arrangement. On a related note, the court rejected the use of perpetual life in the calculation, arguing for limited economic life with no further R&D. Finally, the

72. 133 T.C. No. 14 (9 Dec. 2009).
73. Based on Section 1.482-1(f)(2)(ii)(A) of the Treasury Regulation.

court rejected several other arguments of the IRS that are specific to the case such as the discount rate used, the value of the transferred customer lists and distribution channels, and so on.

The tax court did accept Veritas' CUT valuation that was based on internal comparables (transactions between Veritas itself and unrelated parties), augmenting its position that buy-ins should be evaluated similarly to market license transactions. It again rejected the position taken in the CIP that buy-ins are different from market licenses in that the latter do not include a right to further develop the licensed intangibles. The effect of this decision is very significant. The IRS effectively conceded the case with the hope that the final regulations would effectively reverse it. It was clear that the decision of Veritas was impacted by the government's mistakes in handling the case. The magnitude of the revisions of both the valuation, the supporting assumptions and methods for such valuation, and the lack of explanations may have put the IRS in an irrecoverable position. Further, the IRS' view of buy-ins reflected in the new cost sharing regulations and CIP were successfully positioned by the taxpayer and with no challenge by the government as a radical departure from the common interpretation of buy-ins at the relevant time for the case. The tax court instinctively accepted this positioning as if it inevitably led to a conclusion that the 'new' views presented by the government cannot apply in this case and hence should be rejected. A careful reading of the tax court's opinion must lead to a conclusion that the court genuinely rejected the government's position on buy-ins in favor of the traditional, literal arm's length approach. This means that the now final regulations (although in a temporary form) were exposed to challenges by taxpayers based on the long-standing support of the government itself of the literal application of arm's length in all cases.[74]

In 2011, the Treasury department finalized the regulations, albeit in a softened form.[75] They kept the framework of the investor model as well as the new valuation methodologies including the much criticized income method. The regulations were followed by proposed and temporary regulations that included details primarily regarding the application of the income method.[76] These regulations were finalized without change in 2013[77] despite an ongoing controversy over their appropriateness and even their interpretation. To an extent, the regulations came in response to the court losses, most importantly, in *Veritas*. Yet, especially in light of the obiter in *Veritas*, they were accompanied by the expectation that their compatibility with arm's length would be revisited by the courts.

Indeed, similar cases arose and, recently in *Altera*,[78] the tax court stayed the course and invalidated the 2003 regulations, albeit in a different context. *Altera* was a follow-on to the *Xilinx* case[79] in which the Tax Court held that, under the 1995

74. As I argued in Brauner, *Cost Sharing*, *supra* note 3.
75. T.D. 9568, 76 Fed. Reg. 80082 (12/22/2011).
76. T.D. 9569, 76 Fed. Reg. 80249 (12/23/2011); REG-145474-11, 76 Fed. Reg. 80310 (12/23/2011).
77. T.D. 9630, 78 Fed. Reg. 52854 (8/27/2013).
78. *Altera Corp. v. Commissioner*, 145 T.C. No. 3 (2015).
79. *Xilinx Inc. v. Commissioner*, 125 T.C. No. 4 (2005) http://www.taxnotes.com/worldwide-tax-daily/accounting-periods-and-methods/stock-option-costs-arent-allocable-among-controlled-group-us-tax-court-holds/2005/09/01/8008926, aff'd, 598 F.3d 1191 (9th Cir. 2010).

regulations, participants in cost sharing agreements need not share stock-based compensation costs. *Xilinx* followed an odd path, and its ruling was based on the observation by the courts (Tax Court and the Court of Appeals) that unrelated parties would not share such costs.[80] The 2003 Treas. Reg. sec. 1.482-7(d)(2) was issued in response to the position taken by *Xilinx* and others in similar circumstances. It explicitly required cost sharing participants to share stock-based compensation costs. *Altera* held that the regulation was invalid consistent with the Tax Court's positions in both *Xilinx* and *Veritas* that emphasized that literal Arm's Length is king; that the purpose of transfer pricing is to create parity in treatment between market and non-market transactions essentially regardless of the circumstances, the presence of abuse, etc. Moreover, the decision in *Altera* focused on failures of the government to comply with administrative law standards, primarily the establishment of a factual basis that would necessitate the change in regulations (and in the position taken by the government) about the supremacy of literal arm's length. It is clear that the tax court subscribes to the pseudo economic view of the international tax regime, and, more specifically, that it rejects the view that arm's length should be applied in a systematic, broadly viewed basis with the purpose of countering abuse. This view is clearly opposite to the one apparently taken by the BEPS project. Further, it is expected that, based on similar logic, the new regulations may also be vulnerable.[81]

It should be apparent by now that the issue will not simply go away, and BEPS is the direct outcome of the failures of cost sharing. Extraordinarily, the BEPS project steps in and discusses the same problems that the United States IRS had encountered, namely, the opportunity to very cheaply shift profits from R&D and headquarters locations (typically in high taxed jurisdictions) to low tax jurisdictions via the transfer of intangibles using mere contracts. The overwhelmingly typical cost sharing arrangement involves a United States MNE with headquarters and a robust R&D center solely or almost solely in the United States with a product that produces significant revenues and often dominates its market as well as a newly organized (typically Irish) subsidiary of that corporation designed to participate in a cost sharing arrangement with the parent for the development of the 2.0 or other version of the same product. This subsidiary finances the R&D, all of which is in the United States with money contributed to it (tax free) by the same parent and, in exchange, receives the right to exclusively exploit the intangible worldwide (except for the United States market) from that point onwards. To add insult to injury, the United States courts ruled that the new joint venture is not required to buy into the existing business of the MNE but, rather, merely pay an arm's length royalty for the use of version 1.0 of the product in the development of its version 2.0.

There are some additional wrinkles that make this regime even better than described, yet the above is the most important for the purposes of this chapter. The

80. For criticism, see Brauner, *supra* note 5, 562-563.
81. And, indeed, the same corporation, Altera Corp., filed a new petition to the Tax Court on 18 Dec. 2015, regarding tax years 2010 and 2011 that are subject to the new regulations (when they were in their temporary form), essentially making the same arguments as in the case it won regarding the 2003 regulations.

BEPS project realized all of the above difficulties with cost sharing in the United States and even focused on the most egregious part of the regime: the *ex post* readjustments based on *ex ante* costs. As explained below, although the final outcome is not completely clear about it, it is very clear that the drafters of the final Action 8-10 reports wished to prevent this opportunity, demanding (*ex post*) value rather than historical costs to be used for contractual adjustments. This dramatic reform had not even been seriously considered in the United States. Yet, in the process of doing that, the OECD may have caused other harm, making CCAs more operational, bringing them closer to United States cost sharing and, the original sin, further fortifying Arm's Length as king.

Next, this chapter concisely tracks the CCA regime, the BEPS work, and the final outcome in the form of revisions to Chapter VIII of the TPG.

B. CCAs

As is well known, the TPG, following up on the original OECD transfer pricing report of 1979, were adopted by the OECD in the years 1995-1997. There is no denying the importance and influence of the United States transfer pricing regime and its reforms on the guidelines and the timing of their adoption. Similar to other OECD reports, the TPG are not binding on any country and, technically, have a weak status in support of treaty interpretation. Some commentators and the OECD, however, view them as equal to the OECD commentaries and, as such, as a primary means of interpretation under Article 31 of the VCLT.[82] Nonetheless, there are good reasons why the TPG were not included in the commentary. Article 9 is one of the most problematic articles of the Model, and it is fraught with a history of disagreements over its application. Keeping the guidelines separate from the commentaries permitted their writing in the first place. In practice, many countries have used the TPG (not dissimilarly to the use of the commentaries) as legal prescription, granting the guidelines significant practical force.

The fate of Chapter VIII was somewhat different. It is difficult to understand why it was added to the TPG beyond a mere symmetry with the United States regulations. Unlike the United States' regime, CCAs cover not only the development of intangibles but also all transactions including tangible property joint ventures and services pooling. This difference goes beyond the mere scope since, if anything, the rationale of the United States rules was to establish a safe harbor rule from the complexity and costliness of intangible valuations under the normal transfer pricing rules. The same does not exist for tangible property and services.

Chapter VIII of the TPG simply describes CCAs as arrangements for the pooling of resources and cost allocations (i.e., risks) based on expected future benefits. They are subject to the general arm's length charge and hence, logically, they should be compared to comparable joint ventures among unrelated parties. These are rare, of course and even rarer when intangibles are concerned, hence the United States rules exemption of cost sharing arrangements from the regular application of arm's length. Research joint ventures are few and would rarely be sufficiently comparable to cost

82. See Wittendorff, 246, and para. 1 of the commentary on Article 9.

sharing arrangements. Moreover, no research company would enter into an agreement under which it shares its crown jewel intangibles with another company that brings nothing to the table but cash. Note that, under a CCA (and a cost sharing arrangement), both parties own pieces of the developed properties (or contract in the case of services) and, therefore, may exploit their share independently of their joint venturers. Each participant must be capable of exploiting the product of the venture and benefitting from it; it is not required to actually do so, and it is not required to do so in any particular manner. Similarly, there are no special rules for the contributions made by the parties (unlike the United States buy-in rules mentioned above). Adjustment must be made based on arm's length concepts and preferably on a multi-year basis.

In conclusion, CCAs do not enjoy (nor suffer) any special rules in terms of the application of arm's length. They are simply accommodated and acknowledged by Chapter VIII with some explanations about the application of the regular rules to them. It would, therefore, be wrong to compare them with the safe harbor rules of the United States costs sharing regime.

Yet, Chapter VIII has had some impact, as at least fifteen countries beyond the United States have adopted CCA-type rules beyond the TPG.[83] Germany is notable, having published guidance on CCA in 1999. Its rules follow the TPG, however are tighter overall, less flexible, and vaguer than the current language of Chapter VIII which is very much in line with the proposed changes to Chapter VIII which leads to a thought – if not a conclusion – that they have inspired much of these proposed changes. In general, the German rule follows the idea of the arrangement being a cost pool for whatever purpose is common to the venturers (not just for the development of intangibles) and, as such, it stringently monitors the participants in the pool, yet, once qualified, the allocation of profits is based on cost accounting and not value. Similarly, other countries adopted Chapter VIII into their domestic rules with various modifications but with little meaningful order or structure.[84] Some countries have agreed to

83. Australia; Canada; China; Colombia; Germany; Indonesia; Italy; Japan; South Korea; Malaysia; New Zeland; Poland; Portugal; Slovakia; Slovenia. Source: IBFD Tax Research Platform.

84. *Ibid.* Australia's tax authority, the ATO, in January 2004, finalized its draft ruling on Cost Contribution Arrangements (CCAs), TR2004/1. It generally follows the CCA rules contained in Chapter VIII of the 2010 OECD Transfer Pricing Guidelines, emphasizing economic substance and business sense. Canadian Act defines a qualifying cost contribution arrangement in subsection 247(1). It includes language that seems influenced by the United States cost sharing regulations, yet the limited practice is largely informed by the OECD Guidelines and commentary by the Canadian Tax Authority (CRA) in IC 87-2R. Colombian law indicates in Article 260-3 (2) of the Tax Code, which provides that with regard to CCAs between related parties, the taxpayer must prove the actual provision of services and that the value charged or paid for by those services is in line with the arm's length principle. Article 6 of Decree 3030 defines a cost sharing agreement as an agreement that allows companies to share the costs and risks of developing, producing, or obtaining assets, services, or rights and to determine the nature and extent of the interest of each participant in them. The TPG serve as an interpretative tool only in Colombia as it is not a member of the OECD. In China, the term 'cost sharing agreement' is defined under Article 112 of the EIT Regulations as an agreement reached concerning the sharing of common costs among related parties in accordance with the arm's length principle. Again, the rules are stylized generally but not with direct reference to the TPG. In Indonesia, Article 17A of DGT Regulation PER-32 has specifically recognized Cost Contribution Arrangements (CCAs) as arrangements between related parties to share risks from the development, production, or acquisition of an asset, service, or right and to determine the functions for each respective

treaty provision to the same (but limited to the treaty) effect[85] or to rulings based on the same notion.[86] Other countries are known to approve similar rulings on a case-by-case basis.[87] One could also imagine reliance on the general acceptance of the TPG by domestic courts as support of similar treatment.

C. BEPS

Following the 2014 Actions 8-10 deliverable and other discussion drafts, the OECD released a discussion draft amendment for Chapter VIII of the TPG on 29 April 2015. The draft was released for public comments, and it attracted hundreds of pages of such comments.[88]

The declared purpose of the proposed amendment had been to align the transfer pricing treatment of intangibles as revised by the other work on Action 8 (and 9-10) with Chapter VIII of the TPG because CCAs may be used for the development of intangibles. A potpourri of normative changes also applied to non-development CCAs in what seems to be arbitrary and an after (or no) thought.

The first amendment indeed implements the attitude change towards risk taking. The old Chapter VIII (as well as the United States cost sharing rules) does not require a CCA participant in order to enjoy the benefits of the arrangement in any particular

participant in such an arrangement, much in line with the TPG. There is no relevant case law on CCAs. In Italy, the rules generally follow the TPG, yet there is little guidance on the detailed rules that are lacking at the moment. In Japan, the rules deviate from the TPG in their focus on the development of intangibles which is similar to the United States cost sharing regulations. However, the rules are very rudimentary and do not include details with the likelihood of arm's length measures being applicable, similar to the approach of the TPG. In Korea, Article 6-2 (Tax Adjustment due to an Apportionment of the Arm's Length Price) of the CITL contains rules on Cost Contribution Arrangements (CCA). They loosely replicate the TPG. There is no case law in this area. CCAs are mentioned specifically in the Malaysian Transfer Pricing Guidelines of 2012. They generally follow the TPG, although without direct reference other than to the arm's length standard features. There is no published case law in Malaysia in this regard. In New Zealand, there is little guidance regarding CCAs beyond the TPG (para. 571 of the IR Guidelines) and very little practice and jurisprudence. In Poland, there is no direct domestic legislation regarding CCA, and reference is directly to the TPG, and the Pricing Ordinance (para. 23) provides for specific rules concerning the more limited case of participation in mutually incurred expenses for the production of intangibles. In Portugal, Ruling 1446-C/2001 contains specific rules regarding cost sharing agreements (Article 11) that generally follow the TPG. There is no case law on cost contribution arrangements under the new transfer pricing regime. In the Slovak Republic, Article 17 of the SITA acknowledges the existence of CCAs between entities. The treatment of the CCAs by the tax authorities is in accordance with the TPG. There is very limited case law in this respect. In Slovenia, the definition of a Cost Contribution Agreement (CCA) is prescribed in Article 23 of the Rules on Transfer Prices. In general, it follows the TPG definition with little practice and no case law.

85. See BNA Portfolio 890-1st.: *Transfer pricing: Alternative Practical Strategies*, Chapter 9(III)(B).
86. *Ibid.*, mentioning Brazil's practice, and quoting McLeese et.al., *Tax Treatment of Foreign Payments in Latin America Compared*, 14 Tax Notes International 405, 420 (1997).
87. *Ibid.*, mentioning Spain, and quoting Jose Calderon, *Safe Harbor for Multinational Enterprises Operating in Spain: The New Spanish APA Procedure*, 15 Tax Notes International 1355, 1357-8 (1997).
88. See OECD, *BEPS Action 8: Revisions to Chapter VIII of the Transfer Pricing Guidelines on Cost Contribution Arrangements (CCAs)*, Public Discussion Draft (29 Apr. 2015 – 29 May 2015), Annex, 15.

way or even to enjoy them at all. The amendment would, however, require that participants who share risks (a condition for being considered a CCA participant) to be capable and authorized to control the risks shared, i.e., be able to control, monitor, make decisions, and respond to risks taken.

This reference is clearly directed at the cash-box company example. Such a company does not have the resources (employees) to make such assessments and decisions and hence cannot be considered a participant in a CCA. This change clearly attempts to target this example; an example that may be viewed as extreme, yet it is quite common – definitely among United States MNEs who cost share with their newly organized, wholly owned subsidiaries in low tax jurisdictions. Yet, as a norm, this change is problematic. One way to view it would be to effectively assert that related party CCAs (of the above-described cost sharing type) are so vulnerable to abuse that regular arms' length analysis is simply not appropriate for them. Since risks represent the most manipulable aspects of these transactions, the OECD essentially removes them from the equation for arm's length analysis. This approach seemingly deviates from arm's length and definitely from literal arm's length as we know it. One may consider this deviation as sensible in the CCA context if viewed as just described: if one does not bring anything but cash to the table, one cannot benefit beyond an arm's length return of cash. The problem with such an approach, however, is that it may often be difficult to distinguish the pure abusive structures from the less pure. It is obvious that some co-financing arrangements occur in market conditions, and such arrangements may often represent financial risks that are agreeably larger than other relevant risks in such transactions. The discussion draft's approach to risk does not clarify an exact rule about when would mere financial risks deserve returns. The vague boundaries and the worry about a blunt deviation from literal arm's length in the form of viewing all CCA based on the cash-box benchmark resulted in a strong push back to this part of the draft. This is not surprising to Americans, as an attempt to implement a similar rule in the United States has failed in the face of lobbying and political pressure.[89] Further, CCAs that do not resemble the cash-box example may be difficult to analyze based on this rule that had been written with only that example in mind. However, once leeway is granted in certain circumstances, it is likely to create a slippery slope that would deem the whole change ineffective as it would be relatively simple to circumvent.

A second amendment clarifies that contributions to CCAs must be assessed based on their market value rather than cost. Countries currently vary in their relevant practices where some countries interpreted the requirement to evaluate CCAs based on arm's length to permit valuation of contribution at cost. At the end of the day, these are CCAs. The OECD now clarifies that this would be possible only in rare circumstances where the difference is not meaningful. Of course, this obscurity will surely result in the same slippery slope described above, and it would be difficult to prevent circumvention unless much more detailed rules are written. It is also difficult to fathom how these rules would be written when it is quite clear that there is vast disagreement about what

89. Treas. Reg. 1.482-7(b)(1)(i) of 1995, withdrawn in 1996.

value even means and how it would be measured. Note that the United States costs sharing rules, as well as many other countries' CCA rules, use primarily costs and permits adjustment based on historical costs, making it the most attractive feature of the regime. With coordination being the primary goal of BEPS, it is difficult to understand how the OECD views the incompatibility of rules. It would be unrealistic to expect all of these countries to change the rules; the United States would not.

Yet, the incoherence and vagueness of the rules may be the least of the OECD problems in this context. The more difficult challenge would be to rationalize the change at a more fundamental level. Viewed from the literal arm's length perspective, it does not make sense since it would be easy to demonstrate that market ventures are often accounted for based on costs. One could make the value based rule a rebuttable presumption but then it would be quite simple to empty it of content. Moreover, it is possible that costs-based contribution arrangements represent less, not more, exposure to manipulation. That would be difficult for countries to accept. A more substantive arm's length view would not conduce additional favor to this change. It would view the arrangement as essentially identical to a profit split arrangement: why then would it be treated differently? Moreover, if one believes that the whole purpose of CCAs, at least development CCAs, is to resolve the complexity that some research joint ventures present to the already very serious challenge of valuing intangible transfers, then using value rather than costs achieves nothing. It is quite clear that the United States cost sharing rules are based on this very logic. If costs based arrangements cannot be trusted, then why do we need special rules for CCAs? The real answer is that we do not, yet making this change is sure to add confusion and inefficiency into an already complex issue. Finally, the OECD failed to clarify the difference in application of this change to different types of CCAs that it admits presents different challenges to different contributions: primarily contributions made upon the setting of the CCA (the PCT types) and contributions in the process of developing the product by the CCA.

A third amendment also implements the Action 8 rules, clarifying that the allocation of profits in CCAs should be made based on the new rules for valuation of intangibles, i.e., with an emphasis on people functions (and less on legal ownership and risk taking that is specified in contracts) regarding the development activity including its management and control. This again is colored by the cash-box example. I suspect that, similar to the above issue, it would be difficult to delineate important from unimportant functions other than in the easy cases. This issue would definitely feature prominently in controversy and litigation and would represent significant costs to taxpayers and governments while they attempt to reach workable boundaries between these functions. This would be particularly difficult in firms that are more integrated. Finally, the adjustment would likely occur separately in different countries in the absence of a coordination mechanism. This would clearly result in less compatibility of rules and more of the same that triggered BEPS.

Additional and perhaps less critical changes received somewhat less attention yet they may also introduce further obscurity into the guidance. For example, the attempt to isolate participants from non-participants in CCAs raises questions about the sensibility and feasibility of this distinction in some cases. It is clear that the concept of economic ownership (albeit only some aspects of it) dominates rather than legal structures that would require, for example, distinguishing between contributors who are participants and contributors who are not. With good lawyering, this seems to be very difficult to police, especially in light of the vast differences already among tax jurisdictions on the matter. Another change, if it is a change, provides direct authority to disregard parts or all of the terms of CCAs. This GAAR-type rule would be impossible to consistently implement in the various countries, and it is not clear what it actually adds to domestic and other treaty anti-abuse rules. One would think that minor difficulties should be routinely resolved under proper arm's length analysis and major issues under the regular anti-abuse rules of each country. It also does not discuss why authority does not currently exist in Article 9 or elsewhere in the TPG for this anti-abuse rule. The draft discusses benefits in general with some reference to direct benefits. Again, this received some attention in the comments to the draft due to its obscurity and the lack of explanation of why indirect benefits do not count and how one would distinguish between direct and indirect benefits. This is especially so if the framework is an arm's length framework that must include all benefits. Finally, the draft asserts that new documentation requirements would be necessary without explaining and, more importantly, without specifying how these would fit with the new Action 13 regime.

The discussion draft ignores the most difficult issues that arose in the United States (and elsewhere) in the CCA context: the treatment of buy-in payments[90] and equity compensation costs in cost sharing arrangements. In the United States, these do not have to be shared as ruled (in a very questionable decision)[91] in the test case of *Xilinx*.

The discussion draft also ignores more fundamental issues. It is obvious that it was written as a supplement to the core Actions 8-10 report, yet these changes in the rules raise seminal questions about the role of CCAs. While pre-BEPS Chapter VIII had, at best, been explanatory, it is now directly implementing some substantive rules. It clearly infuses the regime with many more required analyses and uncertainty, and it is likely to result in ample inconsistency in treatment among tax jurisdictions. This requires, at the least, a purpose statement that is better than the current one. For example, does the OECD view this as a safe harbor regime? If so, inconsistency becomes very problematic or, perhaps, is it still merely a guide to the implementation of the rules established elsewhere in the TPG in the particular case of CCAs? If so, then Chapter VIII should be interpreted as adding nothing new to these rules. The draft also does not clarify whether and in what manner Chapter VIII should be interpreted in light of the value creation principle beyond the instrumental rules included in it or what to do when these rules end up being contradictory to this principle.

Finally, nothing is said about the universality of CCAs. It is still the case that only a handful of countries have special, even if varying, rules to regulate them, and a few

90. Veritas, see *supra* note 68. Note that the Veritas issues are not completely resolved by the court. The government and taxpayers continue to struggle with the proper valuation of buy-in payments even after the lengthy litigation. See, e.g., Ryan Finley, *IRS and Taxpayers Still at Odds Over Cost-Sharing Discount Rates*, Tax Notes (Doc 2016-847).
91. See Brauner, *Cost Sharing*, *supra* note 3.

other countries do the same via their adoption of the TPG. Again, coordination, the supposed hallmark of BEPS, is simply ignored from this perspective.

The discussion draft was later adopted in the final report on Actions 8-10 essentially as is. It did establish special rules for CCAs other than repeating why taxpayers may engage in them. It actually reaffirmed the role of Chapter VIII as explanatory and applying the regular rules of arm's length to these transactions. The report also includes confused language about the differences between service and development CCA. It clearly refused to separate the rules applying to them, yet it says that some rules are compatible only with the special features of one of them – always referring to development CCA. The unclear duality that came up often in the comments received by the BEPS project was simply ignored.

It is, therefore, difficult to draw practical conclusions from the changes to Chapter VIII assuming that they would be finalized as is. The safest conclusion would be to treat Chapter VIII as if it adds nothing to the rest of the TPG other than clarifications and examples, i.e., in no instance does it permit deviation from arm's length (whatever one can convince the court it is) as traditionally interpreted. A second conclusion would be that pure cost-based contributions could rarely be compatible with the Chapter VIII framework. To use costs, the taxpayer will have to bear a heavy burden and basically prove that unrelated parties will likely use costs as the basis for their comparable arrangements. A third conclusion would be that cash boxes cannot be parties to CCA as such. The general scheme of BEPS Action Items 8-10 would make an arrangement with a party that merely finances the arrangement too vulnerable under the new Chapter VIII rules, especially if it is a subsidiary of the other parties (such as all well-known United States MNE cost sharing schemes). A fourth conclusion would be that services CCA would require careful drafting or redrafting since, despite their rather ubiquitous use and the lack of serious BEPS concerns about them, the OECD refused to carve them out or somehow specify rules for them. Fifth, it may not be sufficient to have a bona fide business purpose or even an overall resemblance to market joint venture arrangements to qualify as good CCA. Sixth, taxpayers should now be especially careful about which rules apply to which arrangements. Different countries adopt and refer to the TPG very differently. The lack of any coordination devices would likely create some uncertainty about which rules apply when and where and how such rules can be coordinated with incompatible regimes such as the United States cost sharing regulations. Seven, tax authorities should be ready for an increase in disputes, requests for guidance, and likely litigation about all of the uncertainties, real or not, introduced by the new Chapter VIII.

The report was clear about its goal: to prevent abuse by MNE of the tax norms including arm's length as established by the TPG. This was quite apparently problematically in conflict with the general purpose of explaining or implementing the regular rules to CCAs. This is not just a semantic point. Although the focus of BEPS are those CCA that triggered the project, especially if service CCA are included, there are still bona fide CCA, and the current chapter makes it very challenging to them to apply the rules and often treats them unfavorably perhaps based on a general premise that all CCA are abusive in intent.

I have elsewhere expressed my opinion that it would be desirable to get rid of the special rules for cost sharing in the United States, and it seems to me that it would be even more desirable to get rid of Chapter VIII of the TPG. Adding a new anti-abuse rule when other, both domestic law and treaty-based rules are being introduced at an increasing pace worldwide makes little sense. If explanation is required for complex transactions, then it should have been manifestly clear that Chapter VIII adds nothing to the other rules in the TPG and should be interpreted as such. Instead, it added confusion, complexity, and most problematically, compliance and enforcement costs. Much litigation and controversy are to be expected especially over the valuation of contributions. Such costs will be even higher if countries were required to harmonize their treatment, which should not be expected especially when the OECD has not even addressed the issue of standardization of CCA law.

V. CONCLUSION: UNDELIVERED PROMISES

The conclusion of this early review of the transfer pricing regime post-BEPS project is that it achieved little substantive progress. In effect, the OECD has used the BEPS project to effectively continue the work it had started on intangibles prior to the project and unrelated to BEPS.[92] The goal was to protect arm's length and the dominance of the TPG in the face of discontent among the less developed countries and the amounting evidence on the failure of arm's length to accommodate transactions with intangibles.

Business interests should also be relatively content. They have been successful in avoiding dramatic changes to a regime that they have grown to tolerate. Some of the new concepts, however, will be costly and inevitably result in ample litigation and uncertainty. Yet, much of these costs would likely result from the environment created by the BEPS project and not from the content of its final reports.[93] The fragility of the international tax regime and the lack of coordination among countries resulted in a free-for-all audit environment that is already very challenging for MNEs in many countries.[94] The outcome of the transfer pricing work should undoubtedly contribute to this atmosphere. The only ray of hope may be the work on transfer pricing compliance that presents very different prospects and should change this environment; however, the analysis of these aspects is beyond the scope of this session.

Naturally, the BEPS project has not delivered on its promises. Literally nothing was done to improve coordination of tax policies and enforcement that, despite the supposed introduction of the profits, follow value creation principle. Even simple reforms could have done much more, such as an introduction of a consistency

92. See *supra* note 25.
93. See, e.g., Mindy Herzfeld, *News Analysts: A Looming Global Tax War?*, 81 Tax Notes International 467 (8 Feb. 2016); and Steef Huibregtse et al., *Unilateral BEPS Initiatives: The Emperor's New Clothes or How Countries Go to War?*, BNA, 16 Transfer Pricing International Jouranl 16 (30 Jun. 2015).
94. *Ibid.* See also Tax Analysts, *BEPS Project Increasing Audit Scrutiny*, EY Survey Finds, 2014 WTD 197-22.

requirement alluded to in early BEPS documents. A holistic approach was not even attempted since the sole focus was on the preservation of arm's length and, of course, little innovation was introduced.

My conclusion is not much different when CCAs are concerned. On the one hand, it seems that the changes mentioned above are fundamental. The proof may be in the strong resistance to these changes and the ample comments received, and largely ignored, by the OECD on the discussion draft. Some commentators even went as far as declaring the possible death of development CCAs.[95] This conclusion, however, depends on one's view of the actual impact of the rules. If one simply accepts that all CCAs where one party dominates research would essentially lose their tax minimization appeal, then indeed the changes to Chapter VIII may be meaningful. Yet, for this to happen, the obscure rules would have to be consistently and universally interpreted in a very government friendly manner. It is very difficult to believe that it would happen especially when some governments would not desire such an interpretation, for example, for competitiveness reasons. The complete lack of coordination or even thoughts or verbiage about how to coordinate the application of the Chapter VIII rules make these prospects even less realistic. Messiness, inconsistency, and increased controversy and litigation are much more likely.

Significant change may be concluded also based on a different perspective: the empowerment of profit split may result in restructuring opportunities that would seem superior overall to CCAs and not much different in practice. If such an alternative would be simpler to implement and the rules clearer (we still do not know what shape will they take and when will they come along) and hence cheaper to comply with, then it would not be surprising if taxpayers preferred them to the CCA route currently presented by BEPS. This scenario is more likely than the above-mentioned, yet I find it difficult to believe that the same OECD would come up with clearer and more sensible rules for profit split. Profit split is essentially identical to CCA and presents many of the same issues. Indeed, the OECD was not in a position to address it in its BEPS reports. I would say that, regardless of the difficulty for constructing a sensible regime for these complex businesses, a profit split based regime makes much more sense than the obscure CCA regime. It deals directly with the allocation of profits without resorting to unnecessary legal constructs such as CCA that requires additional economic dismantling.

Finally, a few words are due about the differences between CCAs and the United States cost sharing regulations. On the one hand, the OECD has made Chapter VIII of the TPG somewhat more operative than it was pre-BEPS. As already explained, this is ironic, at best, in light of the critical role of cost sharing in permitting the tax structures that triggered BEPS in the first place. Yet, on the other hand, it obscured the nature of Chapter VIII that used to be a framework for approaching joint ventures while applying all of the regular arm's length rules to them and brought it manifestly closer to the United States' cost sharing regime. Close enough that, indeed, some commentators argued that CCAs do not have a meaning other than in the more specific, cost sharing

95. See Ronald van den Brekel et al., *BEPS Action 8: The Death of Development Cost Contribution Agreements?*, 24 Transfer Pricing Rep. 1231 (4 Feb. 2016).

for the development of intangibles context, i.e., modeled after cost sharing. Other commentators refer directly to CCAs and cost sharing as interchangeable terms despite the manifest differences. Such confusion cannot be helpful in providing certainty to taxpayers using such structures unrelated to the United States. It will certainly cause problems for such structures when United States entities are involved. The differences between the cost sharing rules and the rules in Chapter VIII of the TPG are various; the use of cost or value for contributions is the most notable among them. These differences may prevent certain structures from qualifying under one of these regimes and cause double and double-non taxation for no good reason. No coordination of the rules has been discussed in the BEPS documents. It is quite certain that the United States shall not amend its rules to conform them to the BEPS outcome, and the central role of United States MNEs in the clientele of these arrangements ensures that conflicts are imminent. The inherent lack of commitment for policy coordination despite the 2013 commitment to it reveals itself again in this context. It is very difficult to predict the outcome of these discrepancies. Perhaps most countries would simply ignore Chapter VIII to relieve some of the problems, yet, this still leaves BEPS as a prominent available strategy for MNEs. This cannot be a desirable end for the BEPS project.

CHAPTER 5

Interest Deductions and Transfer Pricing Aspects of Intra-group Financing

Antonio Russo

I. THE REPORT ON ACTION 4

On 5 October 2015, the Organisation for Economic Co-operation and Development (OECD) released its final report (hereinafter referred to as 'the Report') on limiting base erosion involving interest deductions and other financial payments (Action 4) under its Action Plan on Base Erosion and Profit Shifting (BEPS).[1]

The report includes a 'best practice approach' for countries to prevent erosion of their tax base through the use of interest expenses and other payments of a financial nature. However, the Report does not cover the transfer pricing aspects of financial transactions that will be addressed in a separate project during 2016 and 2017.

This 'best practice approach' reflects the position reached by the OECD in 2014 (Discussion Draft released on 18 December 2014) in relationship to the various alternatives of rules presented thereto in order to limit BEPS phenomena related to financial deductions. The best practice approach can be synthesized as follows:

(i) A fixed ratio rule which allows an entity to deduct net interest expenses up to an interest coverage ratio (interest/EBITDA) within a corridor comprised between 10% and 30%.
(ii) A group ratio rule (optional) which allows an entity to deduct net interest expenses up to its group's interest coverage ratio if higher than the fixed ratio.
(iii) *De minimis* monetary threshold (optional) to remove low to no-risk entities.
(iv) Rules to address volatility (optional) such as carryforward or carryback rules.
(v) Rules to exclude public-benefit projects (optional).
(vi) Targeted rules to address specific issues/risks.
(vii) Specific rules for the insurance and banking industries.

The policy rationale at the basis of the OECD proposed 'best practice approach' can be summarized as follows:

Money is highly mobile and fungible, and BEPS risks are heightened within Multinational Enterprises (MNEs) that may use intra-group loans to generate interest deductions in excess of the group's actual third-party interest expense and concurrently placing higher levels of third-party debt in high tax countries. Furthermore, groups use third-party or intra-group financing to fund the generation of tax exempt income and, although there is a wide variety of interest limitation rules among countries, these rules often come with layers of complexity without addressing the key underlying issues. Moreover, the OECD is of the belief that additional robust unilateral interest limitation rules may adversely affect the attractiveness of a country to international business and the ability of domestic groups to compete globally.

1. This report was part of a package that included the final reports for most of the fifteen BEPS Actions. See original Action Plan (2013) at https://www.oecd.org/ctp/BEPSActionPlan.pdf.

In this context, a consistent approach using international best practices is needed to eliminate opportunities for BEPS and encourage MNE funding structures whereby allowable net interest expense of an entity is linked to the overall net interest expense of the group and the deductibility is linked to income-producing activities. Risk of 'unintended' double taxation should also be reduced under a uniform approach.

II. THE 'BEST PRACTICE APPROACH': OVERVIEW

A. Recommended Measures

1. *Fixed Ratio Rule*

The main recommendation of the Report is the introduction of a fixed ratio rule which implies that an entity should be able to deduct interest expense up to a fixed percentage of its Earnings Before Interest, Taxes, Depreciation, and Amortization (EBITDA). Using the EBITDA approach (EBITDA as defined for tax purposes) will ensure that a portion of an entity's profit remains subject to tax in a country. It is recommended that countries set their benchmark fixed ratio within a 'best practice' range or 'corridor' of 10%-30%.

Factors that may indicate when a higher benchmark EBITDA ratio (within the 10%-30% range) could be appropriate include the following:

(i) the country intends to operate the fixed ratio rule in isolation rather than operating the rule in combination with a group ratio rule;
(ii) the country disallows the carryforward or carryback of excess interest capacity or of disallowed interest expense;
(iii) the country has higher interest rates compared to other jurisdictions;
(iv) the country has other targeted rules that address BEPS concerns under Action 4; and
(v) the country is obliged for other reasons (e.g., constitutional reasons, European Union (EU) law) to treat different types of comparable legal entities with similar terms even where they pose differing levels of risk.

The underlying benchmark fixed ratio is determined by a country's government and applies to groups in all sectors (with the exception of groups in the banking and insurance sectors) irrespective of the actual leverage of an entity or its group.

However, the OECD recognizes that entities in large groups as well as those in sectors that typically have high levels of financial gearing are in different positions than other entities when raising third-party debt and, therefore, there may be reasons to use a different ratio for them. Similar considerations apply to sectors that benefit from economic rents in which case, according the OECD, there would be policy-based justification to apply the fixed ratio rule more strictly.

2. *Group Ratio Rule*

In order to reduce the impact on highly leveraged groups, in addition to an increase of up to 10% of the interest expenses paid to third parties, the OECD recommends that countries implement a combination of a fixed ratio rule with a group ratio rule. This would allow an entity that exceeds the benchmark fixed ratio to deduct net interest expense up to its group's net third-party interest/EBITDA ratio, if higher than the proposed fixed ratio. Only net interest expense, that exceeds both the benchmark fixed ratio and the ratio of its group, should be disallowed.[2]

Regarding the application of a group ratio rule, a 'group' should include a parent company and all entities which are fully consolidated on a line-by-line basis in the parent's consolidated financial statements.

The OECD points out that countries may also apply alternatives to the group ratio rule by adopting, for instance, an assets-based ratio such as equity/total assets ('equity escape rule'). This would imply that the rule based on the net interest/EBITDA does not apply if an entity can demonstrate that its equity/total assets ratio is equal to or exceeds that of its group. This rule is beneficial for a loss-making entity as it may still deduct its net interest expense if it can prove that the requirements of the rule are met.

3. *Targeted Rules*

The OECD recommends supplementing the fixed ratio rule with targeted rules which will restrict interest deductions on payments made under specific transactions or arrangements that are not subject to the general interest limitation rule. These targeted rules may be required to address situations where entities may attempt to convert interest expense into a different form of deductible expense or convert other taxable income into interest. Entities may also enter into structured arrangements with third parties to increase the amount of net third-party interest expenses taken into account under the group ratio rule, or groups may be restructured, for example, by placing an unincorporated holding entity at the top of a structure to create two groups. The OECD does not provide further guidance on targeted rules, leaving it to the discretion of the countries.

B. Definition of Interest

The aim of the Report is not to recommend a definition of (dis)allowable interest that is applied by all countries for all tax purposes. However, the OECD considers that, in order to address BEPS using interest expense, the 'best practice approach' should apply to: (i) interest on all forms of debt; (ii) other financial payments that are economically equivalent to interest, for example, amounts linked to the financing of an entity and

2. The OECD also proposes the introduction of supplementary provisions to, among others: (i) carve out entities that have a low level of net interest expenses; (ii) exclude interest paid to third-party lenders to fund projects of public interest; (iii) carry forward/back of unused interest capacity and/or disallowed interest.

determined by applying a fixed or variable percentage to an actual or notional principal over time; and (iii) expenses incurred in connection with rising debt.

In deciding whether a payment is economically equivalent to interest, the focus should be on its economic substance rather than its legal form. Therefore, under the economic definition of interest, the following items should be included: capitalized interest; notional interest payments under debt-related derivative contracts; foreign exchange gains/losses on debt; guarantee fees; arrangement fees; payments under profit participating loans; imputed interest on convertible and zero coupon bonds; amounts under alternative financing arrangements (e.g., Islamic finance); and the finance cost element of finance lease payments.

Vice versa, provided they do not form part of an overall arrangement which gives rise to amounts that are economically equivalent to interest, the following items (among others) would not be included: foreign exchange gains/losses on derivative contracts for hedging/assuming currency exposures; amounts under derivative or hedging instruments not related to borrowings, e.g., commodity derivatives; discounts on provisions not related to borrowings; operating lease payments; and royalties.

Notably, deemed deductions for corporate equity (such as the ones provided for under the domestic law of Belgium, Brazil, and Italy, among others) are not treated as interest or an economic equivalent for the purposes of the Report. Incidentally, in relation to this point, one can be critical of the fact that – in drafting the 'best practice approach' – the OECD has not carefully considered taking into account approaches to create a level playing field between debt and equity as this would have eliminated certain distortions without necessarily greatly impairing the attractiveness of a market/jurisdiction to international investors.

C. Ratione Personae

The 'best practice approach' should apply to all entities that are part of a multinational group. However, countries may extend its application to entities that are part of a domestic group and/or standalone entities.

A *de minimis* threshold that is based on the total net interest expense of all entities in the local group may also be introduced to exclude low risk entities from the scope of the fixed and group ratio rules. Countries could also consider introducing anti-fragmentation rules to prevent a group avoiding an interest limitation rule by establishing multiple entities, each of which falls below the threshold.

The OECD has excluded banks and insurance companies from the application of the fixed or group ratio rules. However, further work is being conducted that is to be completed in 2016 that will identify best practice rules to deal with the potential BEPS risks posed by those entities, taking into account the particular features of banking and insurance industries.

D. Addressing Volatility and Double Taxation

There may be cases where the amount of interest expense for an entity exceeds the allowable threshold merely because of a timing mismatch that will correct in a future period. A possible way to address these situations (especially to deal with the impact of losses in a group) is to adopt a multi-year EBITDA (average).

In addition, as the 'best practice approach' relies on EBITDA (as defined for tax purposes), the amount of interest expense an entity may deduct will be impacted by changes in either its group earnings or by differences between the financial statement and taxable income. To address this earnings volatility, the OECD proposes that countries allow an entity to: (i) carryforward only disallowed interest expense; (ii) carryforward disallowed interest expense and unused interest capacity; or (iii) carryforward and carryback disallowed interest expense. The value of carryforwards could reduce over time (e.g., by 10% each year) or could otherwise be restricted.

Interest disallowances that arise under any targeted rules (including hybrid and other BEPS restrictions that are applied in priority to Action 4) should not be carried back or forward.

III. GENERAL COMMENTS AND POLICY CONSIDERATIONS

As already acknowledged in the OECD Thin Capitalization Report,[3] tax policy on the use of debt in financing investments is of particular importance due to the fact that deductibility of interest appears to create a distortion on the choice of capital structure operated by market participants. The OECD, in its final BEPS Report, fails to demonstrate that the internal use of excess cash, having due regard to the most appropriate economic use of financial resources, gives rise to BEPS phenomena in all circumstances which appears to be suggested in its final report.

However, taking into account tax considerations, it can be demonstrated that the question of capital structure is essentially an economic question and certainly even more so when the capital is provided by external investors (shareholders and bondholders or other types of investors).

Since the seminal work of Modigliani and Miller,[4] many studies have been produced on this topic. There is no bright-line test that will determine an optimal capital structure. From a purely economic perspective, an enterprise would have an incentive to increase debt insofar as this reduces the overall cost of capital, subsequently lowering the internal rate of return. Obviously, there is a trade-off; increasing

3. OECD, *Thin Capitalisation*, Paris, 1986, was adopted by the OECD Council on 26 Nov. 1986 ('1986 report). It should be noted that this report still constitutes the basis for the official guidance on the interaction between the arm's length principle and thin capitalization rules. In terms of tax policy analysis, one has to wonder why the OECD in Action 4 has not carefully considered the work done and recommendations issued in the past, especially in connection with avoidance of double taxation.
4. Modigliani, F. & Miller, M. *The Cost of Capital, Corporation Finance and the Theory of Investment*, American Economic Review 48(3) (1958): 261-297, & Modigliani, F. & Miller, M. *Corporate Income Taxes and the Cost of Capital: A Correction*, American Economic Review 53(3) (1963): 433-44.

debt must be sustainable and the tipping point is generally when the increased level of indebtedness in turn increases the cost of debt because of the higher risk of default.

Treasury and financing of operations are core elements of managing an enterprise. Financing choices, therefore, are mainly dictated by propensity to risk and investment opportunities; the operating model itself and the cash flow profile of the individual operating units; the industry; and the competition.

In addition to reducing the cost of capital and thereby increasing the return on invested capital ('ROIC'), choices on optimal levels of indebtedness are also aimed at efficiently allocating resources within the group and increasing the overall flexibility in case of exit or divestitures or in situations of 'trapped income'.

In contrast, the 'best practice approach' favors purely local businesses. A group rule will, in fact, likely result in double taxation if the group is unable to move third-party leverage within the group to match the interest cap with a proposed carryforward of disallowed interest expense to address double taxation. Conversely, a purely local business that does not have cross-border operations will be able to deduct all of its third-party interest expense. The best practice approach may therefore result in the elimination of the (internal) capital efficiency of MNEs. This will cause detriment to market investors as capital will be allocated less efficiently.

There is another element that should be taken into account which is the impact of a group rule on relative competitiveness (advantage/disadvantage) due to the location of operations (and especially the parent company) and access to financing resources depending on the relative level of EBITDA, size of the market, depth and liquidity of the (local) financial market, and the cost of capital which is, in fact, a function of the risk profile of the investment (in this case, the risk profile of the specific MNE which is, in turn, also influenced by the countries/markets where the MNE operates).The OECD pursues the objective of reducing BEPS phenomena linked with excessive use of interest deductions. However, some of the premises or assumptions at the basis of the OECD policy choice are quite sweeping. In the author's view, market distortions can also be created by excessively limiting the possibility to deduct (third party, in addition to intercompany) interest. This – in turn – will result in an increase of the cost of capital for MNEs and market investors alike.

MNEs also fragment their operations in order to rationalize the supply chain. Therefore, it is entirely appropriate from an economic perspective to adopt different capital structures for different segments of the supply chain; typically, stable returns/ cash flows should be financed with debt whereas highly volatile returns/operations should be financed with equity.

The diversification of risk that MNEs can achieve naturally leads to increased leverage which is not a negative consequence, per se. In fact, independent investors benefit from this effect. The OECD seems to sidestep these considerations with no compelling evidence in support of their thesis (the lack of empirical evidence about the actual impact of interest limitation rules on investments is expressly recognized by the OECD in paragraph 5 of the Introduction of the Report).

The OECD laments the high complexity and lack of effectiveness of existing rules dealing with interest deductibility implemented by various jurisdictions (some of which are highly sophisticated, e.g., the Dutch interest limitation rules) but fails to take into account, from a cost and compliance perspective, the practical impact that the various BEPS Actions (2, 3, 4, 6, 9, 12, and 13) which deal directly or indirectly with the capital structure of MNEs may have.

On the contrary, if the best practice approach is to be applied, particular complexity will be brought about by, among others:

(i) Definition of interest and interest equivalent payments.
(ii) Computational aspects related to the determination of interest expenses (e.g., interaction with Action 2).
(iii) Definition of earnings.
(iv) Definition of group and computation of the group ratio/equity escape ratios.
(v) Complexity in dealing with consolidation rules and reporting conventions.
(vi) Interaction with existing rules, both domestic and international, including tax treaties.
(vii) How to deal with the double taxation that will ensue from (an uncoordinated) application of the rule.

Particularly complex and punishing could be the contemporaneous application of the 'best practice approach' and an arm's length test, which was mentioned by the OECD in multiple passages of the Report without any consideration of the practical consequences of such a policy choice. Specifically, no account has been taken of the experience of countries that have attempted the adoption of both sets of rules. Other concerns relate to the apparent lack of sufficient consideration for the work carried out by the OECD on thin capitalization (1986 Report), especially in relationship to the interaction between thin cap regimes and the arm's length provision.

Furthermore, there is lack of consideration for the costs (non-financial and in terms of loss of flexibility as well) that this policy choice will involve for MNEs, possibly distorting competition; regarding flexibility, there is lack of consideration of the fact that equity financing is not only costly but can also lead to 'trapped income' or severe restrictions when capital needs to be repatriated.

The model inspiring the best practice approach is, in fact, the German interest barrier rules, which were introduced in 2008 after the prior thin capitalization regime failed under the test of the European Court of Justice (ECJ, 12 December 2002, Case C-324/00, *Lankhorst-Hohorst*). These rules apply to domestic and cross-border intra-group loans, loans guaranteed by the group, and third-party loans including back-to-back financing. Disallowed interest expense incurred with these loans may be carried forward. The scope of the German interest barrier rules is, in fact, very broad and results in a significant increase in the tax burden on leveraged investments. A study, in particular, has evidenced how these rules do, indeed, affect financing decisions but not in the intended way and not of the intended firms.[5] Furthermore, as recently as 10

5. Reference is made, among others, to Daniel Dreßler and Uwe Scheuering, *Empirical Evaluation of Interest Barrier Effects*, Center for European Economic Research (ZEW) Discussion Paper No. 12-046 (2012).

February 2016, the German Federal Fiscal Court (BFH), in its decision (I R 20/15) expressed doubts as to whether the German interest barrier rules comply with the German Constitution and has referred the case to the German Constitutional Court.

It is relevant to note that the German interest barrier rules have been subject to much criticism, however.

A country that has introduced these rules in domestic legislation similar to Germany is Italy. The rules were introduced in 2008 and it follows the German rules very closely. At the same time, however, Italy introduced mitigating legislation, i.e., an allowance for corporate equity (a.k.a. an interest on equity or notional interest deduction rule).

Interestingly, a 2014 study[6] by the European Commission finds that:

> Overall, [...] one can argue that the Italian system - with its incremental feature and a comprehensive anti-avoidance framework targeting transactions between related parties - seems a more viable option for [...] addressing the debt bias in the corporate sector, while at the same time safeguarding the tax base at the domestic and international level.

The author is of the view that all of the above should have been carefully considered by the OECD in canvassing and proposing the best practice in Action 4.

Finally, one important area of analysis relates to the compatibility of the proposed best practice with EU Law: while acknowledging the relevance of such an analysis, the author has opted for not expanding on the topic in the context of this document.

It is relevant to note, however, that the EFTAS Surveillance Authority (ESA) has, in a letter issued to the Norwegian Ministry of Finance on 4 May 2016,[7] concluded that the Norwegian interest cap rules in the Norwegian Tax Act (NTA)[8] constitute a restriction on the freedom of establishment laid down in Article 31 of the European Economic Area Agreement.[9]

IV. THE FIXED RATIO: BEST PRACTICE OR MISSED OPPORTUNITY?

The OECD indicates that there is a wide array of existing rules which fall into six broad groups that address the deductibility of interest.

Thin capitalization and/or earning stripping rules (often complemented by business purpose tests; characterization rules; and specific targeted rules such as anti-hybrid provisions) generally constitute the main tool for tax authorities to ensure that profits are not artificially shifted from one jurisdiction to another through financial transactions.

6. Zangari, E., *Addressing the Debt Bias: A Comparison between the Belgian and the Italian ACE Systems*, Taxation Papers, Working Paper 44 – 2014, European Commission, EU.
7. Case No: 76153, Document No: 787208, Decision No: 086/16/COL.
8. Section 6-41 of the Norwegian Tax Act. The interest cap rules provide that, for interest expenses over NOK 5 million, interest paid to an affiliated party in excess of 30% of EBITDA is not deductible from taxable income.
9. http://www.efta.int/eea/eea-agreement.

While many jurisdictions have very specific ratio based thin capitalization and earning stripping rules, the approach taken by more and more jurisdictions in applying and enforcing these rules is to consider the simultaneous application of these rules and transfer pricing rules including consideration of the arm's length principle and the parent company debt to equity ratio as potential safe harbors.

The choice of the OECD for a fixed ratio is dictated – among other factors – by effectiveness and efficiency. By the same token, the OECD discards – as a matter of policy choice – the arm's length test as best practice. However, it can be argued that a fixed ratio rule that is based on an interest/EBITDA ratio (or interest coverage ratio) is an approximation of an arm's length test.

As a matter of fact, an appropriate interpretation and application of the arm's length principle to intercompany financing transactions would require that not only the price (represented by the rate) but also the amount of a debenture (loan, bond) would be tested. In other words, the question to be asked is whether a financing transaction would be entered into by unrelated parties having due consideration for the conditions of the transaction, primarily amount and price.

Hence, in a 'debt capacity' arm's length test, analysts would typically synthetically summarize all of the relevant factors in three important financial ratios: debt/EBITDA, interest coverage ratio (EBIT/interest expenses), and overall leverage of the borrower. These are typically benchmarked with the same ratios observed in third-party transactions or distilled from financial information of companies obtaining funding from the market.

Figure 5.1 Interest Coverage Ratio Pre-, Post-credit Crunch (Own Elaborations of Data Points observed in LoanConnector, DealScan®)

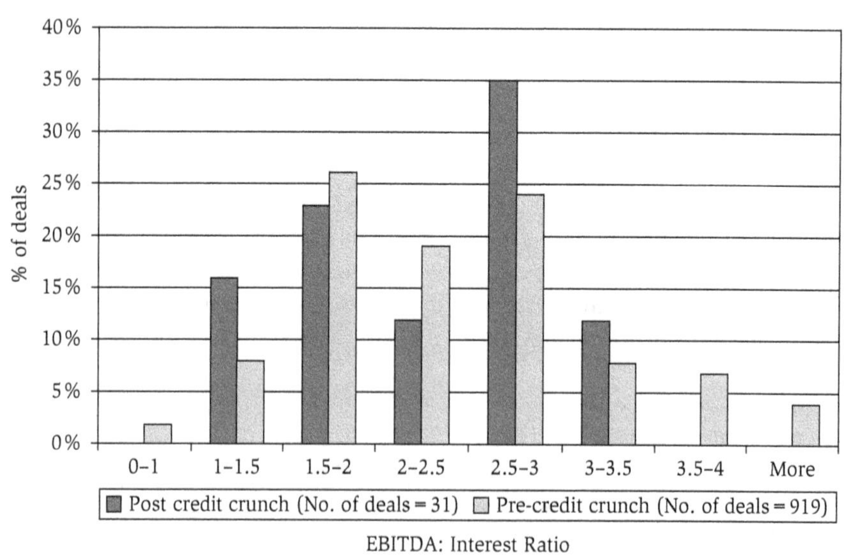

Incidentally, interesting statistics conducted immediately after the credit-crunch (see Figure 5.1) show that, in third-party transactions, the distribution of the interest coverage ratio is significantly skewed towards high percentages, de facto challenging the position of the OECD on the economic rationality of the choice for a low interest coverage ratio.

It appears evident in the view of the author that there is some level of convergence between the test proposed as best practice by the OECD and an arm's length test. It may, therefore, be questioned whether the further work announced by the OECD on financing transactions should, in fact, still be considered of priority especially in connection with loan transactions. A simplified approach (still somewhat close to an arm's length test) can be distilled from the best practice. The OECD, however, suggests that the arm's length test may continue to be applied even by those jurisdictions that will have implemented the 'best practice approach'.

In other words, on the one hand, despite the fact that the 'best practice approach' should be interpreted, in the author's view, as a simplification which, whilst departing from a pure arm's length test, may still be reasonably close to it,the OECD is conceding the possible scenario where countries could conceivably be 'doubling' on rules aimed at limiting interest deductibility.

It is highly doubtful, whether the 'best practice approach' will actually reduce complexity. On the other hand, considering the proximity of the 'best practice approach' test to one of the pillars of the debt capacity test under the arm's length standard, it is questionable why the OECD has not endorsed this latter altogether as, for instance, some countries (e.g., the UK) have done.

In addition, it is surprising to observe that the OECD is silent on the complexity and difficulties that certain countries have experienced in simultaneously implementing (or trying to implement) an interest barrier rule and the arm's length test (e.g., Australia).

Therefore, not only is the assumed reduction in compliance and administrative burden de facto offset by the suggested applicability of the arm's length test in addition to the interest barrier rule, but also the concurrent application of those rules would create a further 'corridor' of levels of interest coverage ratios which would only work to the disadvantage of taxpayers.

Where the proposed 'best practice approach' should have acted as simplification, it appears to actually be the opposite without any regard to providing more certainty to taxpayers. It is, therefore, a missed opportunity where the OECD should have, in fact, preferred to:

(i) either apply the 'best practice approach' as a substitute to the arm's length test (as a safe harbor or an anti-abuse rule);
(ii) apply the arm's length test (also on third-party debt), which is the most comprehensive and most rational approach to testing financing transactions; or
(iii) consider the application of the arm's length principle as a safe harbor rule in order to avoid market distortions or discriminatory results to the disadvantage of specific industries/sectors.

On the last point, it is interesting to report that, for Australia (at the time, this chapter was being written), the arm's length principle is viewed as a safe harbor and debt to equity in excess of 1.5:1 can be sustained if it is shown to be in line with the arm's length principle. The only other exception to the thin capitalization requirement is the group's worldwide debt ratio, which also functions as a safe harbor.

V. THE 'BEST PRACTICE APPROACH': A BRIDGE TO ARTICLE 7?

It is interesting to note how Action 4 is based on the implicit assumption that capital structure should be uniform across a group for policy purposes. Further, by suggesting a group test as a best practice, the OECD also appears to erroneously assume that borrowing is at a constant rate across the MNE.

In the report on the Attribution of Profit to Permanent Establishments[10] introducing the Authorized OECD Approach (AOA) to attributing profits to PEs, a PE is assumed to have the same creditworthiness of the general enterprise. The rationale here is based on the fact that a PE is not a separate entity in spite of the application of the 'separate entity approach'. At the same time, the AOA acknowledges the existence of intra-company 'treasury' dealings where one part of the enterprise may be financing the other part of the same enterprise.

Further, in order to determine the amount of interest that can be deducted at the level of the PE, several capital allocation approaches are considered which acknowledge the possibility of different capital structures. In this context, therefore, one may wonder how it is possible to reconcile Action 4 with other guidance as illustrated above and whether Action 4 will, in fact, automatically lead to the presumption of identical creditworthiness and identical capital structure across the group.

The impression of the author is that Action 4 is an implicit endorsement of a formulary (apportionment) approach that is in contrast with the original 'mission statement' of the BEPS project.

VI. WHAT IS IN STORE FOR THE FUTURE?

In closing this brief commentary to the best practice proposed by the OECD, a few conclusive considerations will be proposed.

Albeit that Action 4 is clearly not aimed at addressing transfer pricing issues, it does still fuel the debate as to which rules are most appropriate to be applied to provide an answer to the 'thin capitalization' question.

The aforementioned 1986 Report might have been the starting point, but the OECD seems to have gone beyond the considerations expressed thereto.

Currently, in the wake of the work the OECD is carrying out on the application of the arm's length principle to financing transactions, the risk is that Action 4 will:

10. Report on the attribution of profits to permanent establishments, OECD, 22 Jul. 2010.

(i) influence the application of the arm's length principle to the point of 'pollution'; and
(ii) provide an opening to formula-based rules.

One should note that the OECD has concluded that the measures suggested in the Report should be considered as best practice which means that they will not necessarily be adopted by all countries participating in the BEPS project. Moreover, the countries adopting Action 4 will have a considerable range of options to achieve the intended objective of the Report.[11]

Hence, one can only derive that Action 4 will, in all likelihood, lead to:

(i) unresolved multiple taxation due to the lack of experience and alignment between different countries on the workings of the proposed 'best practice approach' and the options offered as to a possible implementation; and
(ii) unresolved multiple taxation due to the lack of attention on how the rules should interact with the existing international legal framework.

Finally, during the drafting of this chapter, the EU released the text of a proposed directive laying down rules against tax avoidance practices that directly affect the functioning of the internal market (i.e., the so-defined Anti-Tax Avoidance Directive or 'ATAD').[12] The ATAD includes a proposed rule following the 'best practice approach' in connection with deductibility of interest.

The ATAD, as one of the concerns expressed by the author, however, appears to go beyond the recommendations of the OECD on the introduction of the 'best practice approach'. In fact, as expressed by the think-tank BUSINESSEUROPE:[13]

> by setting a cap of 30 percent of EBITDA, with the possibility for Member States to introduce stricter rules, the interest limitation rule in the draft Directive goes beyond the 10-30 percent of EBITDA corridor recommended by the OECD. It also goes beyond the BEPS proposal in applying interest limitations to intra-country interest payments and not just cross-border payments.

The landscape is rapidly evolving and, considering the high level of uncertainty around future measures with regard to the implementation of Action 4 (and relevant measures and guidance stemming primarily from Actions 2, 3, 6, and especially 8, 9,

11. The UK (HM Treasury) already in late October 2015 launched a public consultation (https://www.gov.uk/government/consultations/tax-deductibility-of-corporate-interest-expense) on the tax deductibility of corporate interest expenses and later (in the Budget presented in March 2016: https://www.gov.uk/government/publications/budget-2016-documents) announced the introduction of an interest barrier rule. The public consultation document clearly evidences, through the multiple questions raised to the public, how the best practice approach lends itself to a number of possible combinations and permutations hence leading to asymmetries between jurisdictions and thus heightening the risk of multiple unresolved taxation. The latest consultation took place on 26 May 2016.
12. Proposal for a COUNCIL DIRECTIVE laying down rules against tax avoidance practices that directly affect the functioning of the internal market COM/2016/026 final – 2016/011 (CNS); the latest draft having been published on 15 Apr. 2016.
13. https://www.businesseurope.eu/sites/buseur/files/media/position_papers/ecofin/2016-03-07_anti-tax_avoidance_package.pdf.

and 10), it could be quite difficult for companies to assess the extent to which the rules might require them to restructure during the transitional period.

In any event, the basic framework of Action 4 should be sufficient in leading MNEs to consider the possible impact, take necessary actions by assessing and, if necessary, altering their current financial arrangements and capital structures.

In consideration of the costs associated with resetting financial arrangements and capital structures, it is to be hoped that countries implementing Action 4 will, in fact, give taxpayers a reasonable period of time to restructure and, more importantly, apply insofar as possible a coordinated approach.

CHAPTER 6

Transfer Pricing Aspects of Low Value-Adding Services

Guglielmo Maisto

I. DEFINITION OF LOW VALUE SERVICES

A. The Characteristics of Low Value Services

Paragraph 7.44 of the Report defines low value intragroup services as: (1) having a supportive nature; (2) not being part of the core business of the Multinational Enterprises (MNE); (3) not requiring use of unique and valuable intangibles; (4) not leading to the creation of intangibles; (5) not involving assumption or control of substantial risk by the service provider; and (6) not giving rise to the creation of significant risk for the service provider.

Some terms and expressions which constitute the rules for identifying the low value services have obscure meaning and would also require clarification. This is due to the fact that they are defined by domestic legislations or administrative practice of some countries either for income tax purposes or VAT purposes. The result is that this domestic law meaning may influence the interpretation of the terms and expressions as used by the Report.

This is certainly valid in regard to the first characteristic ('support') as 'support services' is a defined expression under the law or administrative practice of States for taxes or similar duties.[1] Under VAT EU Regulation 282/2011, 'administrative support' is partly defined by stating that 'where the resources of the fixed establishment are only used for administrative support tasks such as accounting, invoicing, and collection of debt-claims, they shall not be regarded as being used for the fulfillment of the supply of goods or services' (underlined added).

The second characteristic requires the activities not to be part of the core business of the MNE. Reference is made to the MNE as a whole and not to the service provider which is a departure from the old Organisation for Economic Co-operation and Development (OECD) Guidelines which look at the stand-alone affiliate.

The departure, however, is only limited insofar as the simplified approach applies solely to situations in which the affiliate only provides services to other group entities (otherwise, a reliable third party comparable would permit the CUP or other methods to apply).[2,3] It is noteworthy that para 7.46 of the Final Report mentioned only the internal CUP: this seems to imply that only the availability of internal comparables restricts the application of the simplified approach. However, a more careful reading of the Final Report leads to a different conclusion. Indeed, paragraph 7.31 provides that '[a] cost based method would likely be the most appropriate method in the absence of

1. For instance, there is a definition under the laws of India for the purposes of service tax under which support services include 'infrastructural, operational, administrative, logistic, marketing or any other support of any kind comprising functions that entities carry out in ordinary course of operations themselves but may obtain as services by outsourcing from others for any reason whatsoever and shall include advertisement and promotion, construction or works contract, renting of immovable property, security, testing and analysis'. Similarly, the expression 'support services' of business commerce is defined expressly for the purposes of the same tax.
2. The applicability of the CUP method would exclude the applicability of the simplified approach only to the intragroup services covered by the CUP analysis. Indeed, the strict comparability requirements set forth by the OECD Guidelines excludes a broad application of the CUP method to all of the low value.adding services.
3. Paragraph 7.46 of the Report.

a CUP'. Reference is generally made to the CUP method without distinguishing between internal and external. Therefore, the simplified approach should also not be enforced in the case of applicability of the external CUP.

The definition of 'core business' requires some clarification. For instance, within MNEs engaged in IT services as a core business, a service affiliate may provide IT services which are not rendered to third parties and which do not constitute the core (IT) business of the MNE. These intragroup services would meet the test of those services not constituting the core business of the MNE.

In order to assess the satisfaction of this characteristic (core business), it may be helpful to consider the activities of an 'auxiliary and preparatory character' covered by Article 5(4) of the OECD Model Convention (OECD MC).[4] The provision excludes a fixed place of business through which the enterprise solely exercises an activity which has a preparatory or auxiliary character for the enterprise from the definition of PE; these activities are listed expressly by Article 5(4) OECD MC. The rationale for this provision lies with the fact that the activity of the fixed place of business in itself does not form an essential and significant part of the activity of the enterprise as a whole (paragraph 23 of the OECD Commentary to Article 5). The Commentary to the provision also states that such a place of business may well contribute to the productivity of the enterprise, but the services it performs are so remote from the actual realization of profits that it is difficult to allocate any profit to the fixed place of business in question.

The Report describes activities not constituting the core business of the MNE group as 'activities' 'not creating the profit-earning activities or contributing to economically significant activities of the MNE group' (paragraph 7.45). One example may better clarify the interaction between the scope of low value services under the Report, and preparatory and auxiliary activities under Article 5(4) OECD MC. 'Purchasing activities relating to raw material or other material that are used in the manufacturing or processing process' are excluded from low services activities. Article 5(4) (d) OECD MC includes purchasing goods or merchandise in the scope of preparatory or auxiliary activities. Evidently, the Report takes the view that purchase of raw material carries greater value than the one derived from the purchase of goods or merchandise which is consistent with the wording of Article 5(4)(d) OECD MC. It is worth noting that, under old Article 7(5) OECD MC (repealed in the 2010 revision of the OECD MC), no profit is to be attributed to a PE 'by reason of the mere purchase by that PE of goods or merchandise for the enterprise'.

Another consistency between the Report and the activities excluded by Article 5(4) OECD MC may be found by the parallel exclusion of 'warehousing' from low value-adding services in the Report on Actions 8-10 and from the list of auxiliary and preparatory activities under Article 5(4) as advocated by the Report on Action 7.

4. Some inspiration may also be drawn from VAT Directive 2006/112/EC of 28 Nov. 2006 which considers 'incidental' transactions within the scope of exempt or taxable activities for VAT purposes.

II. SERVICES WHICH ARE EXCLUDED FROM LOW VALUE SERVICES

A. Shareholder Activities

In light of the objectives of the simplified approach for low value-adding intragroup services, the Report provides additional guidance on the identification of shareholder costs to be excluded from the pool of costs.

In particular, the Report adds to the existing Chapter 7 guidance examples on costs related to shareholder activities including costs related to stock exchange listings of the parent company; financial reporting and audit costs carried out in the interest of the parent company or related to consolidated financial statements; costs related to investor relations such as communication strategy; costs related to compliance of the parent company with tax laws; and corporate governance costs.

These examples are borrowed from the table provided in Annex 2 of the EU Commission Communication, COM (2011) 16 final of 25 January 2011. The list of activities and costs that can be considered as incurred for the benefit of the parent company according to the OECD approach is now substantially in line with the one provided in Annex 2 of the Communication. The only remaining difference is that the Communication seems to recognize so-called mixed activities (partly shareholder and partly intragroup services rendering benefit) while the Report does not.[5] These particularly include costs of the parent company's audit of the accounts of the subsidiary, costs for the drafting and auditing of the financial statements of the subsidiary in accordance with the accounting principles of the States of the parent, costs of information technology, and costs for the general review of the affiliates' performance if not connected to the provisions of consulting services to the subsidiaries.

With reference to 'costs relating to compliance of the parent company with the relevant tax laws', the question does arise of the characterization of the costs relating to the new Country-by-Country Reporting. Should they be included within the scope of shareholders costs?

Furthermore, the Report provides additional guidance, for instance, with reference to the duplicative activities. The revised guidance makes clear that any consideration of potential duplicative activities should analyze the nature of services in detail. As an example, the fact that a company performs marketing services in-house and is also charged for marketing services from a group company would not, in itself, determine duplication since marketing is a broad term covering many levels of activity.

The following table illustrates the comparison between the examples illustrated by the OECD in the 1979 and 1984 Reports, the 1995 Guidelines, the Communication and the Final Report.

---

5. Also the Dutch Decree of 14 Nov. 2013, No. IFZ 2013/184M issued by the Deputy Minister of Finance clarified that:

> Classifying the activities as group services or shareholder activities may give rise to 'mixed' activities. Mixed activities refer to activities performed by a department or other group of individuals operating within the group, which partly qualify as group services and partly as shareholder activities. Examples of group activities are consolidation activities, merger and acquisition (M&A) activities, activities associated with the implementation and fulfilment of legal corporate governance rules and corporate governance codes of conduct, and activities of the board of directors.

1979 Report	*1984 Report*	*1995 Guidelines*	*EU Communication*	*OECD Final Report*
– cost of the parent's audit of its subsidiaries; – expenses incurred by the parent company in arranging meetings of its own shareholders; – expenses incurred by the parent company for consolidating the results of the members of the group, including the necessary auditing; and – expenses incurred by the parent company in providing finance for the extension of the group itself	(a) costs of activities relating to the juridical structure of the parent company itself, such as meetings of shareholders of the parent, issuing of shares in the parent company and costs of the supervisory board; (b) costs relating to reporting requirements of the parent company including the consolidation of reports; (c) cost of raising funds for the acquisition of its participations; (d) costs of managerial and control (monitoring) activities related to the management and protection of the investment as such in participations.	(a) costs of activities relating to the juridical structure of the parent company itself, such as meetings of shareholders of the parent, issuing of shares in the parent company and costs of the supervisory board; (b) costs relating to reporting requirements of the parent company including the consolidation of reports; (c) costs of raising funds for the acquisition of its participations. (d) costs of managerial and control (monitoring) activities related to the management and protection of the investment as such in participations	(a) costs of activities relating to the juridical structure of the parent company itself, such as: (b) costs relating to reporting requirements of the parent company including the consolidation of reports: (c) costs of raising funds for the acquisition of its [the parent company's] participations; (d) costs of managerial and control (monitoring) activities related to the management and protection of the investments as such in participations unless an independent party would have been willing to buy for or to perform for itself: (e) costs to reorganize the group, to acquire new members or to terminate a division.	(a) costs relating to the juridical structure of the parent company itself [...]; (b) costs relating to reporting requirements (including financial reporting and audit) of the parent company including the consolidation of reports, costs relating to the parent company's audit of the subsidiary's accounts carried out exclusively in the interest of the parent company, and costs relating to the preparation of consolidated financial statements of the MNE; (c) costs of raising funds for the acquisition of its participations and costs relating to the parent company's investor relations such as communication strategy with shareholders of the parent company, financial analysts, funds and other stakeholders in the parent company; (d) costs relating to compliance of the parent company with the relevant tax laws; (e) costs which are ancillary to the corporate governance of the MNE as a whole.

B. Other Services Excluded

The Report expressly excludes, aside from the abovementioned shareholder costs, some services from the scope of low value-adding intragroup services (paragraph 7.47) and in particular:

(a) Research and development services.
(b) Manufacturing and production services.
(c) Sales, marketing and distribution activities.
(d) Financial transactions.
(e) Extraction, exploration, or processing of natural resources.
(f) Insurance and re-insurance.
(g) Services of corporate senior management.

In contrast, services eligible for the simplified regime are listed on an illustrative fashion (these are mentioned as services which are 'likely' to fall under the scope).

The list of excluded services lacks clarity by reason of the uncertainty of the meaning of the terms. For instance, 'marketing services' are excluded while 'internal and external communications and public relations support' – which might fall within the meaning of marketing – are included among low value services. It is worth noting that the Joint Transfer Pricing Forum (JTPF) includes marketing services within the scope of low value services. Comments made in the context of the public consultation have extensively criticized the general exclusion of marketing services from the scope of low value services. Indeed, depending on business-specific circumstances, marketing activities can be considered an intangible generating activity (e.g., in the case of consumer brands), a mid-to-high value service (e.g., creating advertising copy), or a low value-adding service (e.g., printing marketing brochures).

The ambiguity also applies to 'services of corporate senior management' other than management supervision which are regarded as being outside the scope of low value added services. The expression 'corporate senior management' has also been criticized. Indeed 'corporate senior managers' can also be involved in the performance of low value-adding activities. Focus should be on the nature and type of services and not on who provides the services.[6]

Moreover, the expression 'corporate senior management' has no legal meaning and may be interpreted differently within an MNE. For instance, in the US, the expression 'senior executive' means the chief executive officer, chief operating officer, chief financial officer, or anyone in charge of a principal business unit or function. (Model Business Corporation Act which is a model set of law prepared by the Committee on Corporate Laws of the Section of Business Law of the American Bar Association and is followed by twenty-four states.)

6. In practice, it may be wondered the extent to which activities rendered by senior management are enveloped into services taking into account that their responsibilities frequently cover several functions of the group without a clear-cut distinction.

Some criticism was raised as to the exclusion as well as the lack of guidance on the characterization of contract/toll manufacturing activities. The parallel between the low value-adding services and the auxiliary and preparatory activities under Article 5(4) OECD MC indicates that processing activities are not included within auxiliary or preparatory activities which would exclude the existence of a permanent establishment. (Letter c) of paragraph 4 makes it clear that the exclusion is confined to storage for processing by another enterprise.[7]

Finally, certain categories of excluded services are too broad and might well include low value services. For instance, it is doubtful if all services relating to 'financial transactions' fall outside low value adding. The same is true for insurance and re-insurance which for certain businesses may be a routine function.

It should be noted that paragraph 7.48 Final Report clarified that 'the fact that an activity does not qualify for the simplified approach, as defined under paragraph 7.45, should not be interpreted to mean that that activity generates high return'. This admirable statement, however, could not prevent tax authorities from making the simplistic syllogism: excluded services are high value.

III. LIST OF LOW VALUE SERVICES

As mentioned earlier, low value services are listed in an illustrative way which does not rank *pari passu* with the list of excluded services that is conclusive and, in its literal wording, does not appear to permit the MNE to document a contrary characterization under the circumstances. The entire rationale of the simplified approach is to improve certainty and limit disputes and non-efficient use of resources by tax administrations during tax audits. It would, therefore, have been desirable for the Report to establish quite clearly that all of the services listed by the Report have to be regarded as low value services or that, alternatively, burden of proof would lie on the tax administration to document that the services fall outside the simplified approach.

The list of low value services also raises issues of interpretation. For instance, '*training and employee development*' is regarded as falling under low value services. However, these activities might be to create and transfer know-how which is a point made by the Base Erosion and Profit Shifting (BEPS) Report on intangibles (paragraph 1.155).[8]

7. Recently, the Italian Supreme Court – Criminal Section stated that business of toll manufacturers is outside the scope of permanent establishment concept (Supreme Court, Criminal Section, 18 Apr. 2014, No. 17299). The Italian judiciary has given relevance to the absence of decision power and risks at the level of the Italian company. The reasoning of the Italian Supreme Court could lead to the conclusion that toll manufacturer services should be considered low value service as they do 'not involve the assumption or control of substantial or significant risk by the service provider and do not give rise to the creation of significant risk for the service provider' (para. 7.45 of the Final Report). For a comment on the decision of the Supreme Court, see P. Pistone, Italy: No Permanent Establishment for Toll Manufacturing without Participation in Strategic Decision-Making, in Tax Treaty Case Law Around the Globe 2015, p. 115 (Michael Lang et al. eds., IBFD 2016), Online Books IBFD.
8. 'It should be noted, however, that the transfer or secondment of one or more employees may, in some situations depending on the facts and circumstances, result in the transfer of valuable

For some affiliates of the MNE, low value services are included and charged in the scope of broader services in which case the segregation might become difficult and guidance would be required (e.g., a proportionate approach). This might also justify the exclusion of one or more MNE's affiliates from the election 'all in' simplified system or specific rules to be applicable to such situations.

In 2010, the EU JTPF (Guidelines on low value-adding intragroup services, Appendix I to the EU Commission Communication, COM (2011) 16 final of 25 January 2011) provided guidelines on the transfer pricing of low value-adding intragroup services. The guidelines of the JTPF not only show similarities but also include a number of deviations from the list provided by the Report.

Communication of the EU Commission (COM(2011)) 16 Final	**BEPS Final Report Actions 8-10**
List of intragroup services commonly provided that may or may not be within the scope of this chapter	*Services that WOULD LIKELY MEET the definition of low value-adding services*
Information technology	Information technology
Human resource	Human resource
Marketing	Communications and public relations support (but excluding specific advertising or marketing activities as well as development of underlying strategies)
Legal	Legal
Accounting and administration	Accounting and auditing
Technical services	Processing and management of accounts receivable and accounts payable
Quality control	Monitoring and compilation of data relating to health, safety, environmental and other standards regulating the business
Strategy and business development	Activities with regard to tax obligations
Corporate security	General services of an administrative or clerical nature
R&D	
Real estate and facility management	
Logistic	
Inventory management	

know-how or other intangibles from one associated enterprise to another. For example, an employee of Company A seconded to Company B may have knowledge of a secret formula owned by Company A and may make that secret formula available to Company B for use in its commercial operations. Similarly, employees of Company A seconded to Company B to assist with a factory start-up may make Company A manufacturing know-how available to Company B for use in its commercial operations. Where such a provision of know-how or other intangibles results from the transfer or secondment of employees, it should be separately analyzed under the provisions of Chapter VI, and an appropriate price should be paid for the right to use the intangibles'.

Communication of the EU Commission (COM(2011)) 16 Final	BEPS Final Report Actions 8-10
Advice on transport and distribution strategy	
Warehousing services	
Purchasing services and sourcing raw materials	
Cost reduction management	
Packaging services	

Scrolling down the lists of activities, the first main difference between the EU and the OECD is that the latter expressly excludes marketing and R&D services from the definition of low value while the EU does not. This change of approach might be considered in light of the related works on Action 8 ensuring that profits associated with the transfer and use of intangibles are appropriately allocated in accordance with (rather than divorced from) value creation. Indeed, the Report (paragraph 6.56) states that, in considering the arm's length compensation for functional contributions of various members of the MNE group, some 'important functions' (including marketing and R&D activities) will have, in appropriate circumstances, 'special significance' because they usually make a significant contribution to intangible value.

Differently from the JTPF, the OECD does not mention warehousing activities. This is probably due to the possible interaction with paragraphs 11 et seq. of the Report on Action 7 'Preventing the Artificial Avoidance of Permanent Establishment Status' stating that:

> [w]here, for example, an enterprise of State R maintains in State S a very large warehouse in which a significant number of employees work for the main purpose of storing and delivering goods owned by the enterprise that the enterprise sells online to customers in State S, paragraph 4 will not apply to that warehouse since the storage and delivery activities that are performed through that warehouse, which represents an important asset and requires a number of employees, constitute an essential part of the enterprise's sale/distribution business and do not have, therefore, a preparatory or auxiliary character.

As mentioned earlier in this chapter, the inclusion of warehousing in the list of activities that would likely meet the definition of low value-adding services would have been inconsistent with the proposition made under the Report on Action 7 under which warehousing can no longer be regarded as ancillary and preparatory (contributing minimally to the creation of income)

IV. THE DETERMINATION OF COSTS

As per paragraph 7.52, an MNE group electing to adopt this simplified method would, as far as practicable, apply it on a consistent group wide basis in all countries in which it operates. It seems to suggest that an MNE that elects for the simplified approach should – as an initial step – create one global cost pool for all costs incurred by all members of the group in performing any low value-adding intragroup services. Applying such an approach across different countries may create problems, for example, because some countries may allow a charge of costs without a markup for certain activities (e.g., the Netherlands and the United States of America). Moreover, the 'all-in' or 'all-out' approach will likely create issues for low value services which are included in the cost of goods or services charged to other affiliates, in which case segregation might become difficult.

At this stage, the MNE group should identify those costs that should be allocated among members of the group. In this regard, taxpayers should consider that compensation for services rendered to an associated enterprise may be included in the price for other transfers. For instance, the price for licensing a patent or know-how may include a payment for training services performed for the licensee. Even though such services are so closely linked and continuous that they cannot be evaluated adequately on a separate basis, the costs of such services should not be carved out from the price for the rights to use intangible property or transfer of goods. This approach is consistent with paragraphs 3.9 et seq. of the OECD Guidelines.

V. THE 5% MARKUP

Paragraph 7.61 provides for a profit markup equal to 5% to be applied to all pool costs. It is doubtful if one margin for all cost pools will properly reflect the arm's length remuneration. Accounting services may carry profit margins which are different from markups on monitoring safety and environmental matters. Furthermore, the flat markup disregards the location of the cost center and the different labor cost levels which may be found in different countries. Group synergies leading to cost efficiency are also not taken into account (knowledge of business models within the group may result in lower cost compared to an arm's length situation).

Moreover, certain industries carry a profit margin which is less than 5%. Indeed, data provided by the EUJTPF analysis of margins for intragroup services (DOC: JTPF/018/BACK/2009/EN) shows that the profitability of certain service providers is lower than the 5% indicated by the Report.

Category Description	*FCMU Profitability – Median (1999-2007)*
Land transport	2.8%
Air transport	2.5%
Warehousing/Storage	3.3%
HR	3.6%
Travel services	1.6%
Admin/Business support	3.8%

It is clear that it would be odd to obtain remuneration on low value services which are greater than the margins which are derived from the conduct of its core activities.

For these reasons, the fixed margin set out by the Report raised criticism. However, the lack of precision in identifying the proper margin for each class of services is a downside which is rewarded by the simplified approach adopted by the Report. Furthermore, the lack of precision in identifying the proper markup may lead to very negligible profit shifting issues if one considers that a 1% discrepancy between arm's length margin and the 5% fixed margin weighs EUR 10 million taxable income on an aggregated low value cost of EUR 1 billion. The exposure would be even more limited if one considers the overall effect of inbound and outbound services (e.g., in situations in which the 5% markup is too generous or it would generate more deductions for the recipient company and more income for the service provider).[9] The risk of profit shifting is thus very limited and offset by the reduction of cost derived by tax administrations through auditing activities.

It may be wondered if an MNE which elects for the simplified approach and so meets the documentation requirements may do so to protect itself from adjustments in excess of 5% for low value services and, nevertheless, maintain the ability to establish a lower than 5% markup. It is worth noting that the JTPF Report on low value-adding intragroup services does not provide for a fixed markup as it generally refers to experience showing a markup range between 3% and 8% or 'often around 5%'.[10]

It may be discussed at length if a range of marks-up could have been a better alternative to be adopted by the Report (this was indeed the alternative chosen in the preliminary draft report). It is notable that the simplified approach relies on coordination between countries and requires a consistent approach, a target which could hardly be satisfied by a range of margins.

Finally, it may be wondered the extent to which the fixed profit markup may be consistently applied to purely domestic situations which, in some countries, might require legislative changes.

VI. THE THRESHOLD OF THE APPLICATION OF THE SIMPLIFIED APPROACH

The Report provides for a threshold approach (low value services would be subject to audit when overall cost incurred exceeds a certain threshold set out in paragraph 7.63) which may reduce the risk of shifting of income and tax planning techniques.

Indeed, the risk of tax arbitrage exists insofar as the modeling of services may drive low value services compared to ad hoc services which would not fall under the 5% markup simplified approach. This approach enveloping ad hoc services into low value general services, however, may have drawbacks for the MNE insofar as – as mentioned earlier – the increase of the overall amount of low value services may exceed the threshold which would rule out the eligibility for the simplified approach.

9. This is not conclusive as some countries may have an unbalanced ratio between inbound and outbound services such as developing countries which may be essentially inbound with the exception of a few emerging countries which host general services centers of an MNE.
10. Paragraph 63 of the JTPF Report titled '*Guidelines on low value adding intragroup services*' of 4 Feb. 2010 (DOC JTPF/020/REV3/2009/EN).

As mentioned earlier, the simplified approach can be ruled out when the aggregate of costs incurred for low value services exceeds certain amounts determined on the basis of a certain ratio (paragraph 7.63 considers on an illustrative basis proportion of such cost versus total costs or turnover).

It would be desirable for tax administrations to establish more than one ratio to be selected by the MNE in order to permit taxpayers to pick the most suitable ratio which may adequately reflect the peculiarities of the business segment and of the MNE itself (e.g., less efficient MNE which incurs labor costs above average and which may be documented by cost cutting programs).

The difficulty raised by the threshold is the need of coordination between countries as to the qualitative and quantitative features of the threshold. This would avoid situations whereby the country of residence of the service provider accepts the 5% simplified approach and the country of residence of the recipient rules out the 5% simplified approach based on its own autonomous rule on thresholds.

The selection of the threshold is quite broad as the report makes reference to different key (e.g., turnover or cost) amounts (percentage of the relevant ratio) and entities to which the ratio would apply (e.g., the recipient party versus the group).

VII. PROCEDURAL ISSUES AND SCOPE OF THE SIMPLIFIED APPROACH

A. Condition for the Election to Be Applied

It is not entirely clear in the Report if all affiliates belonging to the MNE must participate to the simplified approach. Paragraph 7.53 seems to confirm the all in requisite insofar as it clarifies that failure by one country to apply the simplified approach does not disqualify the other affiliates belonging to the MNE in other countries. Furthermore, the paragraph indicates that the election may be applied at the level of a sub-holding together with all its subsidiaries. Should this all in requisite be confirmed, the possibility to apply the sub-holding limited application of the election should be clarified as the meaning of sub-holding is neither defined nor available in domestic laws of OECD countries.

B. Effects of the Elective Simplified Approach

The effects of the simplified approach also raise some questions and, where the lack of clarity arises, this may reflect the resistance of some countries to surrender their power to assess or disqualify the resident affiliate when the election has so been made by the MNE. The Report indicates that the system is a 'safe harbor' (see the Summary). The Revised Section E on safe harbors in Chapter IV of the Transfer Pricing Guidelines (2013)[11] OECD Report includes, in the definition of safe harbor, situations in which eligible taxpayers are relieved from certain obligations otherwise imposed by a

11. http://www.oecd.org/ctp/transfer-pricing/Revised-Section-E-Safe-Harbours-TP-Guidelines.pdf (accessed 3 Apr. 2016).

country's general transfer pricing rules or are exempted from the application of all or part of these rules.[12] The low value services simplified approach falls within the first class of safe harbors insofar as taxpayers electing for such a regime are not entirely excluded from the application of the rules for the class of eligible transactions.

Indeed, the coverage of the simplified approach does not seem to extend to the benefit test (paragraph 7.54 states that '… tax administrations should generally refrain from reviewing or challenging the benefit test when the simplified approach has been applied…' and that MNE 'should provide sufficient evidence that the benefits test is met'). Finally, the Report indicates that, when the simplified approach does not apply, the tax administrations may undertake a 'full functional analysis and comparability analysis…' (paragraph 7.64).

C. Legal Form of the Simplified Approach

The legal form of the simplified procedure is not covered by the Report. However, it may be envisaged that the implementation may take the form of a memoranda of understanding for competent authorities which are advocated by the Revised Section E on safe harbors in Chapter IV of the Transfer Pricing Guidelines (paragraph 4.119), which has also been implemented in some countries on a bilateral basis.

As the Report makes reference to the MNE's election, it is not clear which legal entity must apply for the simplified approach (the parent company or the sub-holding or each single affiliate). Also, the legal form of the election is not clear. Should it take the form of a specific request to be filed with the tax return, or should it be included in the TP documentation or in the reporting obligation regarding the compliance with documentation requirements? The subject falls within the competence of domestic laws and administrative practice of each State. However, guidance is required insofar as the simplified approach relies on a coordination between more than one State (the cost plus 5% must be simultaneously applied to the country of residence of the recipient of the service as well as to the country of residence of the service provider). The taxable years covered by the simplified approach are also not addressed in the Report. Should such timing rules be different, the simplified approach would have different coverage in the countries involved. For instance, one country might apply the simplified approach from the taxable period in which the election is filed while other countries might apply the simplified approach from the tax period for which the tax return is filed. Furthermore, affiliates may have different financial periods so that an election made simultaneously in the several States might apply to different time intervals. Finally, an entity might join a group in a taxable period for which the deadline for the election has expired so that the simplified approach is no longer available for that taxable period. This might require domestic law or administrative practice to consider retrospective application of the simplified approach under such circumstances.

12. Paragraph 4.100 of the safe HarbourReport.

Some countries might take the view that the simplified approach could also apply, to some extent, during audits regardless of the election. Should the audit focus on services which are rendered by an affiliate which has not filed the election, could the taxpayer apply the 5% markup so that the failure to elect would simply result in more scrutiny of the value of the services during the audit? It would be an odd result under which the arm's length markup for low value services were to be determined at a level greater than the safe harbor level solely because of the failure to elect for the simplified approach. In other words, the rationale of the simplified approach would simply be the limited audit activities on the services and should not result in a departure from the arm's length in the determination of the markup once the tax authority accepts the qualification of the service as a low value service.

Some issues remain obscure such as the MNE's ability to opt out which is one of the concerns of the safe harbors Report (paragraph 4.111).

As to the reaction of States to the Report, the Swedish tax authorities announced in December that the recommendations contained in the Report shall be applied immediately retrospectively regardless of when they shall be incorporated into the OECD transfer pricing guidelines.

CHAPTER 7

Commissionaire Arrangements/Low-Risk Distributors and Attribution of Profits to Permanent Establishments

Giammarco Cottani

I. INTRODUCTION: THE DEVELOPMENT OF ACTION 7 OF THE BEPS PROJECT AND ITS OUTCOME

Action 7 of the Base Erosion and Profit Shifting (BEPS) Action Plan[1] mandated the development of changes to the definition of Permanent Establishment (PE) in order to prevent the artificial avoidance of PE status, including through the use of commissionaire arrangements. Therefore, defining the boundaries of the PE concept becomes of major importance in quantifying the potential tax liability of a foreign person in the source state. Without exaggeration, determining whether a PE is deemed to exist is very likely to be the most frequent tax treaty issue that advisers, government officials, and courts have to deal with.[2]

The significance of the issue is further emphasized by the circumstance that several Multinational Groups (MNEs) have organized their commercial distribution operations through commissionaire arrangements (or other forms of limited-risk distributor arrangements), therefore, depriving the source state, i.e., the state where the selling activities took place, of the opportunity of taxing income arising therefrom, as a literal/legal/formalistic interpretation of the arrangement preventing the commissionaire to fall within the definition of the Agency PE under Article 5(5) of the OECD Model Tax Convention (OECD MTC) (see Section 2).

To this end, it is quite obvious that Action 7 played a pivotal role within the BEPS project. A number of jurisdictions - the United Kingdom on top of all the countries which had an active role in the project - relied heavily on the positive outcome of the discussions. The aim is to enlarge the scope of application of the PE provision under Article 5(5) of the OECD MTC[3] in order to prevent profits arising from any such selling activity from being stashed in a low or no tax jurisdiction where the principal was established.

Looking at the development of Action 7, the Organisation for Economic Co-operation and Development (OECD) published a Discussion Draft containing amendments to the definition of Article 5 of the OECD MTC[4] at the end of October 2014, which significantly caught the attention of the business community. The significance of the issue was witnessed by the more than 800 pages of comments received by the OECD and made publicly available.[5]

1. OECD, *Action Plan on Base Erosion and Profit Shifting*, Paris, 2013.
2. To this end, no other definition in tax treaties is longer than the definition of agency permanent establishment both in the 1963 OECD Draft version of Article 5(4) and 5(5) and in the 1977-2010 version of the OECD Model of Article 5(5) and 5(6).
3. In the author's view, the introduction of the UK's Diverted Profit Tax (incorrectly labeled as the 'Google Tax') arguably targets arrangements that seek to avoid creating a permanent establishment by having as its main purpose of entering into a transaction pursuing a tax avoidance scheme. See L. Cerioni, *The New 'Google Tax': The 'Beginning of the End' for Tax Residence as a Connecting Factor for Tax Jurisdiction?*, European Taxation, 55:5 (2015).
4. See OECD, *Public Discussion Draft- BEPS Action 7: Preventing the Artificial Avoidance of PE Status*, Paris 2014.
5. See OECD, *Comments Received on Public Discussion Draft – BEPS Action 7, Preventing the Artificial Avoidance of PE Status*, and available at http://www.oecd.org/tax/treaties/public-comments-revised-beps-action-7-prevent-artificial-avoidance-pe-status.htm (accessed 23 Mar. 2016).

The relevance of determining with clarity where a commissionaire may fall within the scope of agency PE[6] is a long disputed issue which, over the years, has been further exacerbated by the fact that civil law and common law jurisdictions have dealt differently with the issue of whether or not – and to what extent – commissionaire structures create a PE.

In particular, in civil law jurisdictions, only agents who have a contractual role to act in the name of their principal can trigger an agency PE. Following the principles of indirect representation (see Section 3), a commissionaire should be excluded from the scope of application of Article 5(5) of the OECD MTC, as – by means of the provision – it will only conclude contracts in its own name without creating a legal link between the principal and the party contracting with him. On the other hand, common law jurisdictions stipulate that, should the contracts be concluded on behalf of and with the authority of the principal entity, the relationship between the agent and the principal is not affected by whether the contract is made in the name of the principal or in the agent's own name.

Due to such fundamental differences, the final OECD Report (the '2015 Report') of October 2015[7] triggered some significant changes to Article 5 of the OECD MTC to achieve the following objectives:

I. In order to prevent the artificial avoidance of PE status through commissionaire arrangements and similar strategies, the Report concludes that where activities that an intermediary exercises in a country are intended to result in the regular conclusion of contracts to be performed by a foreign enterprise, that enterprise should be considered as having a taxable presence in the country unless the intermediary is performing these activities in the course of an independent business. This has resulted in changes to Articles 5(5) and 5(6) of the OECD MTC and the Commentary;
II. In order to prevent the avoidance of PE status through specific activity exemptions, the 2015 Report concludes that it should not be possible to avoid permanent establishment status by using the exceptions of paragraph 4 of Article 5 of the OECD MTC in the case of activities that are not preparatory or auxiliary or by fragmenting a cohesive operating business into several small operations in order to argue that each party is merely engaged in preparatory or auxiliary activities that benefit from these exceptions. This has led to changes to Article 5(4) of the OECD MTC and to the Commentary to include: a) 'preparatory or auxiliary' condition applicable to all the subparagraphs of Article 5(4) of the OECD MTC; and (b) a new anti-fragmentation rule;
III. In order to prevent the artificial avoidance of PE status through the splitting-up of contracts in order to take advantage of the exception of paragraph 3 of Article 5, the Report has concluded that the Principal Purpose Test ('PPT rule') should address the BEPS concerns related to the abusive splitting of contracts for purposes of this exception. In addition to the changes to the OECD MTC under the Report on BEPS Action 6, the work has resulted in: (i) the inclusion in the

6. See J.F. Avery Jones & D.A. Ward, *Agent as Permanent Establishment under the OECD Model*, European Taxation, n. 1 (1993).
7. See OECD, *Preventing the Artificial Avoidance of Permanent Establishment Status, Action 7 – 2015 Final Report*, and available at http://www.oecd.org/ctp/preventing-the-artificial-avoidance-of-permanent-establishment-status-action-7-2015-final-report-9789264241220-en.htm (accessed 23 Mar. 2016).

> Commentary of the PPT rule of an example regarding the splitting-up of a contract for work on a construction site; and (ii) the inclusion in the Commentary on paragraph 3 of Article 5 of the OECD MTC of an alternative provision that Member States may use to address such splitting-up of a contract.

Although issues sub (II) and (III) addressed a significant cause of BEPS concerns associated with the (mis)use of the definition of the term 'permanent establishment', this contribution will focus exclusively on the changes to the agency PE definition under Article 5(5) and 5(6) of the OECD MTC.

Based on the above, I will first provide a brief overview of the historical background of how such a provision originated and evolved (in Section 2). I will then address the discussion as to how commissionaire structures are analyzed in both civil law and common law jurisdictions in the wake of the publication of the 2015 Report (in Section 3).

As the debate surrounding the issue of PE is, by definition, two-pronged, i.e., it is not only important: (i) to determine whether a PE is deemed to exist but also – in the case of an affirmative answer – (ii) attributing profits to it in a manner consistent with the arm's length principle, I will analyze (in Section 4) similarities and differences between the approaches of Articles 7 and 9 of the OECD MTC to assess whether the conceptual gap between the two provisions has been narrowed or enlarged after the completion of the transfer pricing Actions of the BEPS project (namely Actions 8,9, and 10).[8]

In the latter regard of the attribution of profits, the preliminary work carried out under BEPS Action 7 focused on whether the existing rules of Article 7 MTC would be appropriate for determining the profits that would be allocated to PEs resulting from the changes included in the PE Report. The conclusion in Action 7 is that these changes do not require substantive modifications to the existing rules and guidance concerning the attribution of profits to PEs under Article 7. However, there is arguably a need for additional guidance on how the rules of Article 7 of the OECD MTC would apply to PEs resulting from the changes triggered by Action 7. I will present my view and try to draw some tentative conclusions in a de iure condito vis-à-vis a de iure condendo approach.

II. COMMISSIONAIRE ARRANGEMENTS AND ARTICLE 5(5) OF THE OECD MTC: HISTORICAL BACKGROUND

Understanding why commissionaire structures cause headaches to tax administrations first and foremost requires having a look in plain terms at the characterization of the commissionaire from a legal standpoint. Afterwards, it has to be established whether the commissionaire may fall within the definition of Agency PE under Article 5(5) of the OECD MTC.

A commissionaire arrangement is a contractual arrangement whereby a foreign enterprise is able to sell its products in a State without technically having a PE to which

8. See OECD Actions 8-9-10 Final Reports, *Aligning Transfer Pricing Outcome with Value Creation*, and available at http://www.oecd.org/ctp/aligning-transfer-pricing-outcomes-with-value-creation-actions-8-10-2015-final-reports-9789264241244-en.htm (accessed 23 Mar. 2016).

such sales may be attributed for tax purposes and without, therefore, being taxable in that State on the profits derived from such sales. As the person that concludes the sales does not own the products that it sells, that person cannot be taxed on the profits derived from such sales and may only be taxed on the remuneration that it receives for its services (usually a commission).

In this respect, Article 5(5) of the OECD MTC literally requires the conclusion of contracts 'in the name of' the enterprise in order for an agency PE to be deemed to exist. Where an agent – such as a commissionaire, indeed – does not conclude the contract in the principal's name but rather in its own name, no PE is deemed to exist.

Against this background, since 1994, the Commentary on Article 5(5) of the OECD MTC envisages the possibility of an Agency PE to arise if the actions of the agent are 'binding' for the principal irrespective in whose name the contract is concluded. In light of the above, the key issue to be addressed, for a commissionaire to be a PE of its foreign principal, was always how to construe from grammatical, historical, and systematic perspectives the term 'binding' vis-à-vis the term 'in the name of'.

In my view, '*binding*', as a term to be read in the context of the OECD's Commentary explanation of the criterion '*in the name of*', can only be construed as a notion creating a legal connection/lien between two parties. In order to corroborate such an interpretation, the League of Nations referred to the term 'on behalf of' in the same conceptual way as '*binding*' and '*in the name of*'.[9] Stated otherwise, the term '*binding*' was historically qualified as a legal concept without alluding to any matters of a commercial, economic, or factual nature (as Action 7 of the BEPS Report now alludes to do).

In particular, the Reports of the League of Nations played a significant role in determining the proper way to construe the term '*binding*'.[10] The 1929 Report was the first text in which the three terms 'on behalf of', '*in the name of*' and '*binding*' were used and – interestingly enough – the Report regarded the terms as expressing the same concept, i.e., bindingness from a legal standpoint. This entails that the only agents to be deemed as dependent to the foreign enterprise are those having sufficient powers to conclude contracts binding upon the enterprise.

Moreover, the Committee of Technical Experts Report of 1927 introduced the concept of '*bona fide agent* of independent status', referring explicitly to brokers and commission agents as typical examples of agents presenting a level of legal and economic independence from their principals to say that they carry on their business irrespective of any influence arising from the principal itself.

Against this background, in the twenty-first century, many countries tended to equate, at least in the application of their tax treaties, the notions of the term '*in the name of*', with '*on behalf of*', the latter notion being understood as '*binding*'.[11] There

9. For a thorough historical analysis of the origin of Article 5(5) and 5(6) of the OECD MTC, see H. Pijl, *Agency Permanent Establishments: In the Name of and the Relationship between Article 5 (5) and (6), Part I*, Bulletin for International Taxation (2013) 1, pp. 7 e ss.
10. See League of Nations, *General Meeting of Government Experts on Double Taxation and Tax Evasion*, Geneva, 1929.
11. See the General IFA Report of 2009, *Is There a Permanent Establishment?*, Cahiers de droit fiscal international, 94a (2009), Online Books IBFD.

were some notable exceptions to this common thread. According to the Austrian branch report, for example, reference was made to the official guidelines whereby 'in the name of' is construed as 'binding' and not whether or not the contract is literally in the principal's name.[12] All of these countries referred to paragraph 32.1 of paragraph 5 (5) of the OECD MTC (in force before the 2015 Report) which explains 'in the name of' as 'binding'.

One likely explanation for such an interpretational issue is due to the fact that, under the agency law of many civil law countries, only the act of concluding contracts 'in the name of' legally bind the principal to the agent. In these countries, there is a substantive and formal identification of the terms 'in the name of' and legal bindingness.

For instance, Belgium adopts a very formalistic tax treaty interpretation whereby 'in the name of' always gives rise to a PE whereas a commissionaire does not. France is a clear example in this respect where the French Supreme Administrative Court (*Conseil D'Etat*[13]) stated that what counts is whether a commissionaire legally engages its principal which, under domestic law, it does not. Other countries, such as South Africa and Switzerland, take a rather substantial/economic approach whereby legal bindingness is not required as the decisive factor is, respectively, whether a transfer of the economic risk to the principal occurred (Switzerland) or whether the agent extensively involves the foreign enterprise in the local economy (South Africa).

Against this background, looking at the answer the OECD gave in the Final Report on Action 7, as a matter of policy, where the activities that a commissionaire/ intermediary exercises in a country are intended to result in the regular conclusion of contracts to be performed by a foreign enterprise, that enterprise should be considered to have a taxable presence in that country unless the intermediary is performing these activities in the course of an independent business.

Therefore, as I am going to further elaborate in Section 3, the OECD seems to have opted for a substantive interpretation of the term 'binding of' in order to prevent BEPS abuses and the artificial avoidance of PE structure, arguably closing the gap with the way in which a transfer pricing analysis between separate enterprises under Article 9 of the OECD model takes place (and, not in the least, by dismissing the historical roots of the notion of Agency PE since the day of the League of Nations).

III. COMMISSIONAIRE STRUCTURES IN LIGHT OF THE ACTION 7 BEPS REPORT: MORE CLARITY OR THE BEGINNING OF THE END?

Article 5(5) of the OECD Model, in its 2010 version, defines a dependent agent as a person – other than an independent agent – who '*is acting on behalf of an enterprise and has, and habitually exercises, in a Contracting State an authority to conclude contracts in the name of the enterprise*'. Paragraph 32.1 of the Commentary on Article

12. Similar interpretations are held for Germany, Ireland, Luxembourg, Russia, Sweden, and the United Kingdom.
13. See *Societé Zimmer Ltd. v. Ministre de l'Economie des Finance et de l'Industrie, Tax Treaty Case La IBFD*; See Section 3 below for further analysis.

5 of the OECD Model (1995) was amended in 1995 to provide that the phrase '*authority to conclude contracts in the name of the enterprise [...]*' applies equally to an agent who concludes contracts that are binding on the enterprise even if the contracts are not actually in the name of the enterprise.

The question, therefore, was whether or not the phrase '*binding on*' should be construed in a legal or an economic manner. In the vast majority of cases, a commissionaire under civil law jurisdictions could never bind its principal and would, therefore, never be an agency PE as it was acting legally *in its own name*.

The world was then turned upside down according to the new wording of paragraph 5 of Article 5 of the OECD MTC as arising from the completion of Action 7 2015 Report where it was stated that:

> Notwithstanding the provisions of paragraphs 1 and 2 but subject to the provisions of paragraph 6, where a person is acting in a Contracting State on behalf of an enterprise and, in doing so, habitually concludes contracts, or habitually plays the principal role leading to the conclusion of contracts that are routinely concluded without material modification by the enterprise, and these contracts are
>
> a) in the name of the enterprise, or
> b) for the transfer of the ownership of, or for the granting of the right to use, property owned by that enterprise or that the enterprise has the right to use, or
> c) for the provision of services by that enterprise, that enterprise shall be deemed to have a permanent establishment in that State [...].

A number of interesting observations arise from the new text of this. First, it seems that a clear substantive/factual approach will be required for a taxpayer or a tax administration to assess the existence of an agency PE. By definition, gathering all the data needed to reach such a conclusion is a very fact intensive exercise which, more often than not (according to the Author's experience) may lead, in particular in a tax audit scenario, to endless disputes as to whether or not certain *behaviors* are significant enough to exceed the threshold of having '*the principal role of leading to the conclusion of contracts*'.

For instance, it is a very frequent scenario within MNE groups that the Principal provides clear guidelines as to the steps to be undertaken to lead to the conclusion of contracts (e.g., the commissionaire can only negotiate within a certain price range or sell within a predetermined amount, etc.). In these circumstances, it is very difficult to determine with clarity whether or not the agent plays a role that 'leads' to the conclusion of contracts.

Moreover, the 2015 Report stated quite significantly that such changes to paragraph 5 of Article 5 of the MTC are not intended to address BEPS concerns related to the transfer of risks between related parties through low-risk distributor arrangements. Indeed, in these arrangements, sales generated by a local sales workforce are attributed to a resident taxpayer which is not the case in the situations that the changes to Article 5(5) and 5(6) to the OECD MTC are intended to address. Given this difference, [...] '*BEPS concerns related to low-risk distributor arrangements are best addressed through the work on Action 9 (Risks and Capital) of the BEPS Action Plan'*.[14] In my view, this is already a significant step ahead in suggesting that a pure Article 9/transfer pricing approach will be required in dealing with issues associated with the potential existence of an Agency PE.

Against this background, I believe that to untie this apparently unsolvable 'Gordian Knot', the interpreter first has to understand where the distinction is between civil and common law jurisdictions as to the notion of 'agency' and then look at the significant input courts have provided on the topic in order to assess whether a commissionaire can effectively fall within the definition of Agency PE.

It is my impression that, despite the clear road traced by the Final Report, taxpayers and tax administration will still keep looking at the issue differently depending on the tax system in which they find themselves operating.

To this end, the main difference between common law and civil law jurisdictions lies in the fact that, in the former, no difference exists between the concept of direct and indirect representation. Indeed, in common law jurisdictions, the agent always binds the principal against third parties irrespective of whether or not the agent discloses who the principal is (so-called notions of disclosed or undisclosed agency).

In civil law jurisdictions, instead, the concept of: (i) direct and (ii) indirect representation exists whereby, according to the former (direct representation), the agent always enters into a contract *'in the name'* and *'on behalf of'* the principal whereas, in the latter (indirect representation), the agent acts in its own name vis-à-vis the third party but without disclosing the name of the principal.

Therefore, the key interpretative issue, according to a common law interpreter, is how to construe, in the former paragraph 5, *'in the name of'* as the agent always binds the principal. On the other hand, a civil law interpreter would rather focus on the exception list of paragraph 6 of Article 5 MTC. In particular, according to the interpretation provided for by A. Jones and D. Ward,[15] paragraph 6 should be treated as an exception to Article 5(5) and therefore, according to the two authors, reference to broker and commission agents is misplaced. In this respect, the authors argue that, should brokers (who are defined as agents who only bring parties together and who do not conclude contracts in the name of others) and commissionaires (who conclude contracts in their own name) not fall under Article 5(5) of the OECD MTC (pre Action 7) and can they be relevant for the exception of paragraph 6?

It is interesting to note that such an interpretation – whereby paragraph 6 is an exception to paragraph 5 – requires that the notion of *'independence'* has to be construed both from a legal and an economic standpoint. Such an interpretation seems, in my view, to be confirmed by the new text of paragraph 6 of Article 5 post Action 7 of the BEPS 2015 Report, whereby [...]:

> a) Paragraph 5 shall not apply where the person acting in a Contracting State on behalf of an enterprise of the other Contracting State carries on business in the first-mentioned State as an independent agent and acts for the enterprise in the

14. See Action 7 Final Report, para. 9, page 15.
15. See J.F. Avery Jones & D.A. Ward, *Agent as a Permanent Establishment under the OECD Model Tax Convention*, European Taxation, n. 5 (1993).

ordinary course of that business. Where, however, a person **acts exclusively or almost exclusively on behalf of one or more enterprises to which it is closely related**, that person shall not be considered to be an independent agent within the meaning of this paragraph with respect to any such enterprise.

b) For the purposes of this Article, a person is closely related to an enterprise if, based on all the relevant facts and circumstances, one has control of the other or both are under the control of the same persons or enterprises. In any case, a person shall be considered to be closely related to an enterprise if one possesses directly or indirectly more than 50 per cent of the beneficial interest in the other (or, in the case of a company, more than 50 per cent of the aggregate vote and value of the company's shares or of the beneficial equity interest in the company) or if another person possesses directly or indirectly more than 50 per cent of the beneficial interest (or, in the case of a company, more than 50 per cent of the aggregate vote and value of the company's shares or of the beneficial equity interest in the company) in the person and the enterprise.

The terms 'acts exclusively' or 'almost exclusively' again seem to confirm that the notion of (in)dependence has to be construed from both a legal and an economic standpoint.

Therefore, my conclusion seems to be that, although the OECD from an Article 5 standpoint now requires a substantive/economic approach, both the historical origin of paragraph 5 of Article 5 of the OECD MTC as well as the approach of civil law jurisdictions will require a formalistic reading of the provision, therefore, excluding the commissionaire from giving rise to an agency PE. This last assertion seems to be confirmed by the interesting analysis proposed by some relevant literature[16] whereby the focus is placed Macurily on paragraph 6 of the provision.

According to such an interpretation, paragraph 6 does not require any condition as to whether the intermediary has to act 'in the name of' and 'on behalf of' or just in its own name but on behalf of the foreign enterprise. In particular, an intermediary does not constitute a PE of its principal if it is:

(i) independent; and
(ii) acts in its ordinary course of business.

With specific reference to the commissionaire figure, this doctrine holds the view that, even though the latter figure would be part of an MNE group, i.e., not be independent, it could never fall within the definition of Agency PE as the criteria of (pre ACTION 7) paragraph 5 would (i) require to act 'in the name of' and 'on behalf of' and because, according to German civil law, a commissionaire can never be granted powers of direct representation.

Indeed, under the law of contracts of civil law jurisdictions (e.g., Italy, France, Germany, Spain, etc.), the commission contract is a form of undisclosed 'mandate' for the purchase and sale of goods. Under a 'mandate' contract, the agent is required to

16. See H.K. Kroppen & S. Huffmeier, *The German Commissionaire as a Permanent Establishment under the OECD Model Treaty*, Intertax 24:4 (1996), pp. 133-136; H. Pijl, *Agency Permanent Establishments: In the Name of and the Relationship between Article 5 (5) and (6), Part One*, Bulletin for International Taxation (2013), pp. 3-25.

execute legal acts on behalf of the principal which may be disclosed (direct representation) or undisclosed (indirect representation). Under an 'agency' contract, the agent is more generally required to act for the principal to promote the conclusion of contracts (typically for the sale of goods and services) within a certain area. In summary, under Italian civil law, a commissionaire is an entrepreneur who acts in its own name but on behalf of a principal in the purchase and/or sale of goods.

The differences between a commission contract and undisclosed agency (the term 'agency' will be used instead of 'mandate' for ease of reference) are such that most scholars consider the former as a specification of the latter rather than as two different contracts. The formal separation between the two types of contracts would be only the consequence of a historical legacy (from the former Code of Commerce in force at the time when an undisclosed agency in the purchase or sale of goods was so common as to require a specific regime) rather than of an actual recognition of the significance of the differences between the two forms of contractual arrangement. In any event, the differences between the two forms of contracts as debated by scholars do not appear to be of significance in the analysis as to whether a commissionaire (rather than an undisclosed agent) may bind its principal. In this specific respect, the analysis applied to the undisclosed agency would apply also to the commissionaire agreement so that, if it can be concluded that an undisclosed agent 'binds' the principal, the same conclusion would also apply under a commissionaire agreement.

The above being said, the question arises as to whether, in the aftermath of the publication of the Final Report on Action 7, a person acting in a civil law jurisdiction as a commissionaire – acting solely in its own name – for a foreign principal would constitute PE of the foreign enterprise from a *juridical standpoint*.

As the legal analysis indicates, a commissionaire may not legally 'bind' its principal as the actions of the commissionaire are binding vis-à-vis third parties only for the commissionaire. On the other hand, a Supreme Court decision in Italy[17] has emphasized the importance of a substance-over-form analysis in determining whether a certain person should be regarded as having the authority to conclude contracts in the name of the foreign person. Even more so, the Supreme Court has taken the position that the 'authority to conclude contracts' will be deemed to also exist when a person based in Italy participates in the meetings in which negotiations take place, regardless of the role of such person.[18] This position seems to be in contrast with the OECD Model Commentary to Article 5 but is followed by the Italian higher courts and should not be ignored.

Hence, the question arises as to whether the interpretation of the Supreme Court on the 'authority to conclude contracts' is such that it implies that a commissionaire should normally constitute an agency PE in spite of the legal analysis. In fact, experience shows that, in the wake of the publication of the Final Report on Action 7, tax authorities will likely increase the scrutiny of commissionaire structures and allege the existence of a PE. However, concluding that a commissionaire is, by definition, an

17. See e.g. Italy's Supreme Court Decision 8488 of 9 Apr. 2010.
18. See the well-known *Philip Morris* Case, decided by the Italian Supreme Court Decisions 3368 of 7 Mar. 2002; 7682 of 25 May 2002.

agency PE would be a conclusion in breach of the definition of 'permanent establishment' as set forth under a number of domestic law regimes and the tax treaties concluded by a number of countries which invariably contain a clause reflecting the older version of Article 5(6) of the OECD Model Convention so that independent agents acting within the ordinary course of their business would not constitute a PE of their foreign principal.

However, in assessing dependency, the question is whether a commissionaire acting solely for one foreign principal, thus being economically exposed to a highly concentrated business risk, would have to be regarded as 'dependent' for purposes of the definition of 'permanent establishment'. While no express indication in this direction has been put forward by either case law or guidelines by the tax authorities, the new wording of paragraph 6 of Article 5 upheld the circumstance that when an agent is acting for only one principal is a strong, although not conclusive, indication that the agent is not economically independent.

Hence, an agent could be regarded as independent only if the contractual agreements, facts, and circumstances of the specific relationship were such that it could be demonstrated that the Italian agent is, by all means, acting independently regardless of the economic subjection to one single foreign principal (this would be the case, for example, of a commissionaire not acting under the instructions of the foreign principal (operational independence) or who could, in principle, also act on behalf of other principals without a breach of any legal agreements or without having to incur any major reconversion costs).

In conducting this analysis, the circumstance that the commissionaire may belong to the same group as the principal could basically be a major fact – in the post-BEPS world – that the entity is not independent for purposes of the exception of paragraph 6. Nevertheless, due distinction should be made between the 'influence' possibly exercised by foreign affiliates on the commissionaire as part of a group from the influence that may be exercised by the principal under the commissionaire relationship. In fact, in determining whether a certain person may constitute the PE of a foreign person, due regard should be applied only to the activities that the alleged agent performs for the benefit of the foreign principal that pertain to the business activity of the foreign principal.

Before moving on to the even trickier question related to the attribution of profits to a commissionaire deemed as an agency PE of its foreign principal, it is worth mentioning that judicial courts of different legal systems have dealt with the issue of whether or not (and to what extent) commissionaire structures create a PE.

The swinging mood which courts have shown over the years in regard to construing a commissionaire as a dependent agent PE of its foreign principal can be demonstrated by referencing a number of cases which confirm subtle bias in favor of a formal/legalistic interpretation of the arrangements aimed at upholding the avoidance of a taxable presence in the State of source. Within this line of reasoning, reference is made to the famous *Zimmer* and *Dell* cases, discussed – respectively – by the French[19] and Norwegian[20] courts.

In the *Zimmer* case, a distributor, Zimmer SAS, which was a related group company, decided to reorganize its business and, from 27 March 1995, Zimmer SAS commercialized Zimmer Limited's products in a commissionaire capacity under a commissionaire agreement. For these purposes, Zimmer SAS sold its assets, inventory, and the balance of the customer's receivables to Zimmer UK. The reorganization involved a reduction in assets, functions, and risks, which, pursuant to internationally recognized transfer pricing principles, resulted in a decrease in the taxable profits of Zimmer SAS in France from 1995 onwards.

The French tax authorities argued that Zimmer SAS constituted a PE of Zimmer Limited in France and assessed, in the hands of the UK company, French corporate income tax (plus a 10% surcharge) and business tax (taxe professionnelle) for the years 1995 and 1996. The UK company objected to the assessment and brought the case before the Court. The key issue was whether the commissionaire (Zimmer SAS) did or did not have authority to conclude contracts 'in the name of' the principal. Therefore, in addition to the other conditions of Article 4(5) of the France-United Kingdom Income Tax Treaty (1968) (equivalent to Article 5(5) of the OECD Model (2010)) being met, it was questioned whether it did constitute a dependent agent of its (UK) principal.

In a 2007 decision, the Paris Court of Appeals decided in favor of the tax authorities. In reaching its conclusion, the Court of Appeals used a substance-over-form approach according to which Zimmer SAS did, in fact, have the authority to bind the foreign principal. The Court noted that, under the commissionaire agreement, Zimmer SAS could accept orders, present estimates and documents within the framework of tender offers, and conclude sales contracts on Zimmer's account without prior approval. In addition, Zimmer SAS could negotiate prices as well as grant discounts and payment facilities to existing or new clients without the prior approval of Zimmer Limited.

According to the Court, the fact that Zimmer SAS acted in its own name as a result of the commissionaire agreement, and thereby could not conclude contracts in the name of Zimmer Limited, did not have any impact on its capacity to engage Zimmer Limited in commercial relationships related to Zimmer Limited's activities. The risks linked to the sales contracts were borne by Zimmer Limited, and Zimmer SAS acted exclusively on Zimmer Limited's account. In conclusion, the Court determined that Zimmer SAS could not be regarded as an independent agent within the meaning of Article 4(5) of the Treaty (i.e., Article 5(6) of the OECD Model (1995)).

The Conseil D'Etat, adopting a mere legalistic approach, dismissed the substance-over-form approach taken earlier by the Court of Appeals and overturned its decision. The Court referred to the definition of 'commissionaire' set out in the Commercial Code

19. See y B. Gouthière, Zimmer, *'Commissionaire' Agent is Not a Permanent Establishment*, European Taxation 50:8 (2010); It is interesting to note that this case sparked the debate within the WP1 to develop the Action 7 targeting commissionaire arrangements.
20. See NO: HS, 2 Dec. 2011, HR-2011-02245-A, *Dell Products v. The State (Tax East)*.

and held that a commissionaire cannot, in principle, constitute a PE of the principal based on the sole fact that, by executing the commissionaire agreement, the commissionaire sells the principals products or services in its own name on the principal's account. For an agency PE to exist, the principal must be personally bound by the contracts concluded by the commissionaire and third parties due to the commissionaire agreement itself or other elements.

According to the Court, since the contracts concluded by Zimmer SAS with its customers did not bind Zimmer Limited to those customers, Zimmer SAS did not constitute an agent of Zimmer Limited within the meaning of Article 4(4) of the Treaty irrespective of the degree of Zimmer SAS' (economic) dependence on Zimmer Limited. In addition, the Court stated that the premises and the staff of Zimmer SAS, which were at the disposal of Zimmer SAS for its commissionaire activities, did not constitute a fixed place of business within the meaning of Article 4(1) and (2) of the Treaty.

Interestingly enough, the *Zimmer* case seems to contradict a previous case of the French Supreme Administrative Court (Interhome)[21] in which the Supreme Administrative Court ruled that 'the exercise of the authority to bind the Swiss parent' could be determined by reference to a legal mandate (legally binding) or by reference to the actual circumstances (economically binding). This was exactly the reasoning that the Court of Appeals followed in its 2007 decision.

In *Zimmer*, the *Rapporteur Public* followed the case law of the Supreme Administrative Court and applied a static approach to the interpretation of tax treaties. Considering that the Treaty was signed in 1968, paragraph 32.1 of the OECD Commentary on Article 5(4) of the OECD Model (1995), which was added in 1995, should not be taken into account in interpreting the Treaty. It is not clear whether or not the Court would have followed a substance-over-form approach rather than a legal approach if the treaty in question had been signed after 1995.

For an agency PE to exist, the principal must be personally bound by the contracts concluded by the commissionaire and third parties due to the commissionaire agreement itself or other elements. In this respect, the tax administration has to prove that the commissionaire agreement has not, in fact, been respected, or that, although it is referred to as a commissionaire agreement, it is not, in fact, a true commissionaire agreement.

In the Norwegian *'Dell'* decision of the Norwegian Supreme Court (Høyesterett), the issue at stake was whether or not a Norwegian commissionaire can create an agency PE for the foreign principal.

Dell AS is a Norwegian tax resident company. Dell Products is incorporated in the Netherlands but is resident in Ireland for tax purposes. Both companies are subsidiaries within the Dell-group. Dell AS sells products in Norway as a commissionaire for Dell Products. The relationship between Dell Products and Dell AS is governed by the Norwegian Commission Act of 1916. According to this Act, agreements concluded by

21. See FR: CE, 20 Jun. 2003, No. 224407 sect., min. c/*Sté Interhome AG*.

the commissionaire with third parties are not legally binding for the principal, i.e., the customers do not have any legal rights towards the principal, only towards the commissionaire.

Dell AS was taxed in Norway on the income derived from the commissionaire business. The Norwegian tax authorities claimed that Dell AS constituted a dependent agent of Dell Products under Article 5(5) of the Ireland-Norway Income and Capital Tax Treaty (2000) and, therefore, Dell Products would be taxable in Norway. The case concerned the 2003-2006 tax years. The tax authorities chose not to assess Dell Products as a PE in 2007 due to an organizational change in 2007. In that year, the responsibility for the employees who worked for Dell Products was transferred from the parent company to Dell Products. The Supreme Court decided in favor of Dell Products and found that whether or not Dell Products had an agency PE in Norway, it had to be analyzed in relationship to Article 5(5) of the Ireland-Norway Income and Capital Tax Treaty (2000), which is identical to Article 5(5) of the OECD Model (in its 2010 format).

The core issue was whether Dell AS was '*acting on behalf of*' and had the '*authority to conclude contracts in the name of*' Dell Products. The tax authorities had put forward that the fact that the agreements concluded by Dell AS with third parties 'in reality' were binding for Dell Products was sufficient in itself to establish an agency PE. This claim was challenged by Dell Products who claimed that the existence of an agency PE required Dell Products to be 'legally bound' by the agreements concluded by Dell AS with third parties. The Supreme Court found that the presence of an agency PE under Article 5(5) of that tax treaty requires the principal to be 'legally bound' by the agreements concluded by the commissionaire with third parties.

According to the Supreme Court, the literal meaning of the expressions contained in Article 5(5) 'clearly indicates' that the principal must be legally bound by the contracts concluded by the commissionaire with third parties. While acknowledging that the OECD Commentaries, in principle, are to be given weight, the Supreme Court found that they do not provide any particular guidance in this case. The Court referred to paragraph 32.1 of the Commentary on Article 5(5) of the OECD Model (2010) and emphasized that, while the first part of the paragraph was inserted to give guidance on common law agency concepts, the second part of the paragraph discussed the evidence required to establish what is 'legal binding' for intermediates other than commissionaires.

The Supreme Court stated that the term 'commission' must be construed, pursuant to Article 3(2) of that treaty, in accordance with its meaning under Norwegian domestic law. The Court mentioned that the expressions used in Article 5(5) of that treaty are to be found in many other tax treaties. It would, therefore, be difficult to establish a reasonable uniform practice to apply a criterion other than 'legally bound'.

Finally, the Supreme Court also considered it relevant to take into account decisions from foreign courts, most notably the decision of the French Supreme Administrative Court in the *Zimmer* case. In this respect, the Supreme Court also made reference to the view of that Court, stating that '*there must be something in the contractual arrangements between the principal and the commissionaire other than the normal commission agreement for the commissionaire to be able to bind the principal in relation to third parties*'.

The Supreme Court seems to put considerable weight on the wording of Article 5(5) of the Ireland-Norway Income and Capital Tax Treaty (2000) which, in the court's view, 'clearly indicates' that the principal must be legally bound by the agreements concluded by the commissionaire with third parties for a PE to exist. The Supreme Court also makes reference to the domestic law meaning of the term 'commission' according to Article 3(2) of the treaty when defining the nature of the arrangement between Dell Products and Dell AS including whether Dell Products can be legally bound by the agreements concluded by Dell AS with third parties. In this respect, the Supreme Court interprets Article 3(2) in a manner that supports its decision on the principles of Norwegian domestic law, specifically the Norwegian Commission Act.

In 2000, the Norwegian Ministry of Finance issued a position paper on the taxation of Norwegian commissionaires of foreign principals concluding that the existence of a PE depends on an overall assessment of whether the principal 'in reality' is bound by the agreements concluded by the commissionaire with third parties. In a letter of 13 January 2012, the Norwegian Tax Directorate, not surprisingly, recognized that this view can no longer be sustained. However, in the same letter, the Norwegian Tax Directorate also concluded that the commissionaire structure cannot give rise to a Norwegian PE for the foreign principal even in cases where the only purpose of the commissionaire structure is to avoid Norwegian taxation. On the other hand, two cases concluded for the existence of a dependent agent PE created by the activities of an entity acting within the group as a commissionaire.

The Spanish Supreme Court decision of 2012 in *Roche Vitamins Europe Ltd* (later named *DSM Nutritional Products Europe Ltd*).[22]

The case relates to a business restructuring whereby significant functions, assets, and risks of a Spanish enterprise were reallocated to a Swiss related company acting as a principal entity. It should be pointed out that the Supreme Court decision cannot be properly understood unless detailed reference is made to the previous decisions of the Lower and Higher Courts, both confirmed but on different legal grounds.

The facts are as follows. The Roche group carried on its business in Spain through a subsidiary company called 'Roche Vitaminas', S.A. (hereinafter, 'Roche Spain') which imports, manufactures, and distributes products therein. In 1999, the Roche group implemented a business restructuring, shifting significant risks and functions associated with the manufacturing and distribution activities to Switzerland.

The new business model was documented in two agreements signed between Roche and DSM Nutritional Products Europe LTD ('DSM', previously, Roche Vitamins Europe LTD), a related Swiss company. According to the first agreement, Roche Spain is obliged to manufacture, in its own factory, the products ordered by DSM, which is the owner of the intangibles and the sole client of Roche. DSM also decides the

22. See, the decision of the Tribunal Supremo, 12 Jan. 2012, Roche, Case 1626/2008; available in the Tax Treaty Case Law IBFD; http://online.ibfd.org/collections/ttcls/html/cl_es_2012-01-12_1-summary.html?WT.z_nav=crosslinks#cl_es_2012_01_12_1 (accessed 23 Mar. 2016).

type and quantity of product to be manufactured by the Spanish related contract manufacturer. DSM is obliged to acquire the whole production. The purchase price between the two associated enterprises is established using the cost-plus method adding a 3.3% margin to manufacturing costs.

By means of the second contractual arrangement, Roche is designated as the 'promotion agent' of DSM's products in Spain and is obliged to represent, protect, and promote the commercial interests of DSM therein receiving, as consideration, 2% of DSM's turnover in Spain on top of the reimbursement of costs incurred to perform those activities. Roche Spain is actually in charge of marketing and logistics in Spain and manages some purchase orders. However, Roche Spain is neither entitled to accept any order nor agreement on behalf of DSM. Moreover, Roche Spain is not allowed to negotiate or change the sale conditions as DSM settles and negotiates all sale conditions and prices. It is important to underline that Roche Switzerland signs and accepts, in its own name, all sales agreements. Through the second agreement, DSM is also allowed to use a warehouse of Roche for an arm's length remuneration.

In 2003, the tax authorities assessed DSM a total amount, including late payment of interest, of EUR 1,420,256.94. The tax authorities relied on two arguments to determine the existence of a PE. First, in the light of the two agreements, there was a dependent agent relationship between Roche and DSM and, as a consequence, DSM carried on an economic activity in Spain through a PE. Second, based on a 'substance-over-form' approach, DSM is the only company that assumed an entrepreneurial risk and that truly carried on an economic activity in Spain by means of Roche's resources.

DSM launched an appeal against the decision of the tax authorities before the Lower Court in Madrid. In its 2006 decision,[23] the Lower Court analyzed the two agreements between DSM and Roche and, following a 'substance-over-form' approach, concluded that both manufacturing and promotion activities were, in fact, carried out by DSM and not by Roche since the former decided how the assets and human resources of the latter should be used for its own benefit and on the basis of an exclusivity agreement. The Lower Court thus considered that DSM bore the entrepreneurial risks and, therefore, carried out such activities through a physical PE under Article 5(1) of the Spain-Switzerland Income and Capital Tax Treaty (1966), i.e., the factory facilities owned by Roche.

DSM appealed the decision of the Lower Court before the High Court. In 2008, the High Court gave its decision[24] in which it confirmed the decision of the Lower Court and the existence of a PE of DSM in Spain. However, unlike the Lower Court, the High Court denied the existence of a physical PE since it considered that the sole fixed place at the disposal of DSM in Spain was the warehouse through which it carried out only auxiliary activities. The High Court, therefore, rejected the idea that Roche's factory facilities were to be regarded as DSM's physical PE.

Still, the High Court considered that the activities carried on by Roche (excepting the pure marketing services) gave rise to an agency PE of DSM under Article 5(4) of the Spain-Switzerland Income and Capital Tax Treaty (1966). The High Court expressly

23. See ES: TEAC, 20 Apr. 2006, Case No. 00/1979/2003.
24. ES: HC, 24 Jan. 2008, Case No. 894/2004.

acknowledged that its conclusion departs from the '*strict*' interpretation contained in the OECD Commentaries which would have led to the conclusion that Roche is not a dependent agent since it does not have any binding authority with respect to DSM.

According to the High Court, the wording '*to conclude contracts in the name of the enterprise*' in Article 5(5) of the OECD Model (1977), which the Court used to construe Article 5(4) of the treaty at issue even though that treaty followed the different wording contained in the OECD Draft (1963), does not entail an indispensable or sine qua non-condition for the existence of an agency PE. It is just one of the many different activities that a dependent agent may perform on behalf of its principal that substantially engages the foreign principal in business activities in Spain. Therefore, the *dependent* character of the agent may be due to an activity other than that of concluding contracts. The binding authority is regarded as an essential requirement only for the purposes of the activity of 'concluding contracts'.

Moreover, the High Court seemed to interpret Article 5(6) of the OECD Model as a negative rule that complements Article 5(5) in such a way that every agent that cannot be considered as 'independent' on the grounds of Article 5(6) must then be considered a 'dependent' agent giving rise to an agency PE. The High Court stated that the 'independence' must be analyzed on a case-by-case basis regarding the legal, economic, and functional aspects of the principal-agent relationship. Due to the specific circumstances of the case, the High Court concluded that Roche had to be regarded as a dependent agent.

The *dependent* nature of the manufacturing and distribution activities performed by Roche was based, according to the Court, on the exclusive client relationship and on the fact that the entrepreneurial risks were assumed by DSM. The *substantial involvement* of DSM in the business activities in Spain was due to the fact that the promotional and manufacturing activities performed on its behalf by Roche were regarded as essential and not as preparatory or auxiliary. In this respect, the High Court considered that both the promotional and the manufacturing activities performed by Roche entailed an active and intense involvement of DSM in business activities in Spain, thus giving rise to an agency PE therein.

As to the (arguably more important) issue associated with the attribution of profits to the Spanish PE, the High Court found that a limited 'force of attraction' was deemed to exist and stipulated that, even though some of the activities performed by the dependent agent could not be regarded as giving rise to a PE (namely, the distribution activities), once the existence of the PE is confirmed, all profits that may derive from the different activities of the dependent agent must be attributed to it.

DSM decided to appeal the High Court decision to the Spanish Supreme Court. On 12 January 2012, the Supreme Court rejected the appeal and confirmed the decision of the lower courts. The Supreme Court acknowledged that there are only two circumstances in which a PE may exist, i.e., if there is a fixed place through which the enterprise wholly or partly carries out its business or if the enterprise acts through a person with authority to conclude contracts in its name. However, the Supreme Court confirmed both the High Court and the Lower Court decisions, acknowledging that each of them relied on different legal grounds (physical PE versus agency PE). In this regard, the Supreme Court basically supported the arguments included in both decisions. The Supreme Court also supported the High Court's ambulatory analysis pursuant to which Article 5(4) of the tax treaty, concluded in 1966, was interpreted in the light of the wording of Article 5(5) of the OECD Model (1977). Finally, the Supreme Court also confirmed the attribution to the Agency PE of profits related to marketing activities.

Notwithstanding the above, the interpretation of the High Court does not correspond to the wording of either Article 5(5) of the OECD Model (1977) or Article 5(4) of the OECD Draft (1963) as it is clear from both texts that the authority to conclude contracts is a fundamental condition for an agency PE to be deemed as existing. It is also remarkable that neither the High Court nor the Supreme Court made any reference in their analysis to decisions issued by the Supreme Courts of other OECD member countries (such as those discussed in this chapter).

This ambulatory approach was also followed by the High Court in justifying the attribution to the agency PE of profits derived from activities (marketing activities) that were not performed by Roche itself in its role as a dependent agent. However, such a limited 'force of attraction' was not envisaged in the wording of the OECD Draft (1963) or its Commentaries.

Another interesting judgment has been delivered by the Italian Supreme Court Decision No. 3769, heard on 29 February 2012 and deposited on 9 March 2012 related to the *Boston Scientific Group* case.[25]

BS IT was a company incorporated in Italy. It was 99% owned by the direct parent company BS NL, and the remaining 1% was owned by the ultimate parent company BS US. Boston Scientific Group is a worldwide developer, manufacturer, and distributor of technologically advanced medical devices. The group manufactures such medical devices in the United States and sells them worldwide. The distribution activities in Europe are undertaken by BS NL which buys the products from the US manufacturing company and acts as a principal for the sale thereof by entering into commissionaire agreements with subsidiaries in various European markets. These subsidiaries are engaged in the marketing and distribution of the above-mentioned medical devices acting in their own name but on behalf of BS NL. As consideration for their activity, the subsidiaries are remunerated on the basis of commissionaire agreements. Apart from being their direct parent company, BS NL was the only principal of the subsidiaries.

On the basis of some functional interviews with several key employees, it became apparent that BS IT was required to observe specific instructions contained in the Boston Scientific group guidelines. Moreover, a letter of patronage issued by BS NL stated that BS IT '*management falls under our direct control and responsibility*'. According to the Italian Tax Authority, these facts were sufficient to claim that BS IT was directly managed by BS NL.

In its capacity as an agent, BS IT was directly sending the clients' purchase orders (by way of an automatic software procedure) to a central depository owned by BS NL: shipment was undertaken by this latter company. According to the Italian tax authori-

25. See Italy's Supreme Court Decision, 9 Mar. 2012, Decision No. 3769.

ties, the fact that BS NL routinely approved the transactions was tantamount to a lack of active involvement on the part of this latter company. However, any complaint by Italian clients was to be addressed to BS IT without BS NL being directly affected.

It was found that BS IT was directly entering into contracts with reference to certain assets owned by BS NL. As the medical devices sold by BS NL required the use of specific machinery, BS NL provided such machinery to clients (e.g., hospitals); sometimes, the machinery was granted for free and other times against the payment of a consideration. Eventually, it was BS IT that eventually decided whether or not to charge the clients for the use of the machinery owned by BS NL and also signed contracts on behalf of this latter company in order to accelerate the contracts signature. Moreover, BS IT autonomously entered into factoring transactions concerning certain trade receivables owned by BS NL without recharging the expenses to this latter company. In addition, BS IT contributed to the group's general expenses (with no consideration), relating to strategic marketing and European civil liability insurance on behalf of the agents.

As both the provincial and the regional tax court had ruled in favor of the taxpayer, the Supreme Court had to decide on an appeal launched by the tax authorities whose claim touched on the following issues:

(1) Independence under Article 5(6) of the OECD Model (2010).
(2) The extent to which an agent must bind its principal to fall under Article 5(5) of the OECD Model (2010).
(3) The scope of the 'ordinary course of their own business under Article 5(6) of the OECD Model (2010).

Under the first part of the claim, the tax authorities alleged that BS IT should not have been considered independent from BS NL on the basis of the following facts and circumstances:

(1) BS NL was the controlling shareholder of BS IT.
(2) In an interview with the sales director of certain divisions of BS IT, the latter had stated that 'the Boston group' was directly involved in how the activity of BS IT was carried out.
(3) In an interview with the general manager of BS IT, the latter had stated that the company 'was due to observe specific instructions provided by the Boston Scientific group guidelines'; a circumstance incompatible with the autonomy of an independent person.
(4) A letter of patronage issued by BS NL stated that BS IT 'management falls under our direct control and responsibility'.
(5) BS NL was the sole principal of BS IT (under paragraph 38.6 of the Commentary on Article 5 of the OECD Model (2010); independent status is less likely if the activities of the agent are performed on behalf of only one enterprise.

Under the second part of the claim, the tax authorities alleged that BS IT habitually exercised powers that allowed it to conclude contracts in the name of BS NL.

According to the tax authorities, such a circumstance did not require BS IT to be granted formal representation powers; the authority was not to be assessed under a strictly civil law point of view but under an economic criterion (substance-over-form). For an agent operating in Italy to be concluding contracts that are binding on the foreign enterprise, it is not necessary that such contracts be effectively entered into 'in the name of' such an enterprise. In this respect, the fact that BS NL routinely approved the transaction orders sent by BS IT was tantamount to a lack of active involvement on the part of the principal even if the agent was acting in its own name.

Under the third part of the claim, the tax authorities alleged that BS IT had been exceeding the scope of the 'ordinary course of their own business under Article 5(6) of the OECD Model (2010) and paragraph 38.7 of Commentary on Article 5 of the OECD Model (2010).

The Supreme Court rejected all three prongs of the tax authorities' position.

The first claim was dismissed by the judges on the basis that all the factual elements appeared to have been adequately considered by the Regional (appeals) Tax Court based in particular on the claim that the criterion of independence is not jeopardized by a parent-subsidiary link even if the parent is involved in the management of an agent, and the parent is the sole principal of the agent.

By dismissing the tax authorities' claim on the grounds of inadequacy, the Italian Supreme Court has managed to avoid addressing the merits of the case on the basis of an inadequate formulation by the tax authorities' position. Having said that, such a case in a post-BEPS scenario could have presented valid arguments to be won by the tax administration in light of the more substantive approach rather than a formalistic one by the tax administrations.

IV. ATTRIBUTION OF PROFITS TO PES: CURRENT GUIDANCE AND FUTURE DEVELOPMENTS

The purpose of this section is to understand to what extent the guidance included in the Authorised OECD Approach (the 'AOA') for the attribution of profits to a PE is applicable with respect to the new approach on commissionaire arrangements in the wake of the publication of Action 7 of the 2015 Report.

In this respect, the legal formulation of the basic treaty rule applicable for determining the profits attributable to a PE have not significantly changed since 1933. On the one hand, according to Article 7(2) of the existing OECD Model, the business profits that are attributable to a PE are those that the PE '*might be expected to make … if it were a separate and independent enterprise engaged in the same or similar activities under the same or similar conditions*'. On the other hand, Article 3 of the 1933 League of Nations' draft multilateral convention[26] referred to the profits that the PE '*might be expected to derive if it were an independent enterprise engaged in the same or similar activities under the same or similar conditions*'.

26. See League of Nations Fiscal Committee, *Report to the Council on the Fourth Session of the Committee*, C.399.M.204. 1933.II.A, Geneva, 15-26 Jun. 1933.

Although the wording of the basic rule has remained almost unchanged for almost a century, countries have adopted different views when interpreting and applying it thereby creating risks of double taxation and non-taxation. The last OECD efforts towards clarifying how the basic rule should be applied have resulted in the development of the AOA which began in 1998 and was finalized in 2008 and resulted in the 2010 Report on the Attribution of Profits to PEs (the '2010 Attribution of Profits Report'). This Report deals with the attribution of profits to PEs in general (Part I) but focuses particularly on PEs in the financial sector (Part II applicable to banks, Part III applicable to global trading, and Part IV applicable to insurance).

Based on the above, it is important to underline that relatively few treaties currently include the new version of Article 7 which was included in the OECD Model in 2010. Through reservations and positions included in the OECD Model, a number of OECD and non-OECD countries have expressly stated their intention to not include the new version of Article 7 in their treaties.[27] Moreover, the inclusion of the new version of the Article in the UN Model Tax Convention (and, therefore, the implementation of the full AOA with respect to Article 7 of the UN Model) has been expressly rejected by the UN Committee of Experts on International Cooperation in Tax Matters primarily because of the differences in the wording of paragraph 3 of Article 7 of the UN Model.

That paragraph includes two sentences that expressly address the issue of notional interest, royalties, and service charges related to dealings between the PE and the rest of the enterprise. The first sentence prohibits the deduction of any profit margin related to such internal transfers (except in the case of notional interest for banking enterprises) in determining the profits of the PE while the second sentence conversely provides that no profit margin should be included in determining such profits with respect to such transfers originating from the PE.

For the sake of this contribution, the 2010 Attribution of Profits Report contains guidance on how to apply Article 7 of the OECD MTC. The 2010 Attribution of Profits Report adopts the AOA as the mechanism to determine the amount of profit that may be taxed in the host country of the PE. The AOA was originally conceived for attributing profits to PEs in the financial sector but was subsequently adapted to have general application. The AOA uses analogy transfer pricing principles, and the Preface to the 2010 Attribution of Profits Report acknowledges that the Transfer Pricing Guidelines are periodically updated and requires that the 2010 Attribution of Profits Report should be applied by taking into account the guidance in the Guidelines as modified from time to time.

Therefore, the AOA approach has to inevitably take into account the revised transfer pricing guidance on risk, capital, and intangibles developed under BEPS Actions 8, 9, and 10 and particularly the revisions to Chapter I of the Transfer Pricing Guidelines which illustrate how to perform a comparability (including functional) analysis.

27. See the reservations of Chile, Greece, Mexico, New Zealand, Portugal, and Turkey in paras. 95, 96, and 97 of the Commentary on Article 7 as well as the positions of Argentina, Brazil, China, India, Indonesia, Latvia, Malaysia, Romania, Serbia, South Africa, Thailand, and Hong Kong in paras. 1, 1.1, and 1.2 of the positions on Article 7.

To this end, the definitional changes made to Article 5 and to the Commentary in the 2015 Report to the dependent agent PE issue involving commissionaire and similar arrangements require an analysis of these arrangements under the lenses of both Articles 7 and 9 of the OECD MTC to assess whether the two provisions lead to the same or differing results in light of the implementation of the BEPS Actions 8, 9, and 10 deliverables. The subject has been discussed previously by WP6 prior to the 2015 changes to Article 5 to the OECD MTC. In the framework of the business restructuring project (leading to the introduction of a new Chapter IX in the 2010 version of the OECD TPG), the WP6 attempted to provide guidance on the application of the AOA to a Dependent Agent Permanent Establishment (DAPE) arising from a sales agency agreement between two associated enterprises. However, WP6 postponed this work stream awaiting finalization by WP6 of the project on business restructuring and finalization by WP1 of its previous work on PE threshold issues.

A. Analysis under Article 7 and Article 9 of the OECD MTC: Key Considerations

In terms of the general process, there is arguably a clear distinction between Articles 7 and 9 of the OECD MTC. According to Article 7, in order to conduct an analysis under the AOA for purposes of Article 7 MTC and attribute profits to the DAPE, a two-step approach should be followed, namely requiring:

(1) Under Step one: hypothesizing the PE as a separate and independent enterprise by performing a functional and factual analysis. Such analysis will determine the attribution of economic ownership of assets, economic ownership of risks, attribution of free capital, and the recognition of dealings.
(2) Under Step two: determining the profits of the hypothesized separate and independent enterprise based upon a comparability analysis applying, by analogy the Transfer Pricing Guidelines.

Under the new guidance provided for by Section D of Chapter I of the Transfer Pricing Guidelines, the general approach requires the so-called real deal approach, i.e., the accurate delineation of the actual transaction or transactions between associated enterprises requires an analysis of the economically relevant characteristics of the transactions which are: contractual terms of the transaction, functional analysis (including risks and assets), characteristics of property or services, economic circumstances, and business strategies.

Some interesting observations already arise at this stage as, in the context of Article 7 OECD MTC, we are legally talking about one single enterprise (of which the PE is an administrative ramification and a 'tax fiction') whereas, in the context of Article 9, we are looking at analyzing the tax ramifications arising between two separate independent enterprises. However, despite the strong opposition of some tax administrations (with specific reference to the United States), it is possible to record a closer alignment of the approach between the two provisions by already looking at some carefully selected terminology in the new Chapter I of the TP Guidelines. I am referring in particular to the notion of 'economically relevant characteristics', a term commonly deployed in the 2010 AOA Report,[28] which is now utilized as a synonym to refer to the notion of comparability factors.[29]

In regard to the approach related to *attribution of assets*, the most striking difference between Articles 7 and 9 of the OECD MTC relates to the concept of economic ownership which serve, in my view, two entirely different aims under the two provisions. To this end, under the AOA (Article 7), the factual position is that no one part of an enterprise own assets as they belong to the enterprise as a whole. In this respect, under the AOA, it is necessary to attribute economic ownership of the assets entailing that, where a PE is treated as the economic owner of an asset, it will typically be entitled to deductions for depreciation and interest; if the PE is treated as a lessee, it will typically be entitled to deductions in the nature of rent.

The attribution of economic ownership of assets is relevant for purposes of attributing capital (free capital and interest-bearing funding) to the PE whereas tangible assets should be attributed based on 'use'. While this is the default rule, the 2010 Attribution of Profits Report also indicates that there may be circumstances in a particular case that warrant a different view, therefore, when appropriate economic ownership of tangible property may be determined based on significant people functions.

On the other hand, under Article 9 of the OECD MTC, the notion of 'economic ownership' – unlike to what has been stated in the United Nations Practical Manual on Transfer Pricing for developing countries[30] – it has been somewhat banned from the transfer pricing jargon applicable to separate independent enterprises in order to avoid that some countries (in particular those representing the developing world) would have claimed the entitlement to profits greater than those attributable to routine functions in all instances where intangibles were exploited for commercial purposes.

I do believe that, conceptually, the notion of 'economic ownership' (referred to in other OECD papers as 'intangible related return'[31]) refers to the opportunity for an associated enterprise to share in the residual return attributable to functions performed, assets used, and risks assumed which exceed those attributable to an independent third party enterprise. On the other hand, it seems that the guidance on

28. See reference to Part I of the 2010, para. 17.
29. See new para. 1.36 of Chapter I TPG as published by the BEPS Report on Action 8-9-10.
30. See Chapter V, para. 5.3.2.15, whereby it is stated that:

> [...] in some cases an enterprise which does not have legal ownership of an intangible may nevertheless be entitled to a share of the returns from its exploitation. Some countries refer to this notion as 'economic ownership.

31. See Section B, para. 65, of the Revised Discussion Draft on the Transfer Pricing aspects of Intangibles, where it is stipulated that:

> although the legal owner of an intangible may initially be entitled to receive the proceeds from exploitation or transfer of the intangible, other members of the owner's MNE group may have performed functions, used or contributed assets, or assumed risks that are anticipated to contribute to the value of the intangible and for which they must be compensated under the arm's length principle.

risk has been somewhat aligned between the two provisions. To this end, if we start by analyzing the attribution of risks under the AOA approach, it is worth noting that, in the context of a PE and its head office, it is the enterprise as a whole which legally bears the risk.

Under the AOA, it is possible to treat the PE as assuming risk even though, legally, the enterprise as a whole assumes the risk, and there can be no legally binding contractual arrangements allocating that risk to a particular part of the enterprise. To this end, the attribution and measurement of risk affects the attribution of capital under Step One of the authorized OECD approach since capital follows risks. The part of the enterprise that performs the significant people functions relevant to the assumption of risks (or that performs the significant people functions relevant to taking over and managing a risk initially assumed by another part of the enterprise) would be attributed to the capital necessary to support these risks. The attribution and measurement of risk also affects the attribution of profits to the PE under the Second Step as the selection and application of a transfer pricing method will take into account risks assumed by the PE and by other parts of the enterprise it has dealings with.

The PE should be considered as assuming any risks for which the significant people functions relevant to the assumption of risk are performed by the personnel of the PE at the PE's location. The significant people functions relevant to the assumption of risks are those which require active *decision-making* with regard to the acceptance and/or management (subsequent to the transfer) of those risks. The extent of the decision-making will depend on the nature of the risk involved. Therefore, this can be a highly fact-specific exercise (see paragraphs 22-26 of the 2010 Attribution of Profits Report).

Under the new guidance in Chapter I of the OECD TP Guidelines, the arm's length allocation of risks first requires to applying the six-step framework,[32] based on the new Chapter I (paragraph 1.60).

In particular, it is necessary to:

(1) *First step*: identify the economically significant risks with specificity;
(2) *Second step*: determine how specific, economically significant risks are contractually assumed by the associated enterprises under the terms of the transaction;
(3) *Third step*: determine through a functional analysis how the parties in a controlled transaction operate in relationship to assumption and management of risks;
(4) *Fourth step*: determine whether the contractual assumption of risk is consistent with the conduct of the parties by analyzing whether: (i) the associated enterprises follow the contractual terms under the principles of Section D.1.1; and, (ii) the party assuming risk as analyzed under (i) exercises control over the risk and has the financial capacity to assume the risk;

32. See new para. 1.60 of Chapter I of the TPG whereby.

(5) *Fifth step*: where the party assuming the risk under Steps 1-4(i) does not control the risk or does not have the financial capacity to assume the risk, then the risk should be allocated to the enterprise that does. If multiple associated enterprises are identified as doing so, then the risk should be allocated to the associated enterprise or group of associated enterprises exercising the most control. The other parties performing control activities should be remunerated appropriately by taking into account the importance of the control activities performed (Chapter I, paragraph 1.98). In exceptional circumstances, it may be the case that no associated enterprise can be identified that both exercises control over the risk and has the financial capacity to assume the risk. As such a situation is not likely to occur in transactions between third parties, a rigorous analysis of the facts and circumstances of the case will need to be performed in order to identify the underlying reasons and actions that led to this situation. Based on that assessment, the tax administrations will determine what adjustments to the transaction are needed for it to result in an arm's length outcome. An assessment of the commercial rationality of the transaction may be necessary (see Chapter I OECD TPG, paragraph 1.99); and

(6) *Sixth step*: price the actual transaction as accurately delineated, taking into consideration the financial and other consequences of risk assumption as appropriately allocated and suitably compensating risk management functions.

In light of the above, it seems that the linkage between the two provisions regarding the attribution/allocation of risks is given by the conceptual similarity between: (i) the notion of 'active decision-making' needed to identify the notion of significant people functions under Article 7 with accuracy and; (ii) the notion of 'management of risk' and control over risk now defined in the 2015 Report on Actions 8, 9, and 10 as [...] ' the capability to make decisions to take on, lay off, or decline a risk-bearing opportunity, together with the actual performance of that decision-making function; and (iii) the capability to make decisions on whether and how to respond to the risks associated with the opportunity, together with the actual performance of that decision-making function. It is not necessary for a party to perform the day-to-day mitigation, as described in (iii) in order to have control of the risks'.[33]

From a practical standpoint, this entails that the notion of control over risk which, in the 2010 version, was a factor to retrieve only in those instances where comparable third-party transactions were lacking now becomes a key component of the six-step approach needed to accurately delineate the economic features of the transaction. It seems to me that this notion resembles, from a substantive standpoint, the same type of analysis required to assess the active decision-making needed to identify where the significant people functions are performed under Article 7 of the OECD MTC.

33. See para. 1.65 of the 2015 BEPS report on Actions 8-9-10 on new Chapter I of the TP Guidelines.

In conclusion, the AOA under Article 7 of the OECD MTC uses the concept of 'significant people functions' for purposes of attributing economic ownership of assets and risks and Article 9 of the OECD MTC Transfer Pricing Guidelines deploys the concepts of 'control over risk' or 'performance and control of functions related to the development, enhancement, protection, or exploitation' in the case of transactions involving the use or exploitation of intangibles. The latter notions are used to determine the assumption of risk and to determine the remuneration of the parties in transactions involving intangibles, respectively.

Example:

The following example - related to attribution of profits to a commissionaire - highlights whether the same or diverging results may be achieved in the event the same fact pattern is analyzed under Article 7 or 9 of the OECD MTC.

Assume the following fact pattern:

Macu is a company resident in Country X. It manufactures widgets in Country X. Macu's widgets are sold to customers worldwide and, in order to do so, Macu uses a network of sales agents. Macu has no physical presence in the countries where its products are sold.

Tedco is a company resident in Country Y acting as a dependent agent for the foreign enterprise Macu. Tedco is engaged by Macu to perform selling activities in Country Y for Macu. It is assumed that, based on the terms of the agreement between Macu and Tedco, the activities performed by Tedco for Macu give rise to a DAPE of Macu in Country Y.

For purposes of this example, Macu and Tedco are associated enterprises. Macu agrees to remunerate Tedco with a sales commission to reward the functions performed by Tedco that is numerically equivalent to a mark-up on the costs incurred by Tedco in providing the agreed services to Macu.

In particular, Tedco acts as a sales agent for Macu under a commissionaire arrangement which involves the following terms and responsibilities:

- Tedco identifies customers, solicits and places customers' orders, and processes customers' orders with Macu.
- Macu decides the marketing strategy and advertising content. Tedco implements the marketing strategy in Country Y and is reimbursed by Macu for all expenses incurred in placing local advertising for the products.
- Macu retains title to the inventory until it is delivered to customers. Macu is responsible for warehousing the inventory and determining the inventory levels of the products to fulfill customers' orders.
- Macu is responsible for arranging and deciding the timing and mode of delivery of the products to customers, and
- Macu manages the credit risk, i.e., Macu legally bears credit risk with respect to customer deliverables, and it also pre-approves every sale to customers made in Country Y after reviewing the client's creditworthiness. Macu also handles collection of customer receivables.

- Tedco's remuneration for services provided to Macu in Country y is determined by means of a cost-plus 10%.

If we consider this fact pattern under *Article 7* of the OECD MTC, there are no profits to be attributed to the dependent agent of Macu in Country Y as there are no functions performed in the host territory other than the functions performed by TedCo for its own account as a sales agent. On the other hand, if we look at the very same fact pattern under the guidance in the new Section D of Chapter I of the TP Guidelines under *Article 9*, the starting point of any transfer pricing analysis is the examination of the contractual terms of the transaction taking into account the further information provided by the other economically relevant characteristics.

In the case at stake, it is observed that the contractual arrangement is one under which Macu appoints Tedco as its sales agent to provide stated service levels. The functional analysis further finds that Macu is the legal owner and controls the risks associated with inventory, marketing intangibles, and receivables and has the financial capacity to assume these risks.

In this example, the contractual assumption of risk is aligned with control of risk, and the sales agent functions of Tedco would be priced taking into account the economically relevant factors. In this example, it is assumed that the arm's length price is determined to be a fee equivalent to cost-plus 10% for Tedco.

V. (TENTATIVE CONCLUSIONS): SHOULD THE DIFFERENT APPROACHES LEAD TO THE SAME OUTCOME?

The analysis carried out shows that the likely outcome of Action 7 is a bias towards a more substantive/economic approach rather than a mere legalistic one. This holds true in particular for the issue of attribution of profits to the commissionaire where, despite the difference of the use of certain concepts (such as that of economic ownership), the economic results tend to align in light of the more nuanced approach required with respect to the analysis on risk as introduced in the new Chapter I of the TP Guidelines. In other words, a variety of results may occur depending on the interpretation of the risk approaches followed by Articles 7 and 9 of the OECD MTC which seem to be closer than ever after the publication of Actions 8-9-10 and 7 of the BEPS Report.

Having said that, it should be noted that a distinction still exists today between these two provisions that can be linked to the contractual allocation of risks. In particular, under an Article 9 scenario, it is undisputable that the risks held by the dependent agent enterprise contractually have to stay with the latter company and not be translated to the DAPE. Should such an assertion be held disputable under Article 7 of the OECD MTC (as under Step 1 of the current AOA, the risks are attributed to the DAPE for purposes of attributing profits to it), a vicious logical circle is created under the new wording of Article 5(6) which could defy the entire attribution of profits exercise. In other words, should the commissionaire (or limited-risk distributor) be attributed actually more significant risks than those allocated contractually, room would exist for a logical interpretation whereby the commissionaire is not acting in the name of the foreign enterprise, but in its own name, therefore dismissing *ab initio* the entire logical analysis under Article 7 of the OECD MTC. Such an approach requires a reading of Article 9 as logically (and hierarchically) preceding the analysis of Article 7 vis-à-vis Article 5 which would require some clarification at the level of the OECD commentary.

Against this background, it is now time to make some considerations on the approach that the author believes is – if not the more correct – the one that produces more logical results. The most logical approach seems to derive from a sum of different factors. First, the definitions used in the risk approach of the PE Report and in the TP Guidelines seem much more aligned than in the past.

Second, if a distinction between the two provisions wants to be retained, a hierarchy between Article 9 and Article 7 should be recognized. More in particular, if Article 9 of the OECD MTC is recognized as a more specialized provision that should not be affected by the rules of Article 7, the arm's length remuneration paid to the subsidiary will not change because such an entity is also a dependent agent. Thus, under the assumption that the transfer pricing analysis was correctly made and the remuneration to be paid to the subsidiary already took into consideration all the risks borne by it, there will be no profit left to be attributed to a PE, if it were found to exist.

Allowing a hierarchy between the provisions avoids a recalculation of the profits to be attributed to the host country – solely for purposes of splitting them between two entities – but does not interfere with the taxing rights of such a jurisdiction as it will still be able to tax exactly the same amount of income arising from the controlled transaction.

CHAPTER 8

Transfer Pricing and Documentation Requirements

Christian Kaeser & Sven Bremer

I. INTRODUCTION

A. International Transfer Pricing Documentation on the Rise

Over the last twenty years, the documentation of transfer prices accompanied by the standardization of Transfer Pricing Documentation (TPD) requirements has been given increased importance in many countries.[1] The proliferation of diverse local TPD rules has made it necessary to create a uniform international standard to reduce both the compliance costs for businesses and potential transfer pricing disputes arising from divergent documentation requirements and inconsistent documentation. However, previous initiatives to standardize TPD have, for several reasons, not fully met the needs of either taxpayers or tax administrations. The most recent harmonization efforts require that new standards for TPD must be developed that enhance transparency for tax administration while taking into consideration the compliance costs for Multinational Enterprises (MNEs).

B. Evaluation of the Current Record-Keeping Obligations

By and large, the vast majority of MNEs can be said to have now accepted the statutory record-keeping obligations. However, criticism can still be levied at the multitude of terms in existence and the abundance of concepts requiring interpretation whose application – as experience shows – frequently leads to disputes in tax audits. This is compounded by the international development and the incredibly explosive increase in documentation standards, especially in developing countries and emerging markets. In industry countries' tax audits, this is leading almost instinctively to a more aggressive inspection, particularly of arm's length documentation. Here, MNEs are caught between having to comply with domestic legislation and also comply with the diverse foreign documentation requirements that are not coordinated internationally and are hence exposed to the unilateral desire for a 'fair' piece of the tax pie.

II. INTERNATIONAL DEVELOPMENTS

A. International Harmonization Efforts

For quite some time now, efforts have been made to harmonize TPD for MNEs in an attempt to avoid costly duplicative work derived from the multiplicity of documentation regulations.

1. OECD, *White Paper on Transfer Pricing Documentation*, Public Consultation, 30 Jul. 2013 (2013), p. 2.

B. Publication of the OECD Transfer Pricing Guidelines in 1995

In 1994, the United States became the first country to introduce documentation regulations for intra-group transfer pricing[2] combined with penalties in the event that transfer pricing turned out to be inadequate and documentation requirements were not complied with. The introduction of penalties led to concerns in other countries that multinational enterprises would henceforth disclose profits primarily in the United States in order to satisfy the IRS. In 1995, the Organisation for Economic Co-operation and Development (OECD) accentuated these fears in its Transfer Pricing Guidelines for Multinational Enterprises and Tax Administrations (OECD TPG) which urge all OECD Member States to observe the principle of proportionality.[3]

1. *Chapter V of the OECD Transfer Pricing Guidelines*

The OECD Transfer Pricing Guidelines (TPG) address TPD in a separate chapter, Chapter V.[4] However, the OECD countries declined to provide an exhaustive list of documents to be included in a TPD package. The TPG merely outline the procedure for furnishing evidence and provide general indications about information and documentation that might be useful.

2. *Importance of the OECD TPG*

The OECD TPG represent a compromise of the OECD members.[5] Strictly speaking, the OECD TPG do not have any direct legal effect. Nonetheless, they do have some significance for the national law of the OECD members even though, according to current knowledge, there are virtually no countries in which the OECD proposals for documentation are enshrined in law; rather, they are part of administrative instructions and pronouncements by the competent national authorities.

Some countries, for example, directly transpose the OECD TPG into national law through national regulations. Others are unmistakably guided by the OECD TPG in their national transfer pricing rules, e.g., the records that are required under German law (§ 90 (3) of the German Tax Code and related German Regulation) largely correspond to the proposals in Chapter V of the OECD TPG.[6]

---

2. See Section 482 of the US Internal Revenue Code, 1994 Final Transfer Pricing Regulations of the United States; See also OECD, *White Paper on Transfer Pricing Documentation*, Public Consultation, 30 Jul. 2013 (2013), p. 7.
3. OECD, *Transfer Pricing Guidelines for Multinational Enterprises and Tax Administrators*, Committee on Fiscal Affairs, OECD, Paris (1995).
4. OECD, *Transfer Pricing Guidelines for Multinational Enterprises and Tax Administrations*, Chapter V: Documentation, Publication Date: 18 Aug. 2010 (2010).
5. See Abstract of OECD Transfer Pricing Guidelines: '*The OECD Transfer Pricing Guidelines for Multinational Enterprises and Tax Administrations Provide Guidance on the Application of the "Arm's Length Principle", Which Is the International Consensus on Transfer Pricing*' (accessed 15 Mar. 2016).
6. See Section 90 para. 3 of the German Tax Code.

Although the OECD TPG can generally be considered a starting point for most national regulations, significant differences between the individual national requirements persist in some cases. This situation is less than ideal for MNEs which are understandably keen to ensure that, as much as possible, documentation prepared for one country can also be used and accepted in another country. In this respect, it is desirable for MNEs that the broadest possible consensus is reached among the individual countries regarding documentation requirements. Similar approaches to standardization can be found not only in the OECD but also among the members of the Pacific Association of Tax Administrators (PATA)[7] – Australia, Canada, Japan, and the United States. The European Union (EU) has likewise stepped up its efforts in this regard under the rubric of the EU Joint Transfer Pricing Forum.[8]

C. PATA

On 12 March 2003, the PATA members attempted to synchronize national TPD regulations. However, the objective of the planned multilateral synchronization of the national TPD obligations is not actually to standardize these documentation requirements but to merely create uniform minimum documentation standards with the (sole) effect that an MNE that complies with these standards in all participating countries is no longer exposed to documentation-related penalties. Yet, the documentation regulations of the individual PATA members differ substantially in scope. This may lead to a taxpayer having to provide more information than required in one country and less in another in order to comply with the minimum standards.

D. EU Code of Conduct

On 10 November 2005, the European Commission adopted a proposal for a Code of Conduct on TPD for associated enterprises in the European Union (EU TPD) that would standardize and partially centralize the TPD that multinational enterprises must provide to tax authorities since, despite the OECD recommendations, the regulations of the EU Member States vary considerably in some cases with regard to the content and structure of TPD.

The EU TPD consists of two main parts: one set of documentation containing common standardized information (the 'master file') and several sets of standardized documentation each containing country-specific information (the 'country-specific documentation') that businesses file with tax administrations in order to report on their pricing for cross-border intra-group activities.[9] The regulations are non-binding for the

7. PATA, Pacific Association of Tax Administrators, *Transfer Pricing Documentation Package*, https://www.nta.go.jp/kohyo/katsudou/shingi-kenkyu/kokusai020617/pdf/01.pdf (accessed 15 Mar. 2016).
8. For more information to the EU Joint Transfer Pricing Forum see http://ec.europa.eu/taxation_customs/taxation/company_tax/transfer_pricing/forum/index_en.htm (accessed 15 Mar. 2016).
9. OECD, *White Paper on Transfer Pricing Documentation, Public Consultation*, 30 Jul. 2013 (2013), p. 8.

Member States; however, each, individual EU Member State must decide on the implementation or form of implementation of the EU TPD at the national level.

E. Evaluation of the Initiatives to Date

In October 2012, the European Commission reviewed the acceptance of the proposed Code of Conduct, concluding that most non-governmental organizations had opted to use the Code of Conduct informally and selectively. In other words, in practice, similar to the PATA initiative, the EU TPD did not achieve the level of importance initially hoped for. There are a variety of reasons for this. For one, there is a lack of acceptance outside the participating EU Member States or PATA countries. For another, complying with the recommendations does not protect taxpayers from being penalized. In addition, the PATA approach assumes a higher level of documentation than the national documentation regulations of the PATA countries.

Even though the OECD elaborations are considered extremely important in international practice, the existing requirements of different countries reveal substantive and formal differences in the general conditions and transfer pricing regulations. Countries whose industry structure is similar to Germany's tend to have more in common than emerging economies (such as BRICS countries) due in part to the economic integration processes and individual interests of the nation states.

III. PRACTICAL EXPERIENCES TO DATE

A. Relevance of the Documentation Requirements in Tax Audits

The continuing trend towards new, diversified national transfer pricing regulations and the heightened scrutiny of transfer pricing issues by national tax authorities have significantly increased the audit intensity of the records prepared by enterprises. In this connection, MNEs encounter heterogeneous country-specific tax audit cultures that range from functional to economic to extremely formalistic approaches. Whereas, in the early years of documentation requirements, it was sometimes sufficient to simply submit documentation to tax auditors, now the arm's length documentation in particular is inspected in detail. Similar trends can be seen in various other countries.

For this, tax audits focus on the comparability analysis which the OECD TPG or individual countries' regulations only touch on but is essential for assessing the arm's length of the transaction in question. A lack of comparable transactions on the market often forces auditors to fall back on database studies. In many cases, the credibility of these studies is called into question by the tax administrations through their own database studies. It is, therefore, no surprise that the issue of 'profit margins of associated enterprises' has led to the highest additional burdens for MNEs in recent years.

In terms of the content, a shift in focus can be observed. Whereas the main focus in the past was on the sale of tangibles and proof of the benefit test for intra-group services, it is now increasingly on documentation of the arm's length character of intra-group financial transactions as well as on the use and documentation of the comparable uncontrolled price method for intangibles. Here, the authorities' conclusions are often reached on the basis of greater knowledge after the fact. Issues such as Location-Specific Advantages (LSAs) have also received considerable attention ever since India and China adopted a position on these in the UN TP Manual.

B. Experience with Documentation Preparation So Far

Whether MNEs apply a centralized or decentralized documentation strategy or a combination of the two strategies plus the introduction of internal worldwide documentation processes for standardization, simplification, and streamlining with simultaneous improvement of global consistency can be disregarded for the moment. MNEs still face manifold challenges of a practical nature in complying with local law requirements. Regarding the internationally accepted use of benchmark studies from databases of external providers, it can be observed that, time and again, at the expense of functional comparability, local tax authorities request benchmark studies exclusively with local benchmark companies and automatically reject comparables found in pan-regional databases. For lack of publicly available data, adjustment calculations (e.g., capital adjustments) to improve the comparability of the benchmark companies used in the benchmark studies, however, are generally not possible. Some countries focus on divergent bandwidths in which they do not provide for a narrowing in an interquartile range as is customary in the United States and Europe. Other topics to be addressed in connection with benchmark studies may arise from benchmark studies being prepared at different times in the context of the price-setting approach and for documentation purposes (outcome testing approach) as well as the question of the required frequency or amplitude of the benchmarks.

There is also the use of one-year or multi-year averages, local deviations in the selection of the Profit Level Indicator (PLI) to be used, and the tax treatment of hybrid entities. Other challenges continuously facing MNEs are different submission deadlines, different fiscal years, and the use of different accounting standards (local GAAP versus IFRSs), submission or translation of the documents in (to) the national language, and varying practices in the admissibility of omnibus transactions or in the method to be used for all of the different forms of financing in the group (e.g., guarantees, loans, factoring, hedging). Individual local specifications still exist that, contrary to the OECD TPG, classify the local company as a tested entity without considering its functional and risk profile.[10]

C. Data Availability

These substantive challenges notwithstanding, most MNEs are rarely able to supply all of the required data instantaneously. IT systems are generally designed for

10. See details in OECD, *Review of Comparability and of Profit Methods: Revision of Chapters I-III of the Transfer Pricing Guidelines* (2010).

performance controlling purposes. For transfer pricing purposes, however, information is generally required for each transaction type. This means that data must be collected and prepared specifically for tax purposes. Although corporate tax departments have now taken steps to set up special reporting systems with operational transfer pricing management, data is often captured and monitored manually which is inefficient and prone to error. In addition, trade-offs between the transfer pricing method used and governance regularly occur. Management policy may also give rise to practical difficulties in procuring information from other units in the group, making systematic data collection and provision difficult. Another challenge is making an efficient transfer pricing concept tailored to the MNE in question compatible with recurring cost saving programs.

IV. TPD ACCORDING TO BEPS ACTION 13

A. Base Erosion and Profit Shifting Project

Recognizing that a common approach in relationship to documentation requirements for businesses and tax administrations would be an advantage, the OECD set out in Action 13 of its fifteen point Action Plan on Base Erosion and Profit Shifting (BEPS) published on 19 July 2013, that new rules regarding TPD would be developed to enhance transparency for tax administration taking into consideration the compliance costs for MNEs. On 16 September 2014, the OECD released its first set of deliverables on the fifteen actions of the BEPS project, including – in compliance with the task from Action 13 – documentation guidance with a model template for the country-by-country report. On 5 October 2015, the final report on BEPS Action 13: TPD and Country-by-Country Reporting (CbCR) was published by the OECD. This report recommends countries to implement a three-tiered standardized approach for TPD and replaces Chapter V of the OECD TPG.

B. Three-Tiered Approach to TPD

The final Action 13 report[11] and the new Chapter V of the OECD guidelines describe a three-tiered standardized approach for TPD. This standard consists of: (i) a master file containing standardized information relevant for all group members; (ii) local files referring specifically to transactions of the local taxpayer; and (iii) a Country-by-Country Report (CbCR) containing information on the global allocation of the group's income and taxes paid as well as other group data.

The master file and local file approach as well as the CbCR template are to be re-examined from a practical viewpoint by 2020. It is assumed that the new standards

11. OECD, *Guidance on Transfer Pricing Documentation and Country-by-Country Reporting*, OECD/G20 Base Erosion and Profit Shifting Project, OECD Publishing (2014) http://dx.doi.org/10.1787/9789264219236-en (accessed 15 Mar. 2016).

will be introduced in most countries with effect from 2016 so that there is adequate practical experience for this re-examination.

C. Master File and Local File

The information to be included in the master file and the local file are set out in detail in Annex I and II to Chapter V of the OECD guidelines. Annex I provides for a comprehensive list of information to be included in the master file; however, this information needs to be interpreted in the light of the wording of the new Chapter V. The master file is intended to give a high-level overview rather than requiring exhaustive listings of minutiae. Thus, taxpayers can limit the content of the master file to the general relevant and important information for the whole group. Nevertheless, taxpayers are faced with a substantial extension of documentation requirements for group-wide information and information related to facts and circumstances outside of the taxpayer's country.

The master file and local file will have essentially the same content as the master file and the country-specific documentation recommended in the EU TPD. In contrast to the EU TPD which sets out that preparation of the master file is optional, the OECD makes preparation of the master file mandatory for MNEs. Nevertheless, the OECD master file and local file approach differs in some respects from the OECD's previous documentation regulations and also those of many countries. Among other things, the OECD requires taxpayers to provide more information and documents than what is stipulated in current domestic laws such as the German Regulations Regarding the Documentation of Profit Allocations (GAufzV).

D. Country-by-Country Reporting

The CbCR is a new, additional element of the documentation that has not been in use internationally until now. Under the new reporting requirements, multinationals are required to annually provide aggregated information that relates to the global allocation of income and taxes paid in each jurisdiction where they do business. Other indicators of the location of economic activity within the group as well as information about which entities do business in a particular jurisdiction and the business activities each entity engages in must also be given.

The CbCR is the major innovation resulting from Action 13 and creates high uncertainty for taxpayers. Appendix III A to Chapter V provides a model template for the report which suggests that it should consist of three tables: (i) the first table provides an overview of allocation of income, taxes, and further group data by tax jurisdiction; (ii) the second table requires information on the main business activities of the group entities residing in each tax jurisdiction; and (iii) the third table permits the taxpayers to provide additional information.

There is an exemption from CbCR for groups with annual consolidated group revenues in the immediately preceding fiscal year of less than EUR 750 million or an equivalent amount in domestic currency. The OECD assumes that this exemption will exclude 85%-90% of groups from the requirement to file the CbCR but that the report, nevertheless, will be filed by groups controlling approximately 90% of corporate revenue.

V. ADDITIONAL CHALLENGES IN LIGHT OF BEPS ACTION 13

A. Increased Documentation Requirements and Enhanced Transparency

In principle, the practical challenges facing MNEs in preparing international documentation as outlined above remain (refer to III) irrespective of the new OECD approach. What is more, the increased requirements exacerbate the currently existing problem of data availability. Particularly the introduction of the CbCR as an additional element in the documentation means that MNEs will have to cope with a significantly higher documentation burden in the future in relationship to the scope and quality of the content as well as enhanced transparency of internal data. The interdependencies between the master file, local file, and CbCR will necessitate greater consistency in transfer pricing practice. On the basis of different performance indicators, the tax administrations will be able to relatively quickly identify potential inconsistencies.

B. Differences in Legislation and Interpretation

By amending Chapter V of the OECD TPG and its annexes, the OECD/G 20 states endeavored, for the first time, to create an internationally accepted standard for documentation requirements in the area of transfer pricing. However, it is important not to overstate this result as yet because key questions concerning the implementation of the new standard still need to be answered. Any differences in requirements of different countries (i.e., diversions from OECD) will make compliance very challenging.

This raises the question of whether the OECD's approach can actually be put into practice if individual countries do not or only partially implement it. In this respect, the OECD TPG fall somewhere between one of the most important changes in transfer pricing standards and a modification of more insignificant detailed regulations in individual countries. The real extent of the implications of the new documentation requirements will only become apparent after publication of further guidance on the implementation of the new regulations. How the respective legislature will adapt the existing documentation requirements based on the OECD guidance and how the tax authorities will interpret these regulations remains to be seen.

As stated in Action 13's report, countries such as Argentina, Brazil, People's Republic of China, Colombia, India, Mexico, South Africa, and Turkey have expressed the view that they might request additional information for each tier. This could result in additional efforts to comply with the documentation. For example, in the recent draft circular issued by the Chinese tax authority, it has proposed to add a fourth document, the Special Issue File, dealing with intra-group services, cost sharing arrangements, and/or thin capitalization. MNEs will need to be extremely aware of any variations in local specific requirements and customize their documentation accordingly in each case, if required. How the tax administration will react if countries formally implement the CbCR earlier or 'localize' it, for example, is also still unclear. So it is hardly surprising that some tax administrations of developed countries are rather skeptical of the more stringent documentation standards now that the initial euphoria has worn off. This is due, among other things, to concerns that the enhanced transparency of groups will lead particularly the BRICS countries to covet the profit allocation of MNEs. Doubts are now arising in other countries as well.

C. Confidentiality

According to the OECD, tax authorities should take all reasonable steps to ensure that there is no public disclosure of confidential information such as trade or scientific secrets and other commercially sensitive information contained in the master file, local file, and CbCR. Tax administrations should assure taxpayers that the information presented in TPD will remain confidential. Confidentiality is not only important for tax-relevant data but also particularly regarding trade secrets, financial data, or other information, for example, family-owned businesses or joint ventures. When sensitive company information is being disclosed, it is imperative to ensure that the foreign tax authorities treat this information as confidential. The principle of proportionality demands that taxpayers are only requested to provide information that is relevant for their taxation or risk assessment. The fear that these data will be made available to competitors is one of the main themes of the comments on BEPS Action 13. Additional concerns about confidentiality arise in the context of international exchange of information between tax authorities. There is no guarantee that all countries will protect the confidentiality of information, and there are considerable differences regarding tax secrecy around the world. In France, Finland, Norway, and Sweden, for example, tax information is publicly available. In cases where disclosure is required in public court proceedings or judicial decisions, every effort should be made to ensure that confidentiality is maintained and that information is disclosed only to the extent needed. This means, however, that information disclosed during a public court proceeding or in a judicial decision is no longer subject to confidentiality. When dealing with confidential information, tax authorities should follow the OECD guide, 'Keeping it Safe'.

VI. CONCERNS ABOUT THE MASTER FILE

A. More Disclosure

Due to the high level nature of the information requested for the master file, most of the requirements were not contemplated in most previous transfer pricing legislations around the world. The new requirements set in the master file as well as the fact that most of the information requested is not directly related to the intercompany transactions of many of the group companies which have to hand in the master file result in important challenges to the MNEs. Several of the requirements ask the MNE to inform regarding the 'principal' or 'most important' parts of different issues. There is no indication or methodology to guide the tax payer in determining which factors should be taken into consideration to determine that a particular fact, contract, asset, etc. should be considered important. This might create a difference in perception between the tax payer and the tax authority on whether the information provided complies with the requirements, resulting in unjust penalties for the tax payer. Moreover, different tax authorities might have a different interpretation on this point which will result in the master file of an MNE group being considered compliant in some countries and not in others. Furthermore, the level of information disclosure ('Taxpayers should present the [master file] information as a whole') means that every group company that is based in a country with transfer pricing legislation as well as the tax authorities of each of the respective countries will have access to the information stated in the group's master file. Since some of the requirements only involve information related to a few of the group companies, it presents the MNE with the dilemma to choose if the information should be disclosed to all of the group companies and their respective tax authorities independently from their involvement in the referred activities/transactions or if the requirement should be complied with by referencing the respective local file and, therefore, only the countries involved in the activity/transactions will have access to this information. A good example of this is found in the last requirement of the MNE's intangible section of the master file: 'A general description of any important transfers of interests in intangibles among associated enterprises during the fiscal year concerned, including the entities, countries, and compensation involved.'

B. Intangibles More in Focus

Due to the delicate nature of transfer of interest in intangibles within a group, the information requested should only be disclosed to the entities and countries involved in the transfer of interest and avoid revealing the sensitive content to unimplicated parties. In this case, the requested information and corresponding transfer pricing analysis should be disclosed in the local files. Furthermore, the second requirement of Section 3 of the master file requests that the tax payer provides 'a list of intangibles or group of intangibles of the MNE group that are important for a transfer pricing purpose and which entities legally own them'.[12] It is interpreted by the text that this requirement includes registered and unregistered intangibles. There is a high level of subjectivity surrounding each of the key factors of intangibles from its definition, the establishment of economic ownership, the methodology of valuation as well as the comparability and key assessment elements of the valuation. This can lead to two or more tax authorities arriving at different conclusions with distinctly different results over the same intangible or countries endorsing greater use of profit split in the future.

12. OECD, *Guidance on Transfer Pricing Documentation and Country-by-Country Reporting*, OECD/G20 Base Erosion and Profit Shifting Project, OECD Publishing (2014) Annex I to Chapter V. Transfer Pricing Documentation – Master File, p. 28, http://dx.doi.org/10.1787/9789264219236-en (accessed 15 Mar. 2016).

The first key factor which can lead to different interpretations of the nature of intangibles is the definition. The OECD definition is one of the most commonly accepted intangible definitions for TP purposes, i.e., 'something which is not a physical asset or a financial asset, which is capable of being owned or controlled for use in commercial activities, and whose use or transfer would be compensated had it occurred in a transaction between independent parties in comparable circumstances'.[13] There is a level of ambiguity in the definition especially in regard to the clause: '...and whose use or transfer would be compensated had it occurred in a transaction between independent parties in comparable circumstances'. Most intangibles and, in particular, IPs owned by MNEs are unique and are rarely sold or licensed to third parties; therefore, the sheer determination if a particular intangible would be compensated by an independent party can already be a subjective exercise with different answers. When comparing which are the main examples of intangibles considered by the OECD related to the ones listed in US legislations, there is a considerable overlap with one noticeable difference, goodwill. However, countries like China and India have very distinct definitions of intangibles which include elements such as locations savings and market premium achieved for conducting business in their countries and believe they should be rewarded as such. The OECD position on this matter is that both local savings and market premium should be dealt with as part of the comparability analysis by using local comparables whose results would also be affected by the location savings and market premium; therefore, there would be no necessity to perform an additional adjustment. China rebuts this by saying that there are not sufficient Chinese-listed companies to make complete local benchmarks; hence, most of their benchmarks are composed of companies in other countries in the region, mainly Japan, for which they expect an additional adjustment in their profits should be made. In the case of India, they do use 100% Indian comparables; nevertheless, they still propose that additional adjustments to the profits should be made. This short example shows the vast difference that currently exists just in the definition of Intangibles which might lead to double taxation for MNEs. The current importance and relevance for finding a common way of understanding the different elements of intangibles can be seen in the number of papers published or drafted in the last two years alone that discuss the subject in a direct or indirect way. This is a step in the right direction for finding a common ground in the definition and valuation of IP. The main problem is that these papers do not have a binding nature to tax authorities which have resulted in tax authorities only following the parts of them they agree with and disregarding the rest. Also, many of the recommendations set up in these papers are very general which still leaves ample opportunity for subjectivity in the matter.

13. Action 8, Assure that transfer pricing outcomes are in-line with value creation; OECD – Revised Discussion Draft on Transfer Pricing Aspects of Intangibles of 30 Jul. 2013, proposed definition of an intangible asset for transfer pricing purposes.

C. Financial Transactions

One aspect of Action 13 has received relatively little attention, i.e., the requirements for disclosure of intercompany financing activities. This section requires taxpayers to prepare new information that one may not expect to see in many of today's transfer pricing reports. The major challenge is a lack of clarity on the level of disclosure required under Action 13. Financing arrangements in MNEs can range from the very simple to the very complex. For example, the first requirement asks about 'important financing arrangements with unrelated lenders'. The wording used here is not restricted to standard-term loans and may include various types of financial arrangements such as bridge loans, equipment leasing, sales/lease-back arrangements, or revolving loans. Financing could also consist of infusions of equity such as venture capital, employee stock option arrangements, or convertible debt. The second requirement requires the 'identification of any members of the MNE group that provide a central financing function for the group'. Central financing functions are not further explained, but common functions might include cash pooling, hedging, treasury management, insurance management, centralized lending, and others. Therefore, this requirement may require special care for those MNEs that derive significant benefits or profits from hedging or other financial activities or MNEs that have located centralized financing functions in low tax jurisdictions. Centralized financing arrangements are often dependent upon contractual arrangements that facilitate risk transfer, and the related profits may be assigned to entities that do not have a significant number of employees or other assets.

A company's annual report may list a substantial amount of required information, and it would be prudent to acknowledge each of these in the master file. Information that is not presented or presented without much detail in the master file may indeed need to be presented in a more granular fashion in the local file.

VII. CONCERNS WITH REGARD TO THE LOCAL FILE

A. Reconciliation

Most requirements of the local file are consistent with the documentation requirements which the majority of transfer pricing legislations have had in place for several years; therefore, the compliance with the local file should generally not represent major challenges for MNEs. The main challenge that the local file will present to some MNEs is related to the second requirement of the financial information which states: 'information and allocation schedules showing how the financial data used in applying the transfer pricing method may be tied to the annual financial statements'. MNEs, especially those that are more influential, use several partially linked systems of accounting and information which can utilize different accounting reporting standards depending on the requirements of each country. It can become a laborious task for MNEs to relate the segmented financial results to the audited local financial statements due to the inconsistency between the different accounting standards and the level of detail required to set the properly segmented financials that are necessary to perform the transfer pricing analysis of particular intercompany transactions. Tying these two together can become even more difficult when special adjustments must be introduced to the segmented financials in order to improve the comparability with uncontrolled parties as well as when assumptions must be made to set up the correct allocation of certain lines of the financial statements that otherwise would not be able to be segmented between related and unrelated transactions.

VIII. CBCR REQUIREMENTS RAISING CONCERNS

A. High Risk of Data Misinterpretation

The significance of the data to be provided in the CbCR is questionable and only partly allows for conclusions about a potential shift of taxable income. The CbCR concept bears a number of inconsistencies and, thus, contains a high risk of misinterpretation potential due to onetime effects or other aspects. For example, on the one hand, the earnings of a Permanent Establishment (PE) are allocated to the country of the head office and, on the other hand, tax payments are attributed locally. The same is true for dividend payments which are not reported as turnover but are included in the 'taxes paid'. Furthermore, the consolidated financial statement only allows a restricted conclusion on the profit (loss) before income tax as the combined result presented in the consolidated financial statement usually does not correspond to the sum of the results of the separate-entity statutory financial statements. Additionally, tax payments are generally based on separate-entity statutory financial statements. Essentially, the definitions provided by the OECD are ambiguous which makes it likely that countries will interpret the reporting requirements differently. It is unclear why the OECD did not follow established international accounting standards. Reconciliations may not always be possible and/or may not be useful, for example, due to differences in currency or temporary, permanent, or local GAAP accounting differences. In addition, the OECD leaves a number of aspects – such as the source of the reported information – to a taxpayer's discretion. This will result in inconsistent implementation, a further limitation of the report's validity, and a considerable risk of double taxation if tax authorities use country-by-country reported data to make an assessment. Therefore, Table 3 which allows companies to provide any additional information or explanation that could be necessary or that could facilitate the understanding of the information provided in the CbCR could become the forth and most important part of the CbCR.

B. Taxes Paid

Additionally, income taxes affecting payments encompass tax prepayments for the current year (versus 'Income Tax Accrued' to the fiscal year only) and also tax prepayments for subsequent years, closing payments for prior periods, and supplementary payments or refunds due to tax audits or legal proceedings. These items consider various periods and do not permit conclusions about whether the amount of tax payments is compatible with the annual result. Furthermore, taxable profits and the profits in accordance with the trade balance sheet are generally not consistent so that income taxes affecting payment have only restricted informative value regarding the annual profit reported in the balance sheet. Another important aspect to be mentioned is the loss carry forward which might result from operational activities of prior years or from tax restructurings. These loss carry forwards have a considerable impact on the tax burden of the taxpayer. The OECD mentioned that the taxpayer does not need to report the loss carry forwards. Hence, it is not clear whether low tax payments despite a potential high income result from the use of loss carry forwards. According to the OECD, the withholding taxes should be included in the taxes paid in order to achieve a complete and comparable picture of the entire tax burden as well as of the regional allocation of taxes. However, the withholding taxes are directly withheld by the contractual parties and paid to the authority abroad. In this case, the receiving company does not have an overview of the taxes withheld by its contractual parties. Furthermore, it also happens that overpaid withholding taxes are not refunded or the refund occurs in the subsequent years. Because of these and many other inconsistencies, the link between the country-specific taxes paid and the profit in a fiscal year is broken. A multiple-year analysis of the annual results and the tax payments might partly correct these effects. Otherwise, a one-year snapshot view only leads to further misinterpretation potential.

C. Dilution of the Arm's Length Principle

The deliverables on Action 13 explicitly point out that a number of emerging markets will demand information in the CbCR over and above the OECD's recommendations. There is reason to fear that the additional information requirements announced in individual cases could broaden the possibilities for analysis based on a formulary apportionment of income instead of the traditional arm's length principle being applied. The OECD states that the CbCR may be used by tax administrations in evaluating other BEPS-related risks and for economic and statistical analysis. However, according to the OECD, the information in the CbCR on its own does not constitute conclusive evidence of whether transfer prices are or are not appropriate and should not be used by tax administrations to propose transfer pricing adjustments based on a formulary apportionment of income. Despite the rhetoric, what exactly the local tax authorities hope to obtain from the information about value drivers, supply chains, and intangible property remains unclear. There would seem to be no clearly defined relationship between this reference data. Frequently, the profits of a group that are primarily attributable to the use of intangibles are difficult to localize and to assess. For this reason, determining the supposed value added based on simple performance indicators appears to be problematic and has the potential for tax administrations to make indecisive assumptions which could result in a formulary apportionment of income from time to time.

D. Role of Technology

Reflecting the CbCR requirements from the IT perspective, the difficulties that MNE programmers face increase significantly when designing effective transfer pricing modules within the group main information system. The best way to obtain complete and consistent data would be with one worldwide and congruent financial reporting system. This could be a consolidation system or an ERP system (Enterprise Resource Planning). Unfortunately, due to size of business, acquisitions, decentrally customized ERP systems possibly in connection with local accounting or legal requirements and, of course, budget constraints, MNEs may face a variety of different data sources ranging from individual SAP solutions and Data or Business Warehouse systems to a mere excel spreadsheet. Interlinked information systems which possess specialized designed transfer pricing modules will play a fundamental role in facilitating an MNE's efforts to comply with the new OECD requirements.

E. Information Exchange

While the master file can be directly collected by jurisdictions, the CbCR will be collected by tax authorities and distributed through tax treaty and information exchange networks. It is commonly understood that the CbCR report should be created and only submitted to tax authorities by the ultimate parent entity and should not be published, for example, in companies' annual reports. Appendix IV of the final guidance contains model legislation that could be used by countries to require the ultimate parent entity of a multinational group to file the CbCR report including backup filing requirements in its jurisdiction of residence. This approach is reasonable as comprehensive overviews about the entire global activities of the group of companies and the corresponding information are available only at the parent company's level. The tax authorities of the parent company should exchange the CbCR reported information on an automatic basis with the jurisdictions in which the group operates through existing instruments such as agreements on automatic information exchange regarding relevant fiscal issues, the twenty-six Tax Information Exchange Agreements (TIEAs), and Double Tax Agreements (DTA). Jurisdictions are encouraged to expand the coverage of their international agreements for the exchange of information which will be an integral part of the ongoing monitoring process.

The OECD included a 'Confidentiality and Data Safeguards Questionnaire' with a checklist of requirements related to legal enforcement and information security. This should be applied as a standard to determine if jurisdictions are not appropriately protecting the information being exchanged. Under the information exchange instruments, data can only be exchanged if both parties have provided safeguards to ensure that information remains confidential. However, the concern is how the presented conditions about the confidentiality are going to be respected in practice by the different jurisdictions.

F. Timing and Secondary Filing Mechanisms

A so-called secondary mechanism would be accepted as appropriate if a jurisdiction fails to provide information to another jurisdiction. Affiliated companies should be in charge of creating the CbCR only if the parent company has no duty to create a report in its particular country, no qualified competent authority agreement for filing the report is in effect, or there has been a systemic failure. This implies that no additional local filing can be required by any local tax authorities if the CbCR submitted to the ultimate parent companies' tax administration is exchanged with the respective country and complies with the OECD requirements set in Action 13. Nonetheless, differences in legislation (or interpretation) of secondary mechanisms could cause a great deal of uncertainty for MNEs. The first years will be a challenge for MNEs particularly where, in the country of the ultimate parent company, the CbCR legislation is delayed or not fully legislated or if there are different filing dates. Inaccuracies should be expected while business systems are refined.

IX. INCREASING THE RISK OF DOUBLE TAXATION

A. Effective Dispute Resolution Mechanisms to Avoid Double Taxation

The new reporting requirements will generate a large amount of additional information for the tax authorities which is, in turn, likely to create more tax audits. This will also lead to additional instances of double taxation, and countries will have to decide whether to fix this through APAs or Mutual Agreement Procedure (MAPs). Both taxpayers and tax administrations have already expressed concern regarding the ability of governments to keep up with BEPS-created transfer pricing disputes. The OECD recognized that the number of treaty-related disputes was increasing even before the BEPS project and that the action plan, particularly Action 13 on CbCR, would likely lead to an increase in those disputes. Already in the pre-BEPS area, the number of pending MAP cases globally increased by almost 100% (between the years 2006 and 2013) with Germany already having the highest inventory of open MAP procedures for several years. Action 14 on improving dispute resolution is seen as an important complement to the work on the BEPS issues. In its final report on that action, the OECD noted that twenty nations have agreed to include mandatory binding arbitration under the MAP in their tax treaties. While this represents more consensus than perhaps anticipated, it will not address double tax disputes in some of the most important jurisdictions, such as China and India, which were not among the twenty countries.

The new documentation standard accompanied by the exchange of more information at an international level will give the tax authorities even greater insight into the transfer pricing structures of MNEs. How tax disputes can be resolved if the use of the master file, the local file, and the CbCR by the tax administrations involved leads to different interpretations and to an adjustment of the transfer prices, however, is still unclear. Experience shows that the resulting economic double taxation can only be effectively redressed through MAP or arbitration proceedings. Yet, this instrument can only be used if a DTA has been agreed upon between the countries in question and whether it is actually possible to conduct a MAP and/or arbitration proceedings. Arbitration proceedings can be conducted effectively without a bilateral DTA on the basis of the EU Arbitration Convention only within the EU. However, even within the EU with an existing arbitration mechanism, the dispute resolution is not always effective (e.g., Italy). This is made more complicated by the cases in which a bilateral DTA does not include a provision that is comparable with Article 9(2) of the OECD Model Tax Convention which, in fact, many older DTAs do not contain. All the same, a number of treaty states currently oppose transfer pricing MAPs if a provision in accordance with Article 9(2) of the OECD Model Tax Convention has not been agreed upon. Against the backdrop of the deliverables from OECD Action 13, therefore, there is a need to clarify, for example, whether tax authorities may also pass the CbCR on to foreign tax authorities when exchanging information, especially if a DTA has not been signed with this country (e.g., Brazil), MAP cannot be conducted (e.g., India, Russia), or there is no compulsion to reach agreement (e.g., China).

Due to these aspects, even today, MNEs are facing significant legal uncertainty and high risks of double taxation (plus interests and/or penalties). Ultimately, the OECD can only achieve its goal if the documentation requirements are accompanied by an effective dispute resolution mechanism for international tax disputes relating to transfer pricing, especially by introducing mandatory arbitration mechanisms in DTAs and making them effective. Without fulfillment of Action Item 14 'Make dispute resolution more effective', the BEPS project will fail in its original context. Additionally, local tax administrations need to establish enough resources to be able to reduce the number of pending cases and be prepared for the increase in disputes.

B. European Council (EC) to Target Tax Avoidance with New BEPS Legislation

Since December 2014, the EC has launched the first steps towards an EU approach and has begun working on an anti-tax avoidance package which will contain legislation to implement the OECD's recommendations on combating BEPS as well as measures targeting tax havens and ensuring that countries outside the European Union implement the guidance on BEPS. The European Commission noted that other planned legislation to ensure fair taxation by multinational companies that is to come in 2016 will include a proposal requiring national tax authorities to share details of multinational country-by-country tax and profit reporting. It will call for an amendment to be added to the EU Administrative Cooperation Directive which already requires EU Member States to automatically exchange interest-bearing bank income as well as details on capital gains and other income of non-residents. A second measure will involve a proposal for resolving tax disputes among EU Member States. The initiative aims at achieving a certain degree of uniformity in implementing the BEPS Action 14 across the EU. The outcome remains to be seen. Ultimately, if implemented, a BEPS directive could insure that every country introduces the same rules. MNEs are more likely to warm to some of the BEPS proposals if given assurances that its rollout throughout the twenty-eight EU Member States will occur equitably and, hence, it could be avoided, for example, that one EU Member State implements the OECD rules but another does not. Otherwise, that would put MNEs at a disadvantage. That being said, there is still a risk of weakening EU competitiveness if the initiatives go beyond what has been agreed upon by OECD BEPS project.

X. REVIEW AND OUTLOOK

Of all of the guidance released under the OECD's Action Plan 13 on BEPS and the corresponding new Chapter V of the OECD TPG, the final report on TPD and the CbCR will undoubtedly impose the greatest compliance burden on large multinational companies and will significantly increase the documentation requirements for large companies. The new TP documentation requirements would require MNEs to accept a shift from a one-sided analysis to a more holistic analysis encompassing consideration of value creation and value chain analysis for the MNE's group operations. Unfortunately, the new reporting requirements do not successfully balance tax authorities' interests and the usefulness of the data.

Emerging markets in particular are expected to implement CbCR requirements beyond those outlined in the new Chapter V. One of the central functions of CbCR is to provide tax administrations with the information necessary to conduct a risk assessment for which an overview of local tax burdens and profits of the group companies are important aspects. However, considering that the relationship between country-specific taxes paid and the profits in a fiscal year is, in many cases, not given, the value of a risk analysis based on this information is rather limited. It remains unclear how national reporting regulations will be implemented through local country legislation or administrative procedures; however, inconsistencies are expected and, unfortunately, the OECD has not used established international accounting standards. There is a considerable concern that it will erode the arm's length principle and that it is a prelude to a formulary apportionment – even this has been explicitly confined by the OECD.

Most of the discussion on the OECD's efforts on transparency has focused on the CbCR which requires companies to produce global blueprints with jurisdiction specific data on employee staffing, facilities, taxable income, and taxes paid. That requirement, with the stated purpose of aiding countries in risk assessment, has been criticized as an administrative burden for taxpayers and a troubling turn toward a formulary-style tax system

Taxpayers must be ready to fulfill the new requirements as well as defend their transfer pricing in light of the new data. Country-by-country data from foreign entities will likely become a challenge in future tax audits; taxpayers should be well-prepared for a discussion with tax authorities and be ready to provide explanations in their TPD for 'unreasonable' country-by-country data such as high profits in a country with a limited number of employees or assets.

The implementation of BEPS in many countries at a different pace and with probably slightly deviating content will lead to inconsistencies in the international tax law environment. While some countries will comply with the BEPS package right away, others will deliberately stall and seek opportunities to raise their competitiveness. All of this will lead to a significant increase in double taxation and international tax controversies. It will be key that all OECD countries really do commit to the measures because, otherwise, loopholes will remain. The United States, for example, has taken a very reluctant stance on this so far and, if some countries do not really commit, this might hold back the whole project. So, the most important aspect for the G-20 ministers will be to fix a firm commitment that all OECD countries will stick to. The explanatory statement does suggest some disagreements on the underlying standards on tax treaties and transfer pricing.

Although the importance is clear of the new requirements in order to accomplish communication that is more transparent between MNEs and tax authorities with the purpose of ensuring that profits are taxed where the business activities are performed and value creation is achieved, it is also clear that the new three-tiered approach will bring several challenges to MNEs and increase the costs of documentation. Achieving the equilibrium between limiting the opportunities of MNEs for BEPS while keeping the cost and effort that MNEs must incur in order to comply with the documentation at a reasonable and achievable level is fundamental for the success of the implementation around the world of the recommendations set in Action 13.

Index

EUCOTAX Series on European Taxation

(1) Peter HJ Essers, Guido JME de Bont & Eric CCM Kemmeren (eds), *The Compatibility of Anti-Abuse Provisions in Tax Treaties with EC Law,* 1998 (ISBN 90-411-9678-1).

(2) Gerard TK Meussen (ed.), *The Principle of Equality in European Taxation,* 1999 (ISBN 90-411-9693-5).

(3) Michael Lang (ed.), *Tax Treaty Interpretation,* 2001 (ISBN 90-411-9857-1).

(4) Pasquale Pistone, *The Impact of Community Law on Tax Treaties: Issues and Solutions,* 2002 (ISBN 90-411-9860-1).

(5) René Offermanns, *The Entrepreneurship Concept in a European Comparative Tax Law Perspective,* 2002 (ISBN 90-411-9887-3).

(6) Michael Lang & Mario Züger, *Settlement of Disputes in Tax Treaty Law,* 2002 (ISBN 90-411-9904-7).

(7) Carlo Pinto, *Tax Competition and EU Law,* 2003 (ISBN 90-411-9913-6).

(8) Michael Lang, Hans-Jörgen Aigner, Ulrich Scheuerle & Markus *Stefaner, CFC Legislation, Tax Treaties and EC Law,* 2004 (ISBN 90-411-2284-2).

(9) Mattias Dahlberg, *Direct Taxation in Relation to the Freedom of Establishment and the Free Movement of Capital,* 2005 (ISBN 90-411-2363-6).

(10) Michael Lang, Judith Herdin & Ines Hofbauer, *WTO and Direct Taxation,* 2005 (ISBN 90-411-2371-7).

(11) Dennis Weber, *Tax Avoidance and the EC Tray Freedoms: A Study of the Limitations under European Law for the Prevention of Tax Avoidance,* 2005 (ISBN 90-411-2402-0).

(12) Félix Alberto Vega Borrego, *Limitations on Benefits Clauses on Double Taxation Conventions,* 2005 (ISBN 90-411-2370-9).

(13) Michael Lang, Josef Schuch & Claus Staringer, *ECJ-Recent Developments in Direct Taxation,* 2006 (ISBN 90-411-2509-4).

(14) Reuven S. Avi-Yonah, James R. Hines Jr. & Michael Lang, *Comparative Fiscal Federalism. Comparing the European Court of Justice and the US Supreme Court's Tax Jurisprudence,* 2007 (ISBN 978-90-411 2552-1).

(15) Christiana HJI Panayi, *Double Taxation, Tax Treaties, Treaty-Shopping and the European Community,* 2007 (ISBN 978-90-411-2658-0).

(16) Dennis Weber, *The Influence of European Law on Direct Taxation: Recent and Future Developments,* 2007 (ISBN 978-90-411-2667-2).

(17) Michael Lang & Pasquale Pistone, *The EU and Third Countries: Direct Taxation,* 2007 (ISBN 978-90-411-2665-8).

(18) Oskar Henkow, *Financial Activities in European VAT: A Theoretical and Legal Research of the European VAT System and Preferred Treatment of Financial Activities,* 2007 (ISBN 978-90-411-2703-7).

(19) Michael Lang (ed.), *Tax Compliance Costs for Companies in an Enlarged European Community,* 2008 (ISBN 978-90-411-2666-5).

(20) Michael Lang (ed.), *Source versus Residence. Problems Arising from the Allocation of Taxing Rights in Tax Treaty Law and Possible Alternatives*, 2008 (ISBN 978-90-411-2763-1).

(21) Ioanna Mitroyanni, *Integration Approaches to Group Taxation in the European Internal Market*, 2008 (ISBN 978-90-411-2779-2).

(22) Rolf Eicke, *Tax Planning with Holding Companies. Repatriation of US Profits from Europe:Concepts, Strategies, Structures*, 2008 (ISBN978-90-411-2794-5).

(23) Peter Essers et al. (ed.), *The Influence of IAS/IFRS on the CCCTB, Tax Accounting, Disclosure and Corporate Law Accounting Concepts: 'A Clash of Cultures'*, 2008 (ISBN 978-90-411-2819-5).

(24) Tonny Schenk-Geers, *International Exchange of Information and the Protection of Taxpayers*, 2009 (ISBN 978-90-411-3142-3).

(25) Raymond Adema, *UCITS and Taxation: Towards Harmonization of the Taxation of UCITS*, 2009 (ISBN 978-90-411-2839-3).

(26) Michael Lang, Jianwen Liu & Gongliang Tang (eds), *Europe–China Tax Treaties*, 2010 (ISBN 978-90-411-3216-1).

(27) Michael Lang, Pasquale Pistone, Josef Schuch & Claus Staringer (eds), *Procedural Rules in Tax Law in the Context of European Union and Domestic Law*, 2010 (ISBN 978-90-411-3376-2).

(28) Sjaak J.J.M. Jansen, *Fiscal Sovereignty of the Member States in an Internal Market: Past and Future*, 2011 (ISBN 978-90-411-3403-5).

(29) Dennis Weber & Bruno da Silva, *From Marks & Spencer to X Holding: The Future of Cross-Border Group Taxation*, 2011 (ISBN 978-90-411-3399-1).

(30) Claus Bohn Jespersen, *Intermediation of Insurance and Financial Services in European VAT*, 2011 (ISBN 978-90-411-3732-6).

(31) Sabine Heidenbauer, *Charity Crossing Borders: The Fundamental Freedoms' Influence on Charity and Donor Taxation in Europe*, 2011 (ISBN 978-90-411-3813-2).

(32) Michael Lang, et al., *The Future of Indirect Taxation: Recent Trends in VAT and GST Systems around the World*, 2012 (ISBN 978-90-411-3797-5).

(33) Harm van den Broek, *Cross-Border Mergers within the EU: Proposals to Remove the Remaining Tax Obstacles*, 2012 (ISBN 978-90-411-3824-8).

(34) Michael Lang, et al. (eds), *Tax Treaty Case Law around the Globe – 2011*, 2012 (ISBN 978-90-411-3876-7).

(35) Dennis Weber (ed.), *CCCTB: Selected Issues*, 2012 (ISBN 978-90-411-3872-9).

(36) Daniël Smit, *EU Freedoms, Non-EU Countries and Company Taxation*, 2012 (ISBN 978-90-411-4041-8).

(37) Rita de la Feria, *VAT Exemptions: Consequences and Design Alternatives*, 2013 (ISBN 978-90-411-3276-5).

(38) Karin Simader, *Withholding Taxes and the Fundamental Freedoms*, 2013 (ISBN 978-90-411-4842-1).

(39) Madeleine Merkx, *Establishments in European VAT*, 2013 (ISBN 978-90-411-4554-3).

(40) Carla De Pietro, *Tax Treaty Override*, 2014 (ISBN 978-90-411-5406-4).

(41) G.K. Fibbe & A.J.A. Stevens (eds), *Hybrid Entities and the EU Direct Tax Directives*, 2015 (ISBN 978-90-411-5942-7).

(42) Gerard Staats, *Personal Pensions in the EU*, 2015 (ISBN 978-90-411-5953-3).

(43) Michael Lang & Ine Lejeune (eds), *VAT/GST in a Global Digital Economy*, 2015 (ISBN 978-90-411-5952-6).

(44) Massimo Basilavecchia, Lorenzo del Federico & Pietro Mastellone (eds), *Tax Implications of Environmental Disasters and Pollution*, 2015 (ISBN 978-90-411-5611-2).

(45) Cristina Trenta, *Rethinking EU VAT for P2P Distribution*, 2015 (ISBN 978-90-411-6137-6).

(46) Marie Lamensch, Edoardo Traversa & Servaas van Thiel (eds), *Value Added Tax and the Digital Economy: The 2015 EU Rules and Broader Issues*, 2016 (ISBN 978-90-411-6612-8).

(47) Raffaele Petruzzi, *Transfer Pricing Aspects of Intra-Group Financing*, 2016 (ISBN 978-90-411-6732-3).

(48) Mario Grandinetti (ed.), *Corporate Tax Base in the Light of the IAS/IFRS and EU Directive 2013/34: A Comparative Approach*, 2016 (ISBN 978-90-411-6745-3).

(49) Bruno da Silva, *The Impact of Tax Treaties and EU Law on Group Taxation Regimes*, 2016 (ISBN 978-90-411-6905-1).

(50) Michael Lang, Alfred Storck & Raffaele Petruzzi (eds), *Transfer Pricing in a Post-BEPS World*, 2016 (ISBN 978-90-411-6710-1).

www.ingramcontent.com/pod-product-compliance
Lightning Source LLC
LaVergne TN
LVHW021727021026
849161LV00004BA/761